Street by Street

BRISTOL

lst edition May 2

© Automobile
Limited 2001

This product includes map data licensed from
Ordnance Survey® with the permission of the
Controller of Her Majesty's Stationery Office.
© Crown copyright 2000. All rights reserved.

Licence No: 399221.

Published by AA Publishing (a trading name
of Automobile Association Developments
Limited, whose registered office is Norfolk
House, Priestley Road, Basingstoke,
Hampshire, RG24 9NY. Registered number
1878835).

Mapping produced by the Cartographic
Department of The Automobile Association.

A CIP Catalogue record for this book is
available from the British Library.

Printed by GRAFIASA S.A., Porto, Portugal

The contents of this atlas are believed to be
correct at the time of the latest revision.
However, the publishers cannot be held
responsible for loss occasioned to any person
acting or refraining from action as a result of
any material in this atlas, nor for any errors,
omissions or changes in such material. The
publishers would welcome information to
correct any errors or omissions and to keep
this atlas up to date. Please write to
Publishing, The Automobile Association, Fanum
House, Basing View, Basingstoke, Hampshire,
RG21 4EA.

Ref: MN059

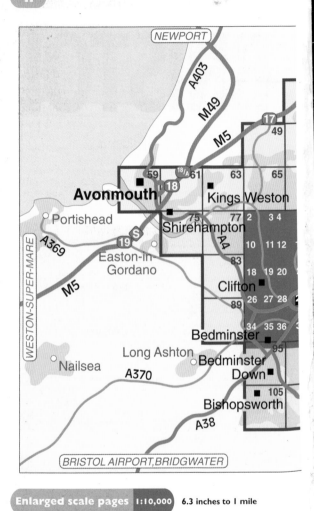

NEWPORT

A403

M49

M5

17
49

59   18/A 61   63   65
Avonmouth   18   Kings Weston

Portishead   75   77 2   3 4
Shirehampton

A369   19 S   10   11 12

Easton-in-
Gordano   83

M5   18   19 20
Clifton

89   26   27 28

34   35 36
Bedminster

95

Long Ashton   Bedminster
Nailsea   A370   Down

105

Bishopsworth
A38

BRISTOL AIRPORT, BRIDGWATER

WESTON-SUPER-MARE

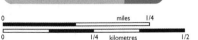

Enlarged scale pages 1:10,000   6.3 inches to 1 mile

0   miles   1/4
0   1/4   kilometres   1/2

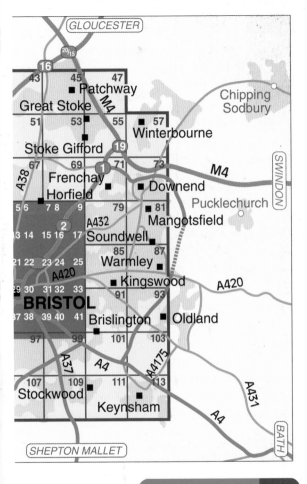

GLOUCESTER

20/15

16

43   45   47
Patchway
Great Stoke

M4

Chipping
Sodbury

51   53   55   57
Winterbourne

Stoke Gifford

19

SWINDON

67   69   1 71   73
Frenchay
Horfield

A38

M4

Downend
Pucklechurch

5 6   7 8   9   79   81
2   A432   **Mangotsfield**
13 14   15 16 17   **Soundwell**

21 22   23 24 25   85   87
A420   **Warmley**

29 30   31 32 33   **Kingswood**
91   93

A420

BRISTOL
37 38   39 40 41   **Brislington**   **Oldland**

97   99   101   103

A37   A4   A4175

107   109   111   113
Stockwood   **Keynsham**

A431

A4

BATH

SHEPTON MALLET

3.6 inches to 1 mile   **Scale of main map pages 1:17,500**

0   miles   1/2

0   kilometres 1/2   1

iv

Junction 9	Motorway & junction
Services	Motorway service area
	Primary road single/dual carriageway
Services	Primary road service area
	A road single/dual carriageway
	B road single/dual carriageway
	Other road single/dual carriageway
	Restricted road
	Private road
	One way street
	Pedestrian street
	Track/ footpath
	Road under construction
	Road tunnel
P	Parking

P+	Park & Ride
	Bus/coach station
	Railway & main railway station
	Railway & minor railway station
	Underground station
	Light railway & station
++++++	Preserved private railway
LC	Level crossing
•—•—•—	Tramway
- - - - -	Ferry route
....	Airport runway
— - — - —	Boundaries- borough/ district
▼▼▼▼▼▼	Mounds
93	Page continuation 1:17,500
7	Page continuation to enlarged scale 1:10,000

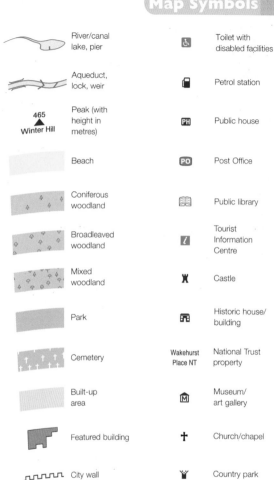

	River/canal lake, pier	♿	Toilet with disabled facilities
	Aqueduct, lock, weir	⛽	Petrol station
465 ▲ Winter Hill	Peak (with height in metres)	PH	Public house
	Beach	PO	Post Office
	Coniferous woodland	📖	Public library
	Broadleaved woodland	i	Tourist Information Centre
	Mixed woodland	♜	Castle
	Park	🏛	Historic house/ building
	Cemetery	Wakehurst Place NT	National Trust property
	Built-up area	M	Museum/ art gallery
	Featured building	†	Church/chapel
⊓⊔⊓⊔	City wall	♉	Country park
A&E	Accident & Emergency hospital	🎭	Theatre/ performing arts
🚻	Toilet	👥	Cinema

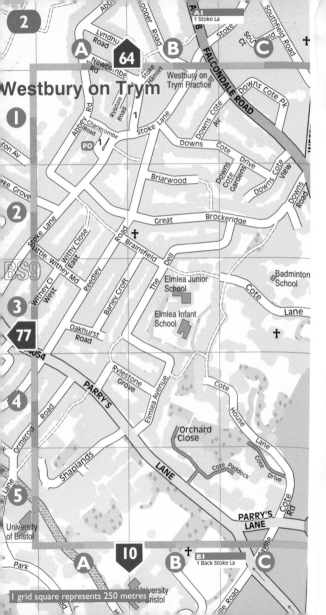

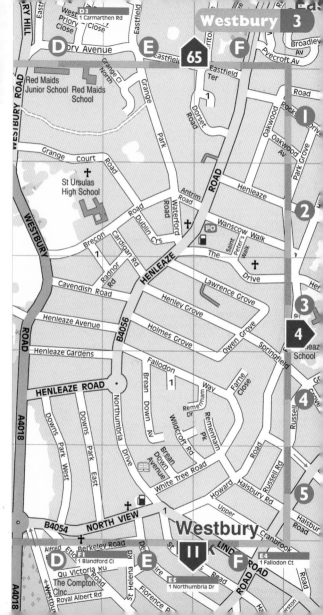

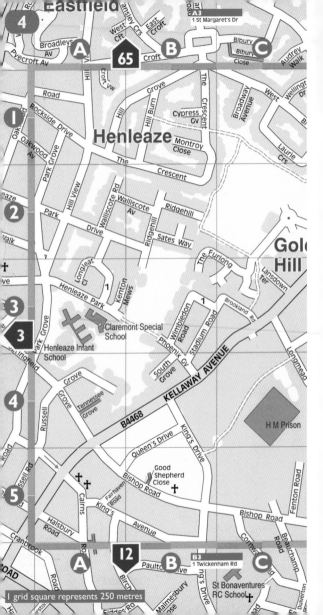

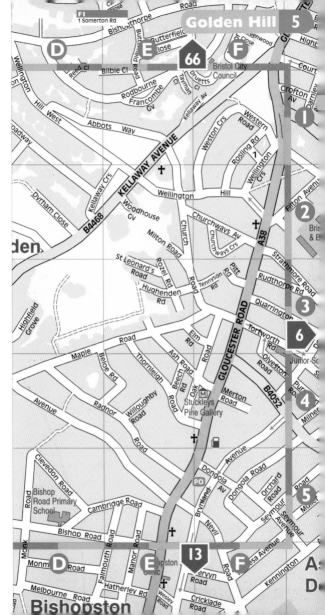

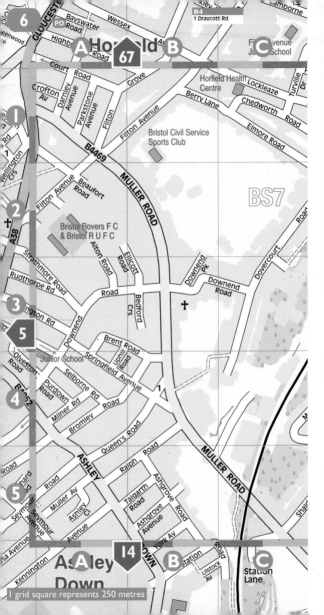

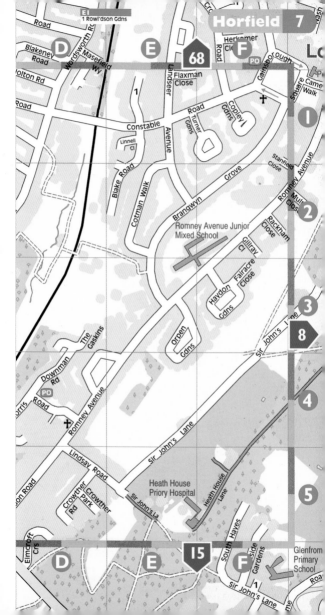

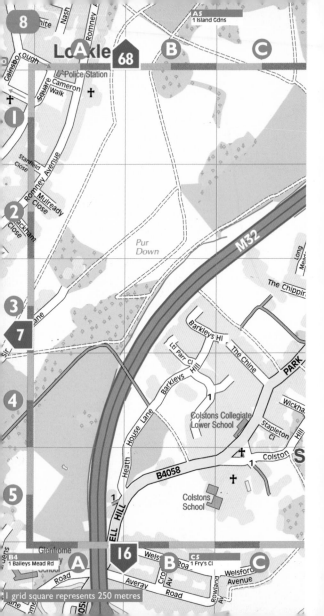

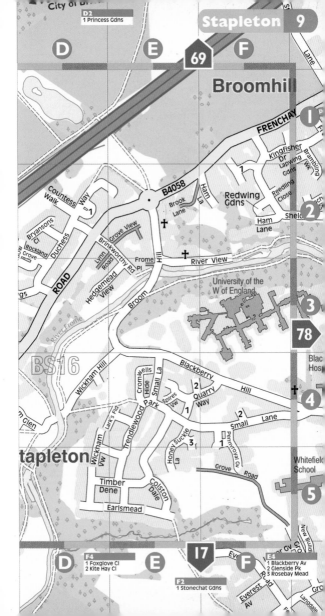

City of Br...

D2
1 Princess Gdns

D

E

F

69

Broomhill

FRENCHAY

I

Kingfisher Dr
Lapwing Gdns
Reedling Close
Brambling Wk

2

Redwing Gdns

Sheld...

Ham Lane

Countess Walk

Way

B4058

Brook Lane

Ham La

Bryansons Cl

Rockland

Grove

Duchess

Grove View

Brinkworthy Rd

Lynn Road Pl

Frome H...

River View

ROAD

Hedgemead View

Broom

University of the
W of England

River Frome

3

78

BS 16

Wickham Hill

Cromwells Hide

Small La

Blackberry

Blac
Hos

m Glen

Spires Vw

Park

2
Quarry Way

1

Hill

4

Lark's Fld

Trendlewood

Honey Suckle La

3

2

Small

2

Lane

1

Pennyroyal Gv

tapleton

Wickham Vw

Timber Dene

Colston Dale

Grove

Road

Whitefield
School

5

Earlsmead

New Build...

D

F4
1 Foxglove Cl
2 Kite Hay Cl

E

17

F

F2
1 Stonechat Gdns

EV...

...or Gv

E4
1 Blackberry Av
2 Glenside Pk
3 Rosebay Mead

Everest Av

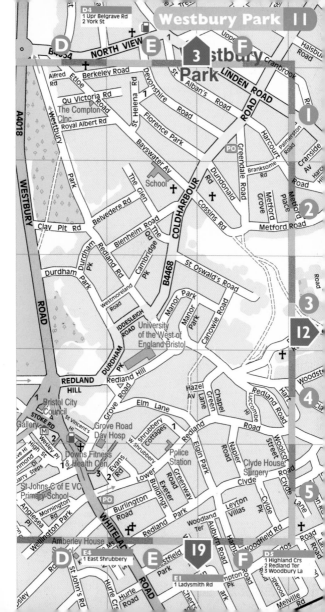

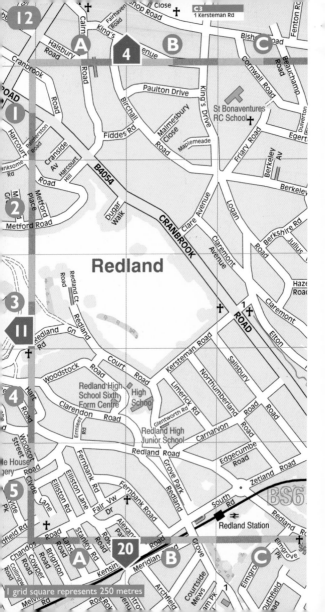

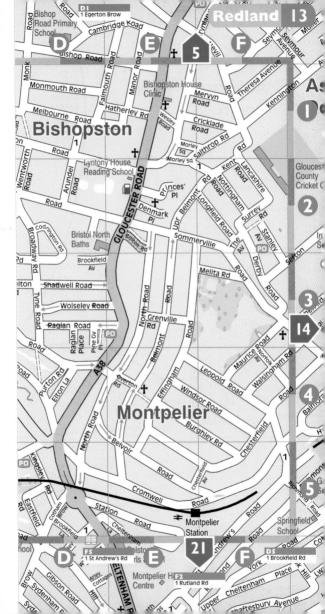

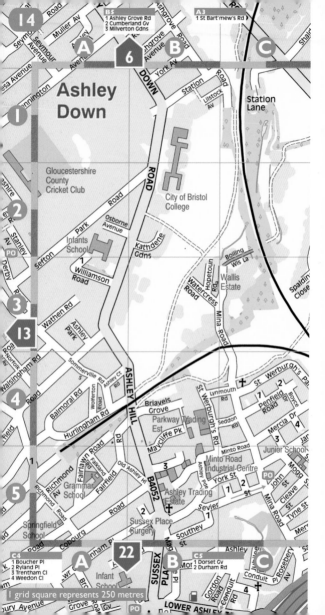

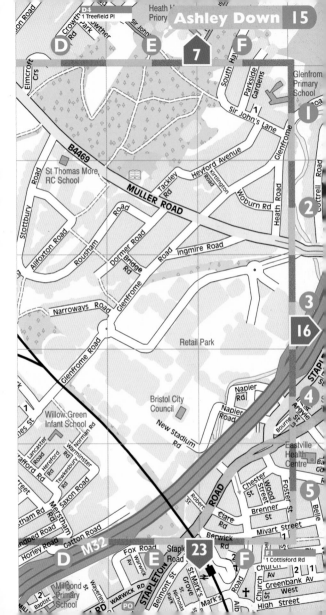

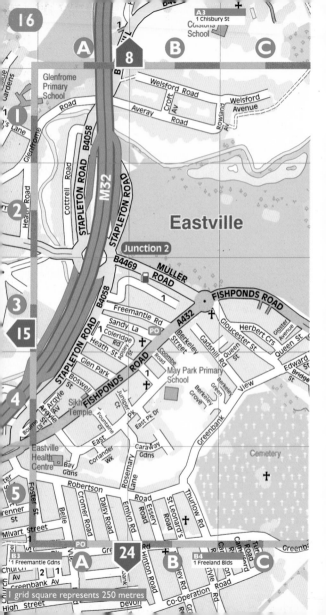

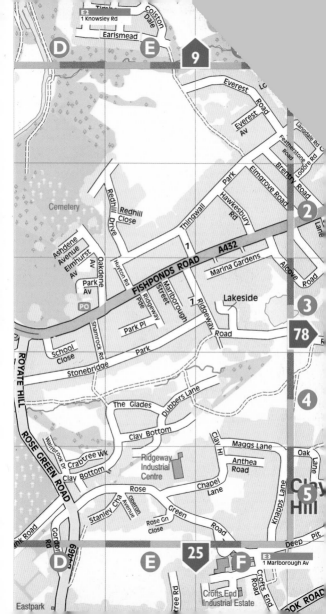

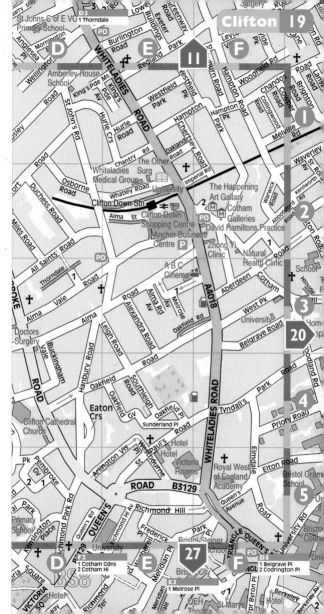

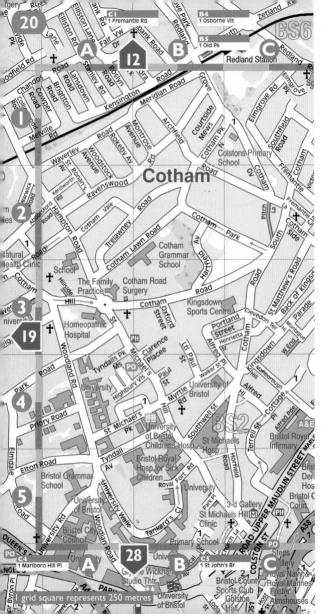

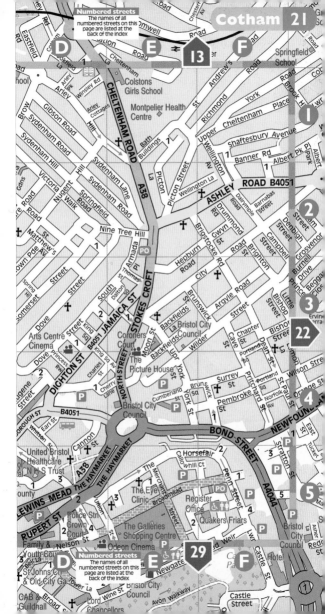

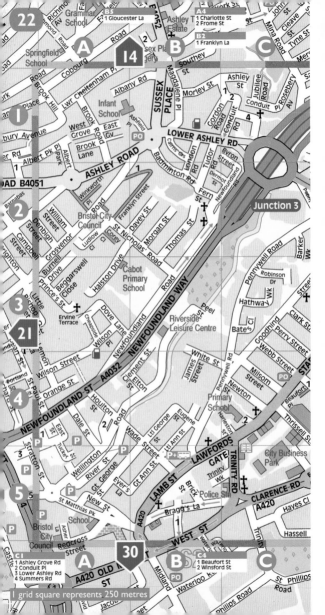

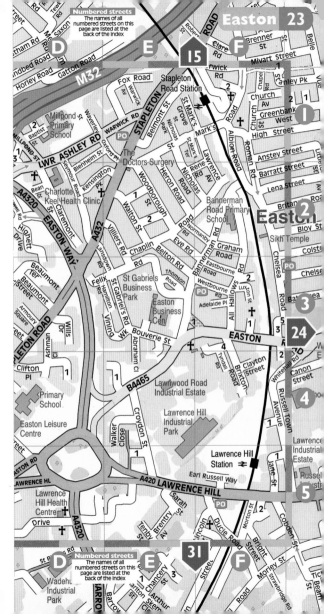

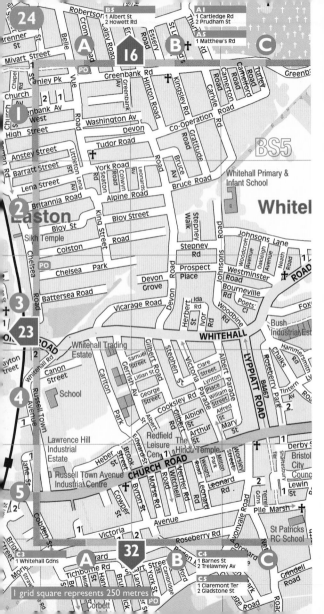

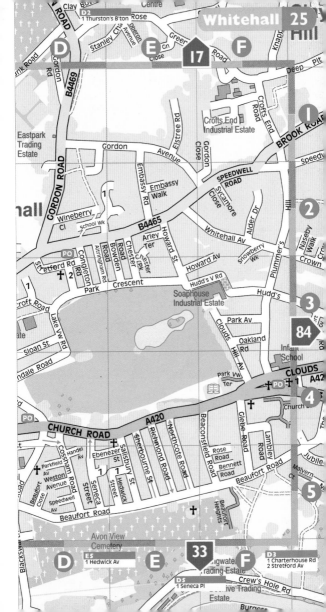

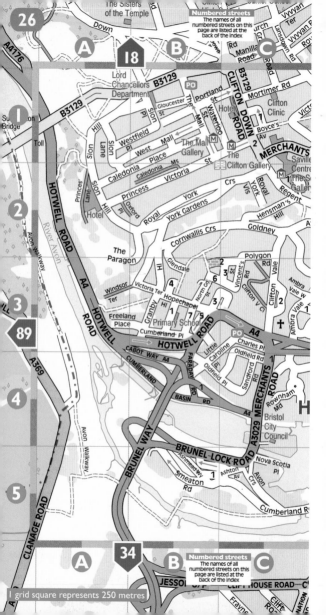

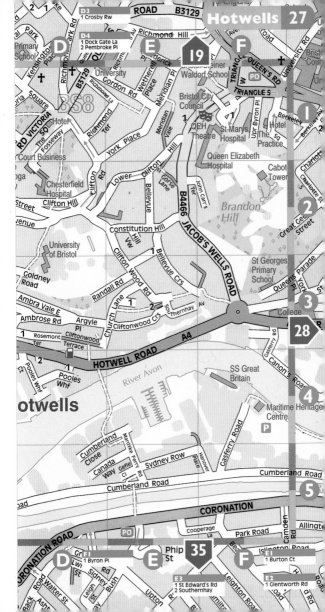

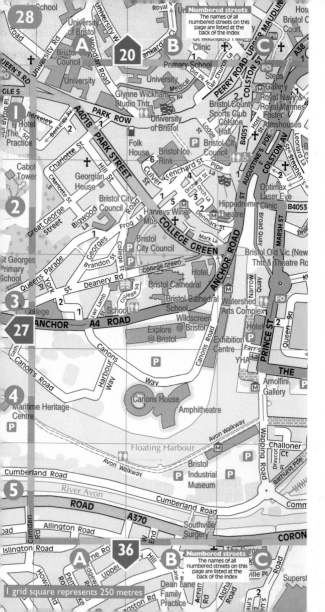

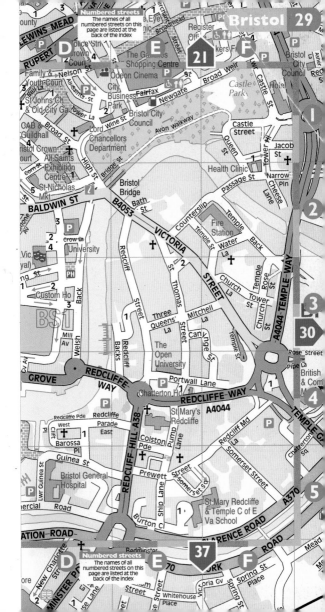

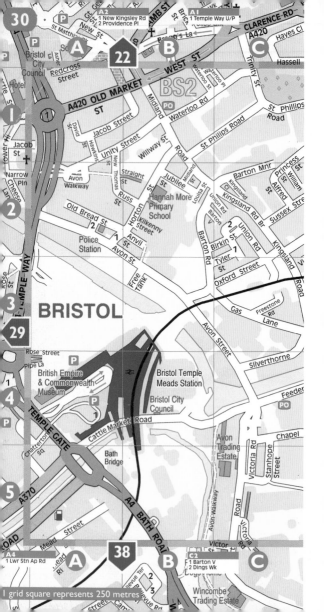

BRISTOL

Bristol Temple Meads Station

Bristol City Council

British Empire & Commonwealth Museum

Hannah More Primary School

Police Station

Avon Trading Estate

Wincombe Trading Estate

Bath Bridge

BS2

1 grid square represents 250 metres

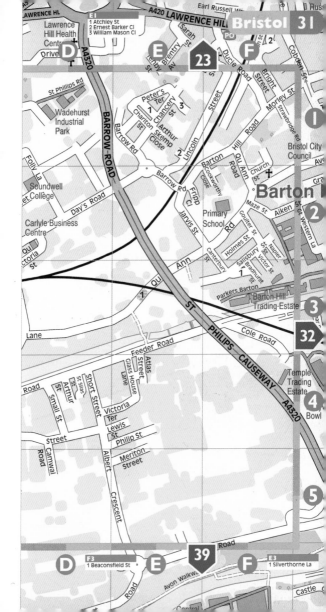

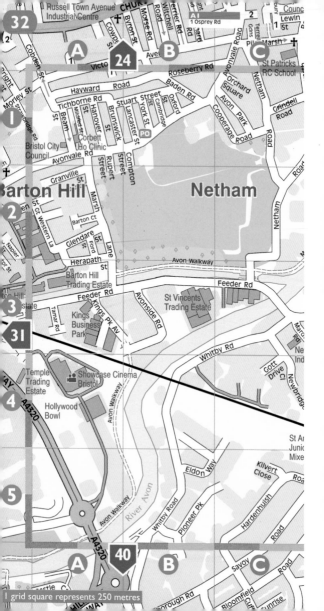

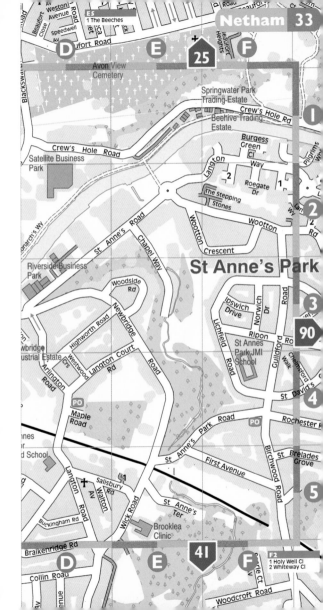

Avon View Cemetery

Springwater Park Trading Estate

Crew's Hole Rd

Beehive Trading Estate

Satellite Business Park

Crew's Hole Road

Burgess Green Cl

Langton Way

Roegate Dr

The Stepping Stones

Wootton

Wootton Crescent

St Anne's Road

Chapel Way

St Anne's Park

Riverside Business Park

Woodside Rd

Newbridge

Ipswich Drive

Norwich Dr

Ripon Rd

St Annes Park JMI School

Lichfield Road

Guildford Rd

Chelmsford Walk

St David's

Highworth Road

Langton Court Rd

Newbridge Industrial Estate

Westwood Crs

Arlington Road

Road

St Anne's Park Road

Rochester R

PO

Maple Road

First Avenue

Birchwood Road

St Brelades Grove

nnes or d School

Langton Road

Salisbury Rd

Walton Av

Wick Road

St Anne's Ter

Buckingham Rd

Brooklea Clinic

Braikenridge Rd

Collin Road

Woodcroft Road

D **E** **F**

I

2

3

90

4

5

41

D **E** **F**

F2
1 Holy Well Cl
2 Whiteway Cl

E5
1 The Beeches

Beaufort Close

Weston Av

Speedwell Av

Beaufort Road

Blackswarth

Monarch's Wy

Blackswarth Rd

Pilgrims

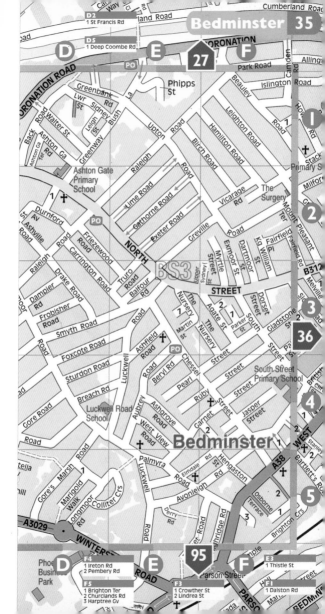

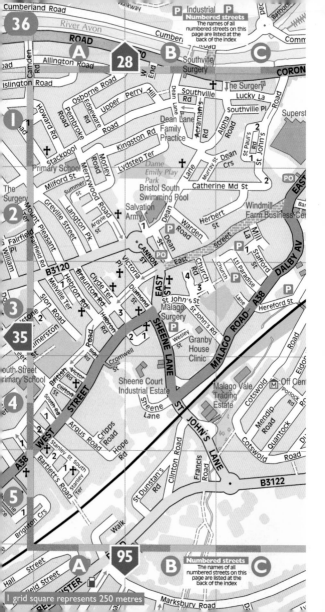

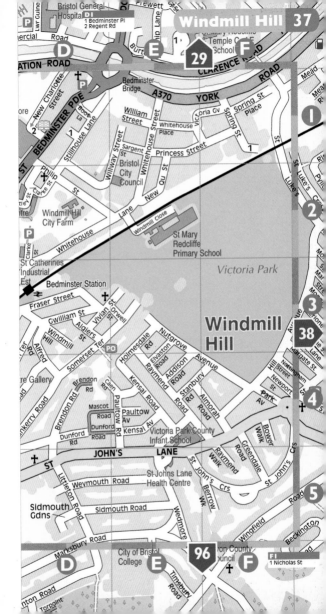

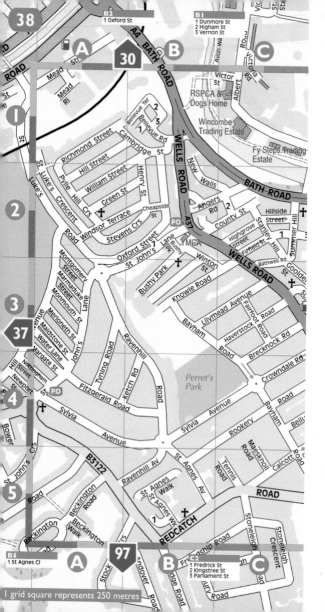

38

B2
1 Oxford St

B1
1 Dunmore St
2 Higham St
3 Vernon St

A **30** **B** **C**

ROAD
A4 BATH ROAD

Victor St
Albert
Victoria Rd

Mead St
Mead Rd

RSPCA & Dogs Home

Wincombe Trading Estate

Fy Steps Trading Estate

1

Bellevue Ter
Bellevue Rd
2
3

WELLS ROAD

New Walls

BATH ROAD

St Luke's
Richmond Street
Hill Street
Pyle Hill Crs
William Street
Cambridge St
Green St
Henry St
Windsor Terrace
Cheapside St
Stevens Crs

Angers Rd
County St
2
Highgrove Street
Hillside Street
Stanley Hill
Firfield St
1
Summer Hill

A37
PO
Oxford Street
St John's Lane
Bushy
YMCA
Winton St
Bathwell Rd
WELLS ROAD
Cooldge

Luke's Crescent
Road
Windsor Terrace

2

Bushy Park
Knowle Road

Montgomery Street
Marmaduke Street
Monmouth St
Merioneth St
Maidstone St
Water Lane
Margate St
St John's
Lane
Ravenhill Road

Lilymead Avenue
Bayham Road
Haverstock Road
Fairfoot Road
Brecknock Rd
Crowndale Rd

3
37

Perret's Park

Nottingham St
Newport St
PO
Fitzgerald Road
Ketch Rd
Tyning Road
Ravenhill Road

Sylvia Avenue

Sylvia Avenue
Rookery
Bayham Road
Belli'
Maesknoll Road
Calcott Road

4

Bower
St John's Crs
Road

5

B3122
Beckington Road
Beckington Walk
Ravenhill Av
St Agnes Walk
St Agnes WLK
7
St Agnes Av
Tennis Road
REDCATCH
ROAD
Stoneleigh
Stoneleigh Crescent

Beckington Walk

B5
1 St Agnes Cl

A **97** **B** **C**

C2
1 Fredrick St
2 Kingstree St
3 Parliament St

Stock
Andover Road
dge Road
ury Road

I grid square represents 250 metres

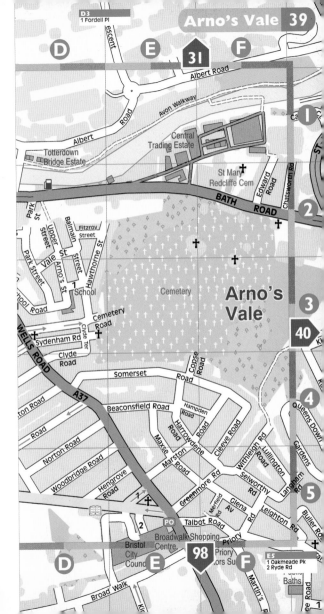

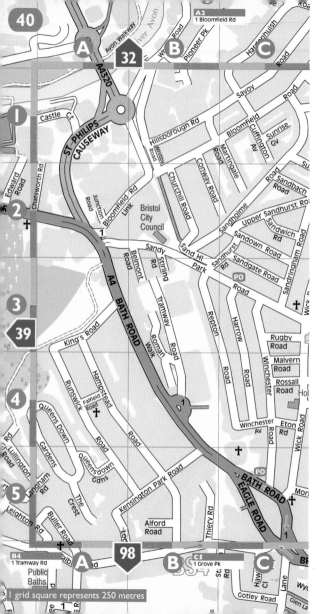

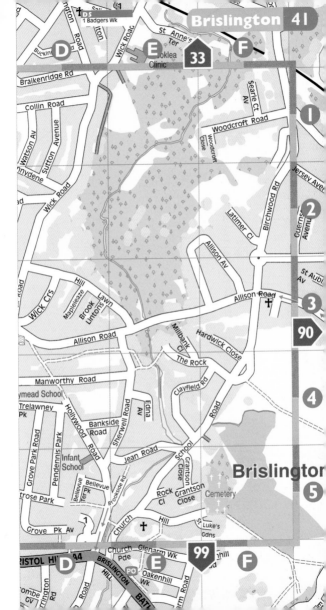

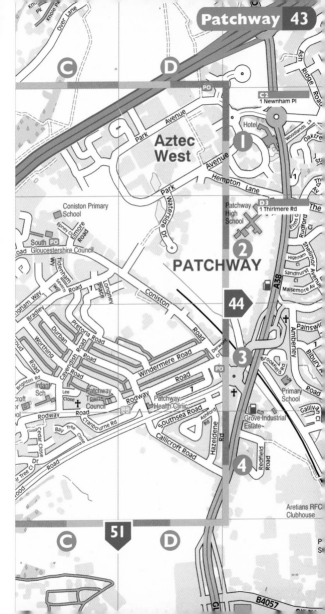

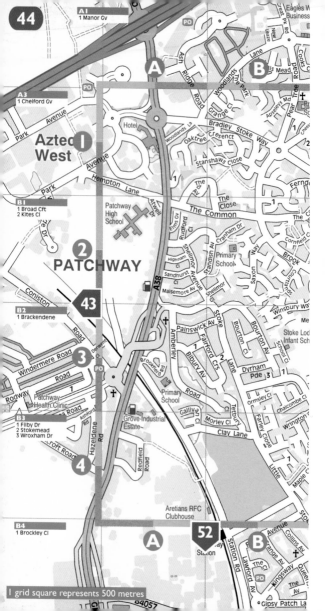

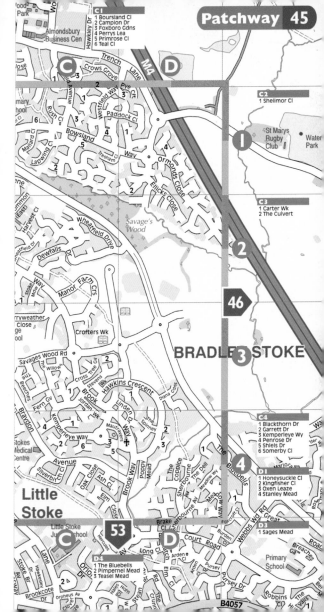

C1
1 Boursland Cl
2 Campion Dr
3 Foxboro Gdns
4 Perrys Lea
5 Primrose Cl
6 Teal Cl

C2
1 Shelimor Cl

St Marys Rugby Club • Water Park

C3
1 Carter Wk
2 The Culvert

46

BRADLEY STOKE

C4
1 Blackthorn Dr
2 Garrett Dr
3 Kemperleye Wy
4 Penrose Dr
5 Shiels Dr
6 Somerby Cl

D1
1 Honeysuckle Cl
2 Kingfisher Cl
3 Oxen Leaze
4 Stanley Mead

D2
1 Sages Mead

Little Stoke

53

D4
1 The Bluebells
2 Pimpernel Mead
3 Teasel Mead

B4057

Primary School

Almondsbury Business Cen
M4
Trench Lane
Crows Grove
Pye Cft
Westfield Way
Paddock Cl
Bowsland Way
Tresham
Ormonds Close
Ellicks Close
Savage's Wood
Wheatfield Drive
Dewfalls
Manor Farm Crs
Crofters Wk
Savages Wood Rd
Hawkins Crescent
Diana Cl
Linden Way
Kemperleye Way
Maufravers
Brook Way
Poppy Mead
Avenue
Oak Close
Ash Cl
Elm
Little Stoke Jun School
Court Road
Webbs Wd Rd
Pursey Dr

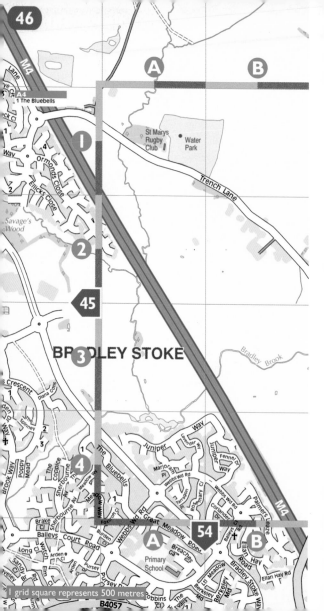

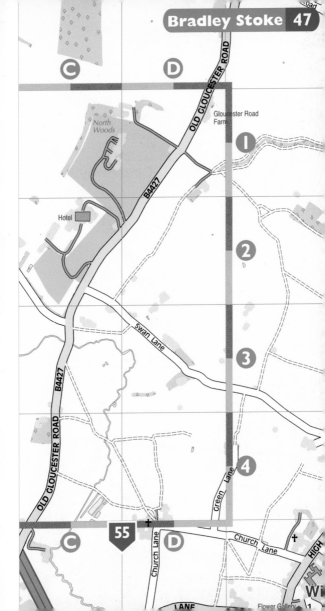

C D

OLD GLOUCESTER ROAD

Gloucester Road
Farm

North
Woods

1

B4427

Hotel

2

Swan Lane

3

B4427

OLD GLOUCESTER ROAD

Green Lane

4

55

C D

Church Lane

Church Lane

HIGH

Wi

Flower Gallery

LANE

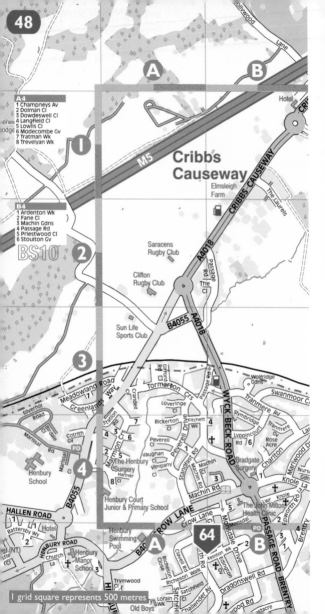

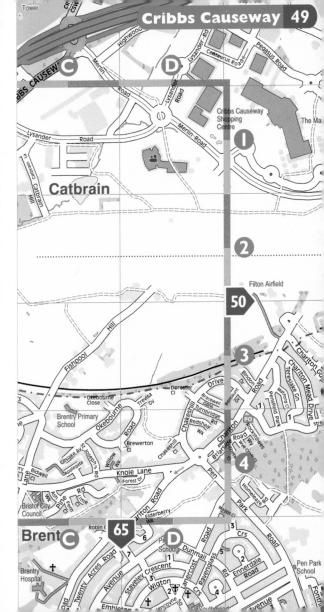

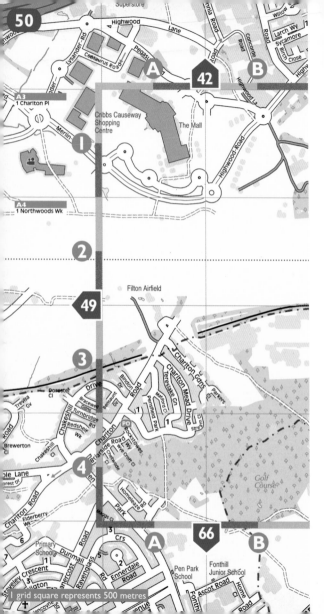

50

Superstore

Highwood Lane

Willow

Larch Wy

Sycamore

Birch Close

A **42** **B**

1 Charlton Pl **A3**

Cribbs Causeway Shopping Centre

The Mall

Merlin

Highwood Road

Highwood La

1

1 Northwoods Wk **A4**

2

Filton Airfield

49

Charlton Gdns

Charlton Mead Drive

Parkes

3

Drive

Dorset Cl

Bindon Dr

Trevisa Gv

Bracewell Gdns

Pleasant

Chakeshill Dr

Turnbridge Rd

Redshelf Wk

Charlton Rd

Teresake Cn

Mkt

Penfield Park

Penfield Park

Brewerton Cl

Chakeshill Cl

PO

Boxstowes

Briarside Road

Nye Croft Cl

Homestead Rd

Avon Croft Cl

D M Street

Golf Course

4

ole Lane

Forest Dr

Elderberry Wk

Park

Mogg St

Charlton Road

3

A **66** **B**

Primary School

Dunmail Road

Crs

Pen Park School

Fonthill Junior School

6

1

Ravenglass Rd

Ennerdale Road

Ascot Road

Staveley Crescent

Sedbergh

Fonthill

Home

1 grid square represents 500 metres

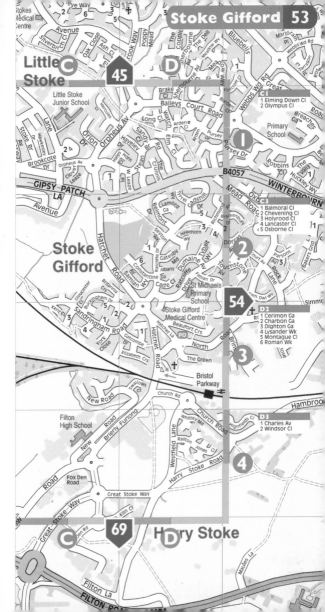

47

C   D

Old Gloucester R

Green Lane

Church Lane

†

Church Lane

†

HIGH S

R
S

I

Wi

Flower Gallery

1

Flax

LANE

BEACON

B4057

PO

M

Green

Bradstone

Dragon Rd

3

WINTERBOURNE HL

2

Cedar Wy

Harc

Dragon Road

56

Perry Cl

Mill Road

3

Quarry Barton

BRISTOL ROAD

Pye Corner

Hambrook Sports Club

Moorend

Whiteshill

†

Hambrook CE School

4

Worrel's Lane

WHITESHILL

OLD GLOUCESTER ROAD

Players Close

Sturden Lane

B4427

Road

71

C   D

M4

Hambrook

Gloucester Road

The Stream

de

Brom

Watley's End

BS36

Hicks Common

Doctors Surgery

Winterbourne Down

Kendleshire

Down Road

River Frome

Frome Valley Walkway

Frome Valley Walkway

Park Lane

Nightingale Close

Park La

Huckford La

A432

Coalsack Lane

Ruffet

BADMINTON ROAD

Cuckoo

Hill

Dingle

Frome Lane

The

End

2

North

Saint Francis Drive

St Francis Dr

Cloisters

Road

Manor

Factory Rd

Beaver Cl

The Gully

Sallys Ww

Masons Vw

Harris Barton

Frome Vw

Park La

Park Av

Park Lane

Wayside Cl

Medway Dr

Heather Av

Kelbra Cres

St Saviour's Rise

Beesley

Wood

1

2

3

4

C

D

C

73

D

M4

Iw Brook Rd

Ⓐ **Ⓑ**

B2
1 East St

❶

Docks

LC

King St

Richm

Napier St
Cliff St
Clifton

Meadow
St

Gloucester Rd

Bristol City
Council

Avo
Stat

❷

Sea Bank Road

River Road

❸

The Royal
Portbury Dock

Road

❹

Marsh La

St

Portbury Sawmills
Industrial Estate

Royal

Portbury

Marsh Lane

Redland Rd

Ⓐ **Ⓑ**

1 grid square represents 500 metres

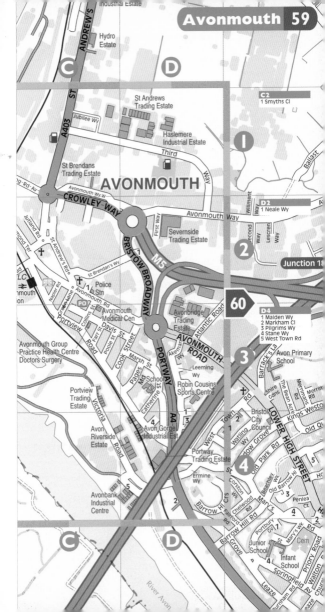

A4
1 Antona Ct
2 Antona Dr
3 Kilminster Rd
4 Orchard Crs
5 Penpole Cl

Haslemere
Industrial E

I

Third

BS11

Ballast

Lane

Kings Weston Lane

Junc

Willment
Way

Avonmouth Way

Fifth Wy

Fourth Way

Way

B3
1 Bangrove Wk
2 Humberstan Wk

First Wy

vonmouth Way

Severnside
Trading Estate

Second
Way

Lescren
Way

M5

RISTOW BROADW

2

Junction 18

59

B4
1 Broadleaze
2 Grainger Ct
3 Penpole Pk

Atlantic

AVONMOUTH
RD

3

Leeming
Wy

Avon Primary
School

Barrack's La

Shire
Gdns

Merrimans
Rd

Merrimans
Rd

Playford
Gdns

Windcliff Crs

Marsh St

Pages
Rd

School

Robin Cousins
Sports Centre

M5

The Bean Acres

Kings Weston Avenue

Old Quarry Rd

Nigel
Rd

Catherine

A4

Avon Gorge
Industrial Est

PORTWAY

West

Town
Wy

Bristol
City
Council

Old Quarry Road

Shirehampton

Watling
Wy

Meadow Grove

Old Park Rd

Home

Gnd

Portway
Estate

Ermine
Wy

Corston
Wy

Beachley
Wk

Old Barrow Hill

Penlea
Ct

Oaktree Ct

Per

Portway
School

Barrow

Barrow Hill Crs

Chetwood
Wk

Fairford
Rd

Mary's

The Hermitage

HIGH

Clifford Gdns

74

A

Portway
Gv

Mary's Wk

Junior
School

Cem

Priory
Rd

Health
Cen

B

Pembroke Rd

Penpole

PO

PAR

Park
Baths

Infant
School

Springfield

Walton Rd

Church Leaze

Priory

Bradley

Bradley Av

Primary
School

Avonwood

Woodwell

urnham Way

Av

St Bernard's

Road

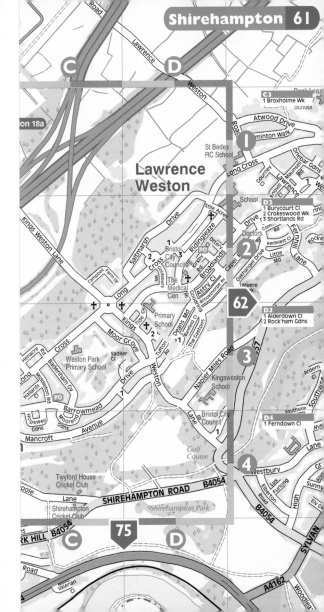

Road

Lawrence

Weston

Weston

C

D

C3
1 Broxholme Wk

Back Leaz

School

Atwood Drive

minton Walk

St Bedes
RC School

Long Cross

Courney
Cl

Knowll
Cl

Onebar Gdns

Lawrence

Rd

Hauesele

We

Rocky

I

on 18a

Kings Weston Lane

**Lawrence
Weston**

Drive

School

Drive

Doctors

D2
1 Burycourt Cl
2 Crokeswood Wk
3 Shortlands Rd

Fernhill

Lane

istle Acres

Ridinleaze

ottery

Capel Rd

Oakhanger Drive

Comm
Rd

Awdelett Cl

Little
Md

2

Saltmarsh

Long

Campbell Farm Dr

1

Bristol
City
Council

2

Cross

Goldsbury

PO

kwkby
3

Broadlands

Astry Cl

Brookmorde Rd

Gooding

**Meere
k**

62

Drive

The
Medical
Cen

Cross

Kings

Tilse Ove

Primary
School

Moor Gr ove

2

Deans Md

Banfield Cl

Tutton
Av

The Castors

D3
1 Alderdown Cl
2 Rock'ham Gdns

Ardern
Cl

Southvie

3

357

Napler Miles Road

Kingsweston
School

Henacre
Rd

Long

Baddenham Cv

Middleton Rd

Hallards Cl

Weston

Drive

Lane

Bristol City
Council

D4
1 Ferndown Cl

southside

Lane

Nys

PO

Hopewell
Gdns

Moorend
Gdns

Barrowmead

Avenue

7

Golf
Course

Westbury

Lux
Furlong

Elberton
Road

High

Gr

Sunny

Elv G

Mancroft

4

**Twyford House
Cricket Club**

Lane

SHIREHAMPTON ROAD B4054

Shirehampton Park

B4054

SYLVAN

pole

Shirehampton
Cricket Club

K HILL

B4054

75

C

D

Road

Valeran
Cl

A4162

Woodlea

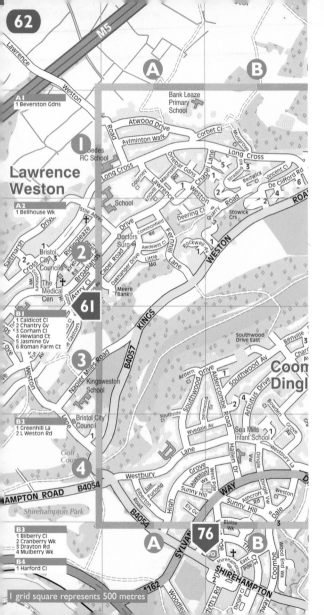

M5

Lawrence

Weston

A1
1 Beverston Gdns

Bank Leaze
Primary
School

Atwood Drive

Aviminton Walk

Corbet Cl

Long Cross

Musgrove

**Lawrence
Weston**

Bedes
RC School

Long Cross

Orlebar Gdns

Courtney

Chapel Lane

Knowle

Lawrence

Weston

Stradling

Redwick

Vincent Cl

De Clifford Rd

A2
1 Bellhouse Wk

Stile Acres

School

Maunsell

Road

Deering Cl

Quarry Road

Stowick
Crs

Ridingleaze

Drive

Doctors
Surg

Commonfield
Rd

Fernhill

WESTON

Saltmarsh

Cross

Bristol
City
Councils

Broadlands

Capel Road

Awdelett Cl

Oakhanger Drive

Little
Md

Rockwell Av

Lane

The
Medical
Cen

61

Meere
Bank

B1
1 Caldicot Cl
2 Chantry Gv
3 Corham Cl
4 Hewland Ct
5 Jasmine Gv
6 Roman Farm Ct

KINGS

B4057

Southwood
Drive East

Benville

3

Napier Miles Road

Kingsweston
School

Ardern

Southwood Drive

Abercombe Road

Southwood Av

Dentwood

Arbutus Drive

Bowden

Grove

**Coom
Dingl**

B2
1 Greenhill La
2 L Weston Rd

Bristol City
Council

Southside

Wyedale Av

Lane

Grove

Hallen Dr

Sea Mills
Infant School

Westbury La

Weston

Dingle

4

Golf
Cou

Westbury

West Dene

WAY

Sunny Hill

Ashcroft
Rd

Dingle Vw

Weston

Dale

HAMPTON ROAD   **B4054**

Shirehampton Park

High

Luke

Furlong

Elberton Road

B4054

Grove

Ely Gv

Sunny Hill

Blaise
Wk

B3
1 Bilberry Cl
2 Cranberry Wk
3 Drayton Rd
4 Mulberry Wk

B4
1 Harford Cl

SYLVAN

76

SHIREHAMPTON

The

East

Coombe

Wood End Wk

Avenue

A   **B**

Woodle

rth's Rd

Dingle

I grid square represents 500 metres

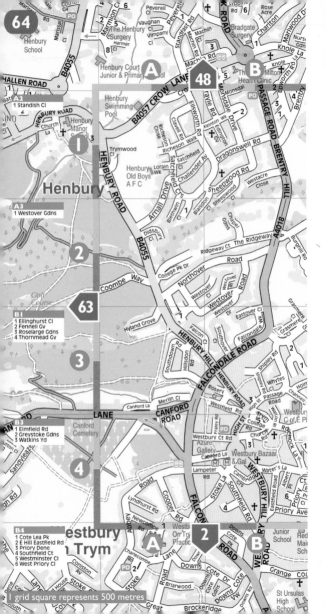

I grid square represents 500 metres

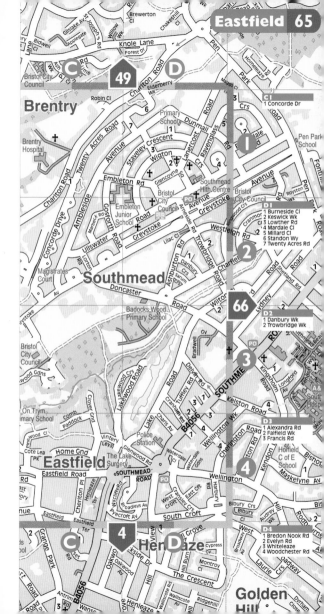

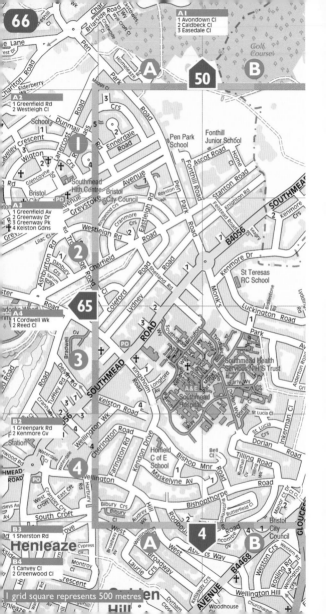

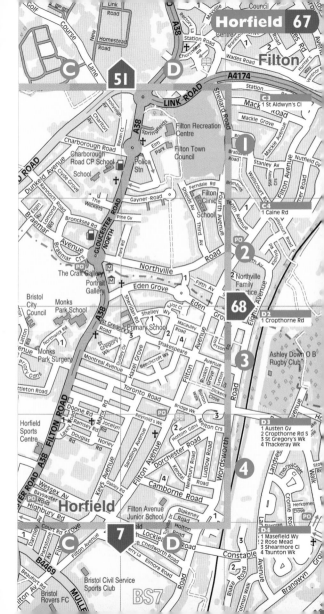

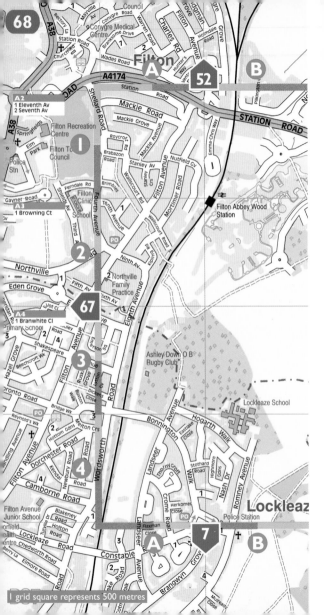

I grid square represents 500 metres

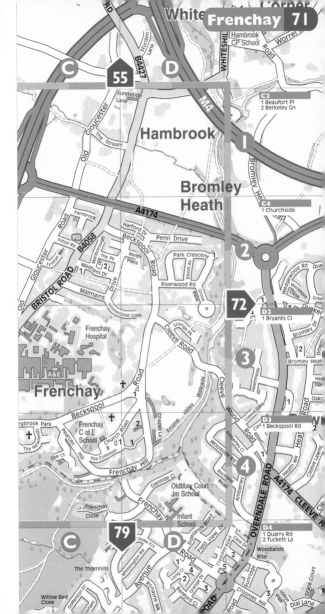

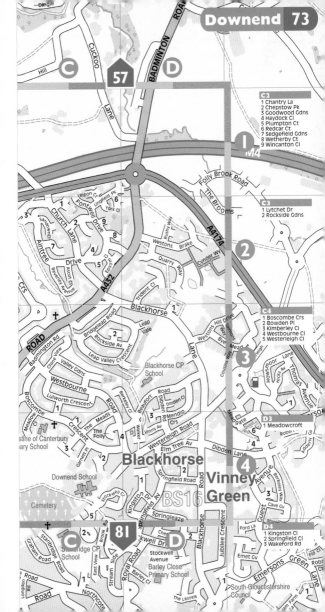

C
57
BADMINTON ROAD
D

C2
1 Chantry La
2 Chepstow Pk
3 Goodwood Gdns
4 Haydock Ct
5 Plumpton Ct
6 Redcar Ct
7 Sedgefield Gdns
8 Wetherby Ct
9 Wincanton Cl

I
M4

Folly Brook Road
The Brooms

C3
1 Lytchet Dr
2 Rockside Gdns

Church Lane
Fonthill Drive
Lingfield Pk
York Cl
Aintree Drive
Ascot Cl
Beverley Avenue
Westons Brake
Quarry Way
Cynder Wy
A4174
2

Trident Cl
Blackhorse
Leap Vale
Bridgeleap Road
Rockside Av
Leap Valley Crescent
Westons Hill Drive
Symonds
Bye Mead
Cousins Way

C4
1 Boscombe Crs
2 Bowden Pl
3 Kimberley Cl
4 Westbourne Cl
5 Westerleigh Cl

Howsmoor Lane
Hicks Av
Thomas Avenue
3

Badminton Rd
Chiltern View
Valley Gdns
Westbourne
Lulworth Crescent
Berkeley Cl
Beaufort
Road
Dibden Cl
Dibden Rd

Blackhorse CP
School

ROAD
Boscombe
Crescent
Meadow
The Meads
The Folly
Garnett's Pl
Walter
Vinny Av
Mendip
Crs
Westerleigh Road
Elm Tree Av

D3
1 Meadowcroft

Meadgate
Dibden Lane
4

Downend School

Cemetery

Blackhorse
BS16
Springfield Road
Springfield
Springleaze
Vinney
Green
Cave Gv
Guest Avenue
Berkeley Way
Ford La

D4
1 Kingston Cl
2 Springfield Cl
3 Wakeford Rd

C
81
D
Stanbridge CP
School
Stanbridge Road
Graham Road
East View
Stream Side
Brook
Royal Road
Barley
Northcote
The Laurels
Stockwell Dr
Cherry
Stockwell
Avenue
Barley Close
Primary School
Jubilee Crescent
Blackhorse Crescent
Emet Gv
Emersons Green
Emersons Green Lane
South-Gloucestershire
Council

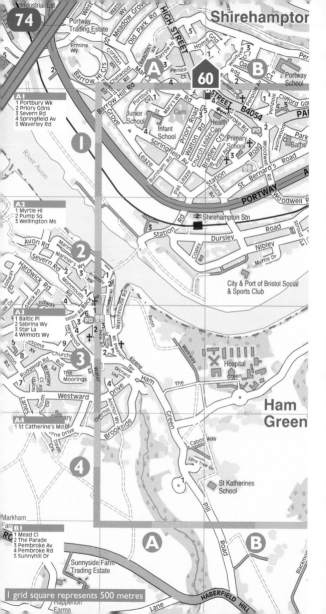

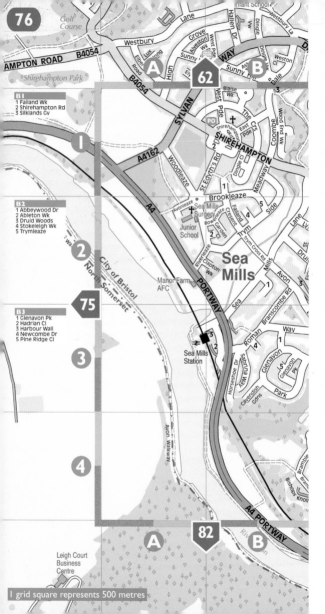

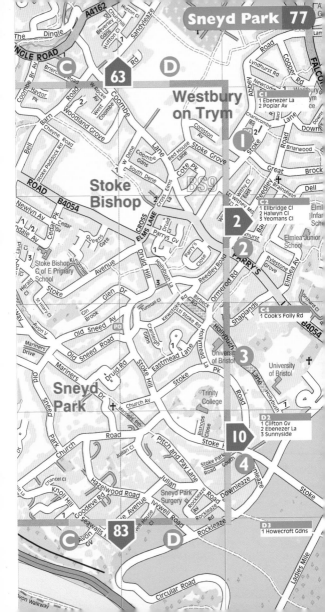

78

70

A1
1 Curlew Cl
2 Lapwing Gdns
3 Ronald Rd
4 Whinchat Gdns
5 Witherlies Rd

A3
1 Adelaide Pl
2 Albert Ter
3 Featherstone Rd
4 Langdale Rd
5 Wharf Rd

A4
1 Balaclava Rd
2 Drummond Rd
3 Halstock Av
4 Lodore Rd
5 Midland Ter
6 Stoke View Rd

B2
1 Claverham Rd
2 College Av
3 Guinea La

B3
1 Hinton La
2 Hockey's La

B4
1 Acton Rd
2 Ivy La
3 Justice Rd
4 Poplar Pl

Frenchay Village Museum **A**

PARK ROAD

Kynges Mill Cl

Clark Dr **B**

Stanbury Av

Sterncourt Rd

Pendleton Grove

FRENCHAY

Nuthatch Drive

Wren Drive

Nuthatch Gardens

PO

Alberton Road

Bragbrook Lane

Brockworth Cres

Frome Valley Road

Driflease Road

Begbrook Dr

Brambling Walk

Sheldrake Drive

Ham La

Brook La

Stonebridge Gdns

River View

Begbrook Primary School

Perrymans Close

9

2

Fromeside Clinic

Blackberry Hill Hospital

Blackberry Hill

Small La

Quarry Wy

Small Lane

Frenlelwood Park

Ismea

Cuckoo La

Road

Fishponds

College Road

University of the W of England

College House

Elfin Rd

Infant School

Oldbury Court Road

Victoria Park

Manor Road

Snowdon Road

Pound Dr

Pound La

N Devon Rd

Eastbury

Lambrook Road

3

Everest Road

Everest Av

Whitefield Fishponds School

New Buildings

Snowdon Close

Channon's Hill

Courtney Rd

Guinea La

Beechwood

PO

Coronation Av

Brook

Dr Bells C of E School

Station Road

New Station Road

Graeme Cl

17

4

ONDS

Elm

Brentry Road

Grove Road

Stoke View Business Park

PO

B4048

Lwr Station Rd

Ernest Wlk

Dunkirk Rd

Station Way

station Way

Parnall Road

Parnall Road Industrial Estate

Ridgeway

Redhill Cl

Thingwall

Park

84

Lodge Causeway Trading Estate

Balaclava Industrial Estate

Dominion Road

Ridgeway Road

Vera Road

Avon Business Park

Goodneston Road

Mendip View Avenue

Primary School

Abingdon Road

Enfield Road

Honiton Rd

Rowan Close

Cla **A** **Hill**

Clay Hill

Maggs La

Anthea Rd

Oak

Tiverton Wlk

Dorlands Rd

Atlas Close

B

Mayfield Park North

Mayfield Park South

Holly Lodge Road

Ridgeway Industrial Centre

WHITEFIELD ROAD

1 grid square represents 500 metres

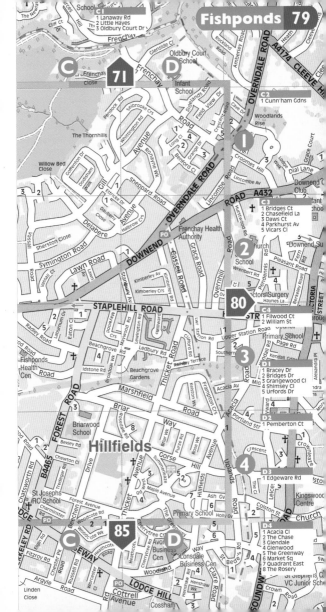

72

B

A1
1 Chestnut Rd
2 Conifer Cl
3 Edmund Cl

A2
1 Christchurch Av
2 Christchurch La
3 Downend Pk Rd
4 Nelson Rd
5 Tyler's La

I

A3
1 Alexandra Cl
2 Kensington Rd
3 Nelson Rd
4 North Vw
5 Pendennis Av

2

79

A4
1 Beazer Cl
2 Colston Cl
3 Leicester Sq
4 Portland Pl
5 Wesley Cl

B1
1 Buckingham Pl
2 Westerleigh Rd
3 Woodlands

3

B2
1 Clarence Gdns
2 Heathcote Rd

4

B3
1 Byron Pl
2 Eastleigh Cl
3 Fiennes Cl
4 Irving Cl
5 James Cl
6 Saunders Rd
7 Shipnran Ct
8 Teewell Cl

Staple Hill

Soundwell

86

B

B4
1 Gladstone Dr
2 Gloucester Rd
3 St Stephens Cl
4 Wiltshire Pl
5 Woodchester

1 grid square represents 500 metres

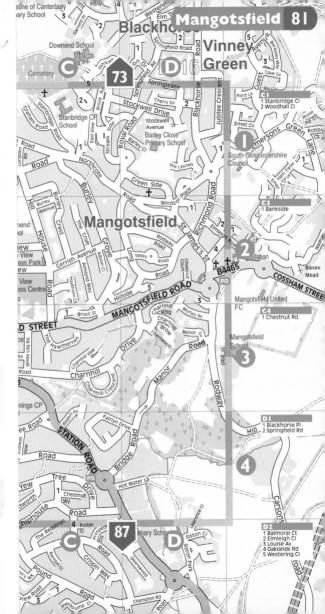

A

76

B

A4 PORTWAY

River Avon

Leigh Court
Business
Centre

I

2

Church
Rd

Church Rd

Church Road

Monarch's Way

3

Abbots
Leigh

Monarch's Way

The Mnr Cl

A369

Home Farm Road

4

Manor
House

ABBOTS

Ashgrove Av

LEIGH

Clifton
College
Sports Club

Valley Rd

ROAD

BS8

A

88

B

B312

Upper
Farm

Leigh

Cumm Park
Rugby Club

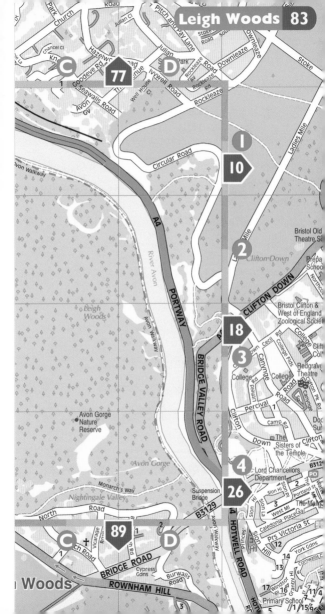

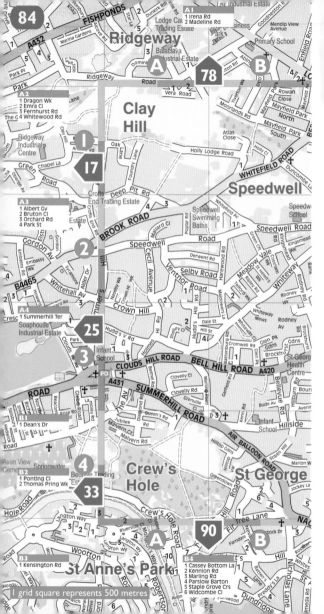

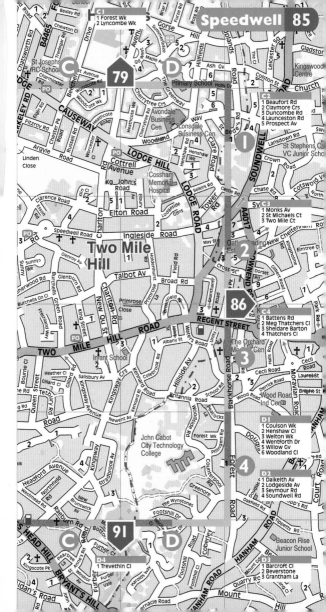

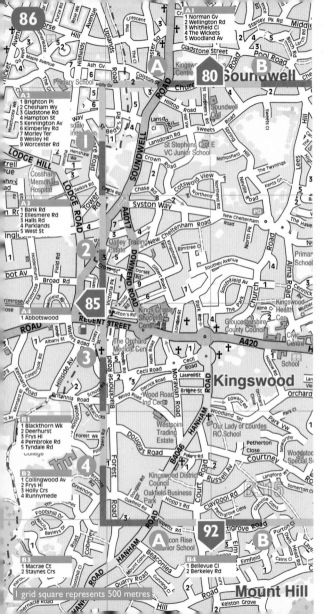

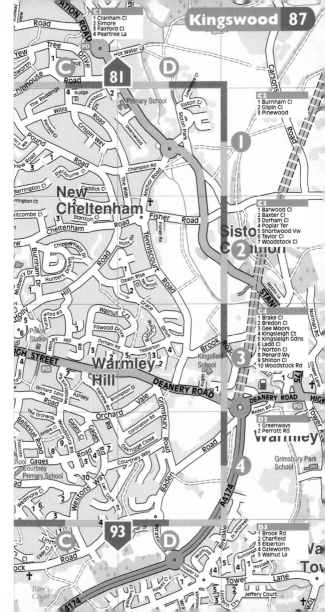

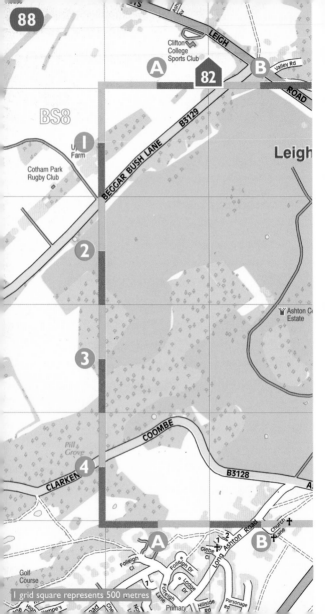

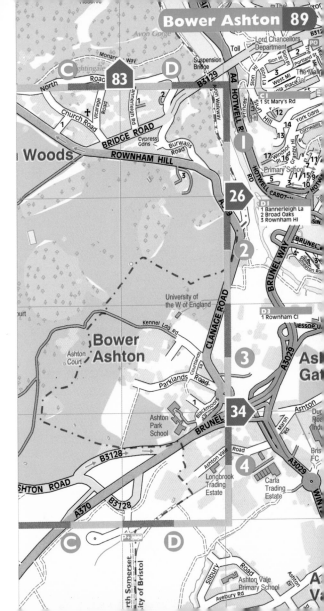

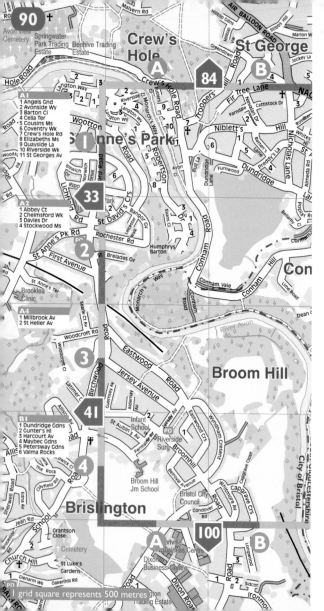

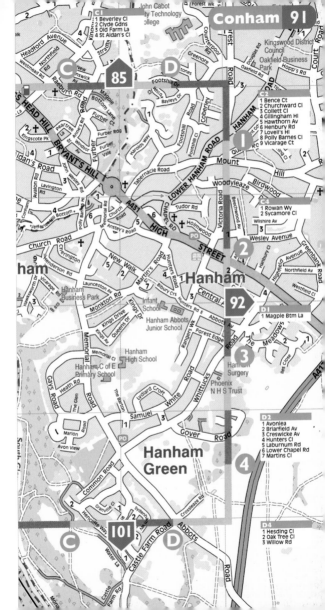

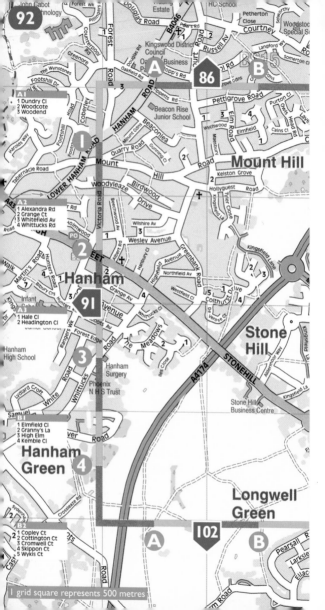

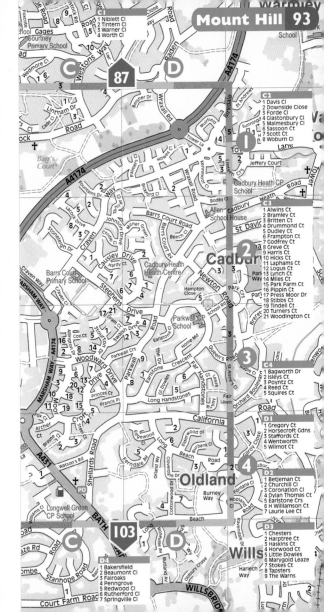

C1
1 Niblett Cl
2 Tintern Cl
3 Warner Cl
4 Worth Cl

87

C2
1 Davis Cl
2 Downside Close
3 Forde Cl
4 Glastonbury Cl
5 Malmesbury Cl
6 Sassoon Ct
7 Scott Ct
8 Woburn Cl

Cadbury Heath CP School

Cadbury
1 Alwins Ct
2 Bramley Ct
3 Britten Ct
4 Drummond Ct
5 Dudley Ct
6 Frampton Ct
7 Godfrey Ct
8 Greve Ct
9 Harris Ct
10 Hicks Ct
11 Laphams Ct
12 Logus Ct
13 Lynch Ct
14 Miles Ct
15 Park Farm Ct
16 Pippin Ct
17 Press Moor Dr
18 Stibbs Ct
19 Tindell Ct
20 Turners Ct
21 Woodington Ct

C4
1 Bagworth Dr
2 Isleys Ct
3 Poyntz Ct
4 Reed Ct
5 Squires Ct

D1
1 Gregory Ct
2 Horsecroft Gdns
3 Staffords Ct
4 Wentworth
5 Wilmot Ct

D2
1 Betjeman Ct
2 Churchill Cl
3 Coronation Av
4 Dylan Thomas Ct
5 Earlstone Crs
6 H Williamson Ct
7 Laurie Lee Ct

D3
1 Chesters
2 Harptree Ct
3 Haskins Ct
4 Little Dowies
5 Margold Leaze
6 Stokes Ct
7 Tapsters
8 The Warns

Oldland

Wills

103

C4
1 Bakersfield
2 Beaumont Cl
3 Fairoaks
4 Penngrove
5 Redwood Cl
6 Rutherford Cl
7 Springville Cl

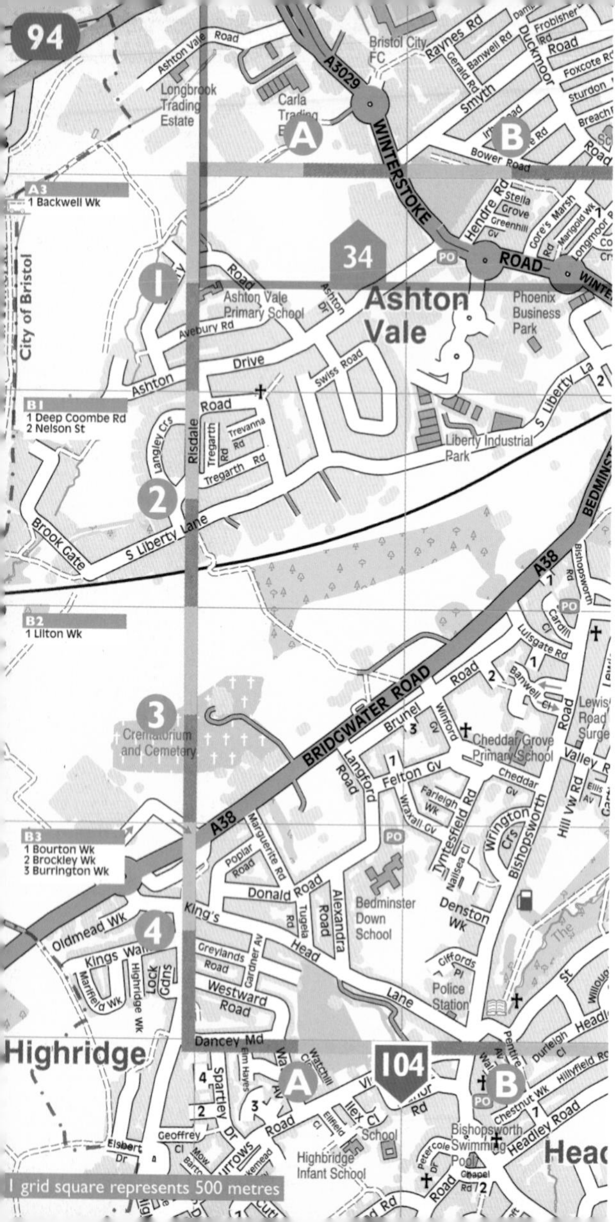
Ashton Vale Road
Longbrook Trading Estate
Carla Trading Estate
Bristol City FC
A3029
Raynes Rd
Gerald Rd
Banwell Rd
Duckmoor Road
Frobisher Rd
Foxcote Rd
Sturdon
Smyth
Bower Road
Winterstoke Road
A3
1 Backwell Wk
City of Bristol
34
Hendre Rd
Stella Grove
Greenhill Gv
Gore's Marsh Rd
Marigold Wk
Longmoor
PO
Ashton Vale
Ashton Vale Primary School
Ashton Dr
Phoenix Business Park
Avebury Rd
Ashton Drive
Swiss Road
B1
1 Deep Coombe Rd
2 Nelson St
Risdale Road
Langley Crs
Tregarth Rd
Trevanna Rd
S Liberty La
Liberty Industrial Park
Brook Gate
S Liberty Lane
B2
1 Lilton Wk
Bishopsworth Rd
Cardill Cl
Luisgate Rd
A38
Bridgwater Road
Bedminster
Crematorium and Cemetery
Banwell Cl
Lewis Road Surgery
Brunel Road
Winford Gv
Cheddar Grove Primary School
Langford Road
Felton Gv
Farleigh Wk
Wraxall Gv
Tyntesfield Rd
Cheddar Gv
Wrington Crs
Bishopsworth
Valley Rd
Hill Vw Rd
Ellis Av
B3
1 Bourton Wk
2 Brockley Wk
3 Burrington Wk
Marguerite Rd
Poplar Road
Donald Road
Alexandra Road
Tugela Rd
Bedminster Down School
Nailsea Cl
Denston Wk
King's Head Lane
Oldmead Wk
Kings Wk
Marfield Wk
Highridge Wk
Lock Gdns
Greylands Road
Gardner Av
Westward Road
Giffords Pl
Police Station
St
Headley
Durleigh Cl
Pentire Av
Dancey Md
Highridge
Elm Hayes
Watchill
104
Spartley Dr
Ilex Cl
School
Hillyfield Rd
Chestnut Wk
Headley Road
Geoffrey Cl
Elsbert Dr
Ellfield Cl
Highbridge Infant School
Bishopsworth Swimming Pool
Petercole Dr
Chapel Rd
Head
1 grid square represents 500 metres

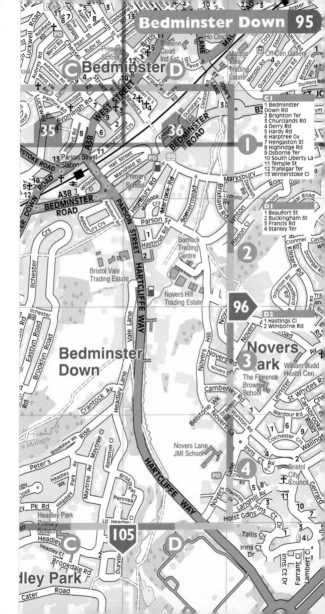

Bedminster C D

35 36

Bedminster Road I

C1
1 Bedminster Down Rd
2 Brighton Ter
3 Churclands Rd
4 Derry Rd
5 Hardy Rd
6 Harptree Gv
7 Hengaston St
8 Highridge Rd
9 Osborne Ter
10 South Liberty La
11 Temple St
12 Trafalgar Ter
13 Winterstoke Cl

D1
1 Beaufort St
2 Buckingham St
3 Francis Rd
4 Stanley Ter

2

96
D2
1 Hastings Cl
2 Wimborne Rd

Novers Park 3

The Florence Brown School

William Budd Health Cen

Bristol City Council

4

Bedminster Down

Bristol Vale Trading Estate

Novers Hill Trading Estate

Barnack Trading Centre

Novers Lane JMI School

Headley Park Primary School

105

Headley Park C D

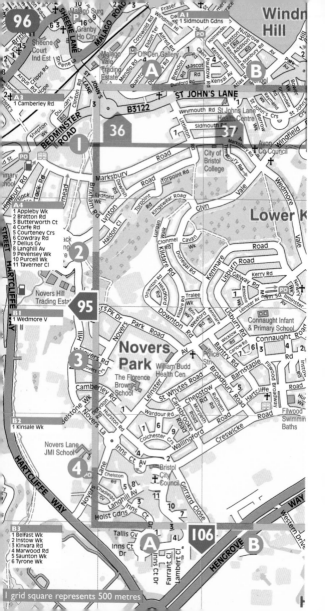

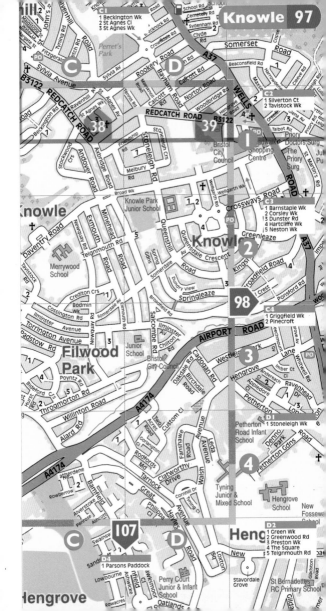

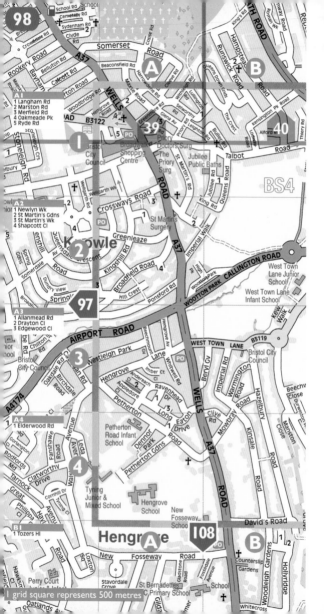

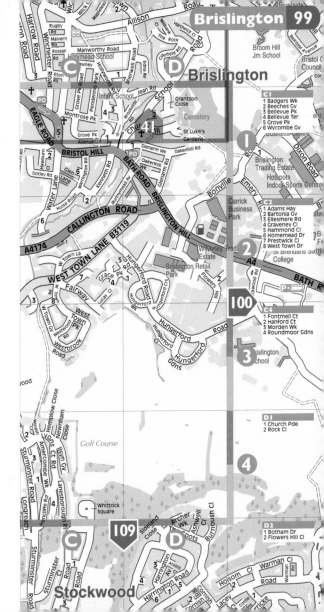

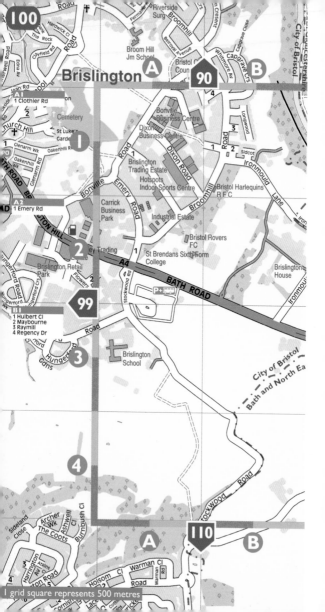

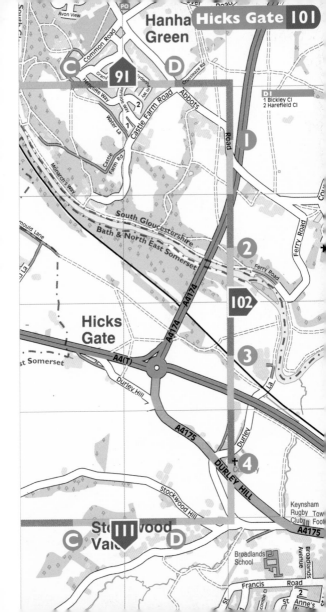

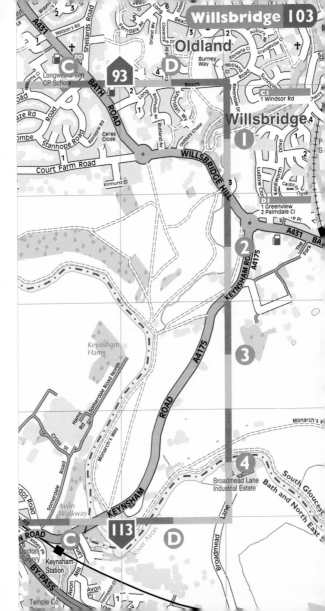

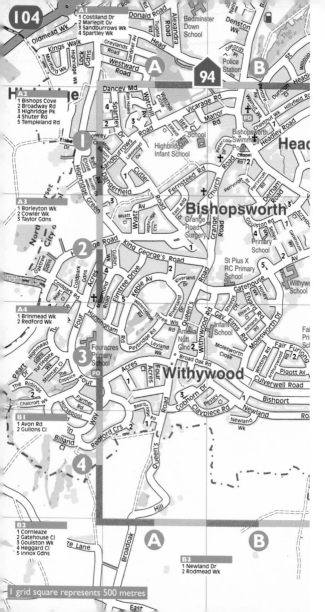

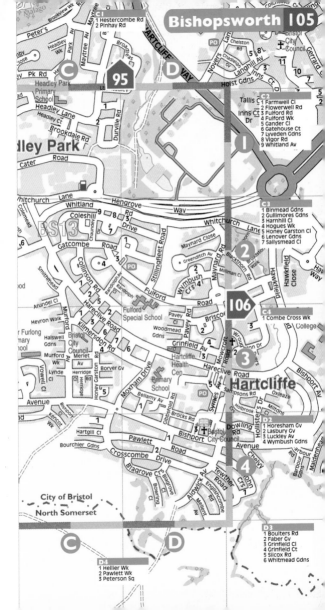

Bishopsworth 105

C1
1 Hestercombe Rd
2 Pinhay Rd

C2
1 Farmwell Cl
2 Flowerwell Rd
3 Fulford Rd
4 Fulford Wk
5 Gander Cl
6 Gatehouse Ct
7 Lyveden Gdns
8 Vigor Rd
9 Whitland Av

C3
1 Binmead Gdns
2 Gullimores Gdns
3 Harnhill Cl
4 Hogues Wk
5 Honey Garston Cl
6 Lenover Gdns
7 Sallysmead Cl

C4
1 Combe Cross Wk

D2
1 Horesham Gv
2 Lasbury Gv
3 Luckley Av
4 Wymbush Gdns

D3
1 Boulters Rd
2 Faber Gv
3 Grinfield Cl
4 Grinfield Ct
5 Silcox Rd
6 Whitmead Gdns

D4
1 Hellier Wk
2 Pawlett Wk
3 Peterson Sq

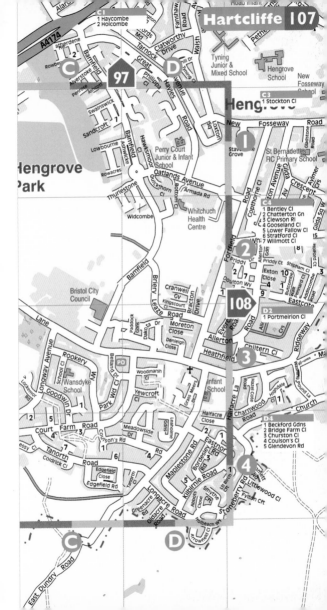

C1
1 Haycombe
2 Holcombe

A4174

Tyning Junior & Mixed School

Hengrove School

New Fosseway School

97

C

D

C3
1 Stockton Cl

Heng.ove

New Fosseway Road

Stavenine Grove

St Bernadettes RC Primary School

Perry Court Junior & Infant School

Oatlands Avenue

Armada Rd

Whitchurch Health Centre

Hengrove Park

C4
1 Bentley Cl
2 Chatterton Gn
3 Clewson Rl
4 Gooseland Cl
5 Lower Fallow Cl
6 Stratford Cl
7 Willmott Cl

2

Priddy

Exton Close

Doulton Wy

108

Bristol City Council

cranwell Gv

Kingscourt

Moreton Close

Denleigh Close

Eastcote

D2
1 Portmeirion Cl

3

Allerton

Heathfield

Chiltern Cl

Ridgeway

Rookery

PO

Woodmarsh

Infant School

Halfacre Close

Halfacre Road

Charnwood Road

Church

Wansdyke School

Yewcroft Cl

D4
1 Beckford Gdns
2 Bridge Farm Cl
3 Churston Cl
4 Coulson's Cl
5 Glendevon Rd

Court Farm Road

Tanorth Road

Edgefield Close

Edgefield Rd

4

Maplestone Rd

Kilmindle Road

Longacre Road

Stonebery Rd

Littlewood Cl

C

D

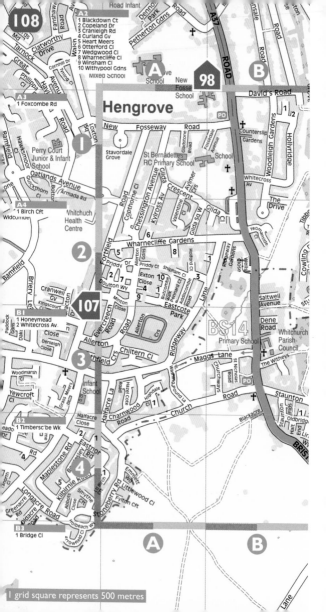

108

98

107

Hengrove

1 grid square represents 500 metres

A2
1 Blackdown Ct
2 Copeland Dr
3 Cranleigh Rd
4 Curland Gv
5 Heart Meers
6 Oterford Cl
7 Wedgwood Cl
8 Wharncliffe Cl
9 Winsham Cl
10 Withypool Gdns

A3
1 Foxcombe Rd

A4
1 Birch Cft

B1
1 Honeymead
2 Whitecross Av.

B2
1 Timbersc'be Wk

B3
1 Bridge Cl

Perry Court Junior & Infant School

Whitchurch Health Centre

Stavordale Grove

St Bernadettes RC Primary School

Eastcote Park

Dene Road

Whitchurch Parish Council

BS14

Mixed School

New Fosse School

New Fosseway Road

David's Road

Countership Gardens

Woodleigh Gardens

Hollyridge

Whitecross Av

The Drive

Saltwell Avenue

Allerton Crs

Infant School

Church Road

Staunton

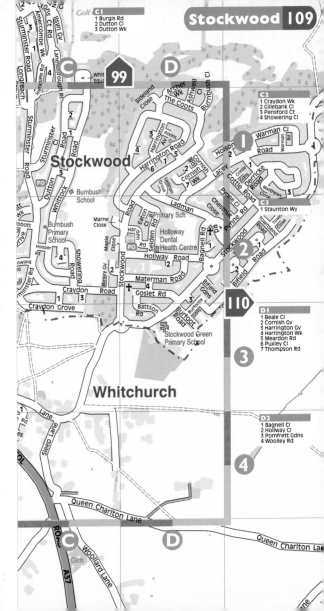

Golf **C1**
1 Burgis Rd
2 Dutton Cl
3 Dutton Wk

99

C2
1 Craydon Wk
2 Gillebank Cl
3 Pensford Ct
4 Showering Cl

Stockwood

Burnbush School

C3
1 Staunton Wy

Burnbush Primary School

Primary Sch

Holloway Dental Health Centre

Ladman Road

Craydon Road

Craydon Grove

Goslet Rd

Battson Rd

Stockwood Green Primary School

110

Whitchurch

D1
1 Beale Cl
2 Cornish Gv
3 Harrington Gv
4 Harrington Wk
5 Meardon Rd
6 Puxley Cl
7 Thompson Rd

3

D2
1 Bagnell Cl
2 Hollway Cl
3 Pomfrett Gdns
4 Woolley Rd

4

Queen Charlton Lane

Queen Charlton La

Woollard Lane

Cem

A37

Sleep Lane

Cemetery

OURLEY HILL

Keynsham
Rugby Town
Club Foot

101

Stockwood
Vale

C

D

Dog Hill

Sto

D3
1 Acacia Ct
2 Cherry Tree Cl

5

Broadlands
School

Broadlands
Avenue

St Ladi

1

Francis Road

St Anne's
Avenue

2

Mendip Close

Whitcombe Cl

Welcombe Grove

St George's Rd

Park
Close

Wheathill
Close

Ashurst Rd

Charlton

Charlton

Heathfield
Close

Staple Grove

Westfield
Close

Keynsham
Co Primary
School

2

Lays Drive

Caernarvon Road

Tennyson Close

Ludlow Close

Barnard
Walk

Kelston
Road

Road

Lays
Farm

Lincoln
Close

Kenilworth Cl

Durham Grove

Tenby Rd

Berk

112

PO

Fairleigh

Caroline

Warwick Road

Keens

3

Norfolk
Grove

Norton Close

Richmond Rd

Longmeadow
Walk

Birch Cl

2

Maple
Close

Coronation

Willow
Walk

Newlands Rd

1

Holmoak Road

Cedar Dr

Oak Tree
Wk

Holly Wk

Bramble

Castle
School

Walnut
Close

4

Queen
Charlton

C

D

Lane

Parkhouse

Road

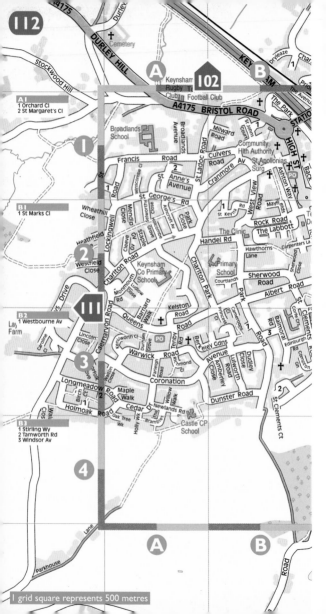

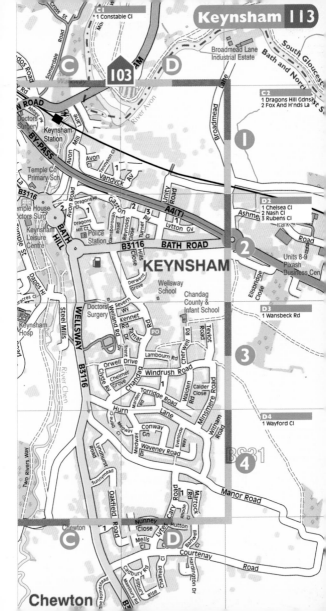

Arno's Vale	39 F3	Kendleshire	57 D4
Ashley Down	14 A1	Keynsham	113 D2
Ashton Gate	34 B2	Kingswood	86 B3
Ashton Vale	34 A5	Knowle	97 D2
Avonmouth	59 C1	Lawrence Weston	61 C1
Aztec West	43 D1	Leigh Woods	88 B1
Barton Hill	31 F2	Little Stoke	45 C4
Bedminster	35 E4	Lockleaze	68 B4
Bedminster Down	95 C3	Longwell Green	92 B4
Bishopston	13 D1	Lower Knowle	96 B2
Bishopsworth	104 A2	Mangotsfield	81 C2
Blackhorse	73 C4	Montpelier	13 E4
Blaise Hamlet	63 C1	Moorend	72 B1
Bower Ashton	89 C3	Mount Hill	92 B1
Bradley Stoke	45 D3	Netham	32 B2
Brentry	65 C1	New Cheltenham	87 C2
Brislington	41 F5	Novers Park	96 A3
Bristol	30 A3	Oldland	93 D4
Bromley Heath	71 D1	Over	42 A1
Broomhill	9 F1	Patchway	43 D2
Broom Hill	90 B3	Pye Corner	56 A4
Cadbury Heath	93 D2	Redland	12 A3
Catbrain	49 C1	Ridgeway	78 A4
Clay Hill	84 A1	St Anne's Park	33 E3
Clifton	18 C4	St George	84 B4
Conham	90 B2	Sea Mills	76 B2
Coombe Dingle	62 B3	Shirehampton	60 B4
Cotham	20 B2	Siston Common	87 C3
Crew's Hole	84 A4	Sneyd Park	77 C3
Cribbs Causeway	48 A1	Somerdale	102 B4
Downend	72 A4	Soundwell	80 B4
Eastfield	65 C4	Southmead	65 C2
Easton	23 F2	Speedwell	84 B1
Eastville	16 B2	Staple Hill	80 B3
Filton	52 A4	Stapleton	8 C5
Filwood Park	97 C3	Stockwood	109 C1
Fishponds	78 A2	Stockwood Vale	111 C1
Frenchay	71 C3	Stoke Bishop	77 C1
Golden Hill	4 C2	Stoke Gifford	53 C2
Great Stoke	54 B2	Stone Hill	92 B3
Hambrook	71 D1	Two Mile Hill	85 C2
Ham Green	74 B3	Vinney Green	73 D4
Hanham	91 D2	Warmley Hill	87 C3
Hanham Green	91 D4	Westbury on Trym	77 D1
Harry Stoke	69 D1	Westbury Park	3 E5
Hartcliffe	106 A3	Whitchurch	109 C1
Headley Park	104 B1	Whitehall	24 C2
Henbury	63 D1	Whiteshill	55 D4
Hengrove	107 D1	Windmill Hill	37 F3
Hengrove Park	106 B1	Winterbourne	56 A1
Henleaze	4 A1	Winterbourne Down	57 C3
Hicks Gate	101 C3	Withywood	104 A3
Hillfields	79 C4		
Horfield	67 C4		
Hotwells	26 C4		

USING THE STREET INDEX

Street names are listed alphabetically. Each street name is followed by its postal
town or area locality, the Postcode District, the page number, and the reference
to the square in which the name is found.

Example: **Abbey Ct** *BRSG/KWL/STAPK* BS4 ....**90** A2 🔟

Some entries are followed by a number in a blue box. This number indicates the
location of the street within the referenced grid square. The full street name is
listed at the side of the map page.

GENERAL ABBREVIATIONS

ACC	ACCESS	FM	FARM
ALY	ALLEY	FT	FORT
AP	APPROACH	FWY	FREEWAY
AR	ARCADE	FY	FERRY
ASS	ASSOCIATION	GA	GATE
AV	AVENUE	GAL	GALLERY
BCH	BEACH	GDN	GARDEN
BLDS	BUILDINGS	GDNS	GARDENS
BND	BEND	GLD	GLADE
BNK	BANK	GLN	GLEN
BR	BRIDGE	GN	GREEN
BRK	BROOK	GND	GROUND
BTM	BOTTOM	GRA	GRANGE
BUS	BUSINESS	GRG	GARAGE
BVD	BOULEVARD	GT	GREAT
BY	BYPASS	GTWY	GATEWAY
CATH	CATHEDRAL	GV	GROVE
CEM	CEMETERY	HGR	HIGHER
CEN	CENTRE	HL	HILL
CFT	CROFT	HLS	HILLS
CH	CHURCH	HO	HOUSE
CHA	CHASE	HOL	HOLLOW
CHYD	CHURCHYARD	HOSP	HOSPITAL
CIR	CIRCLE	HRB	HARBOUR
CIRC	CIRCUS	HTH	HEATH
CL	CLOSE	HTS	HEIGHTS
CLFS	CLIFFS	HVN	HAVEN
CMP	CAMP	HWY	HIGHWAY
CNR	CORNER	IMP	IMPERIAL
CO	COUNTY	IN	INLET
COLL	COLLEGE	IND EST	INDUSTRIAL ESTATE
COM	COMMON	INF	INFIRMARY
COMM	COMMISSION	INFO	INFORMATION
CON	CONVENT	INT	INTERCHANGE
COT	COTTAGE	IS	ISLAND
COTS	COTTAGES	JCT	JUNCTION
CP	CAPE	JTY	JETTY
CPS	COPSE	KG	KING
CR	CREEK	KNL	KNOLL
CREM	CREMATORIUM	L	LAKE
CRS	CRESCENT	LA	LANE
CSWY	CAUSEWAY	LDG	LODGE
CT	COURT	LGT	LIGHT
CTRL	CENTRAL	LK	LOCK
CTS	COURTS	LKS	LAKES
CTYD	COURTYARD	LNDG	LANDING
CUTT	CUTTINGS	LTL	LITTLE
CV	COVE	LWR	LOWER
CYN	CANYON	MAG	MAGISTRATE
DEPT	DEPARTMENT	MAN	MANSIONS
DL	DALE	MD	MEAD
DM	DAM	MDW	MEADOWS
DR	DRIVE	MEM	MEMORIAL
DRO	DROVE	MKT	MARKET
DRY	DRIVEWAY	MKTS	MARKETS
DWGS	DWELLINGS	ML	MALL
E	EAST	ML	MILL
EMB	EMBANKMENT	MNR	MANOR
EMBY	EMBASSY	MS	MEWS
ESP	ESPLANADE	MSN	MISSION
EST	ESTATE	MT	MOUNT
EX	EXCHANGE	MTN	MOUNTAIN
EXPY	EXPRESSWAY	MTS	MOUNTAINS
EXT	EXTENSION	MUS	MUSEUM
F/O	FLYOVER	MWY	MOTORWAY
FC	FOOTBALL CLUB	N	NORTH
FK	FORK	NE	NORTH EAST
FLD	FIELD	NW	NORTH WEST
FLDS	FIELDS	O/P	OVERPASS
FLS	FALLS	OFF	OFFICE
FLS	FLATS	ORCH	ORCHARD

OV	OVAL
PAL	PALACE
PAS	PASSAGE
PAV	PAVILION
PDE	PARADE
PH	PUBLIC HOUSE
PK	PARK
PKWY	PARKWAY
PL	PLACE
PLN	PLAIN
PLNS	PLAINS
PLZ	PLAZA
POL	POLICE STATION
PR	PRINCE
PREC	PRECINCT
PREP	PREPARATORY
PRIM	PRIMARY
PROM	PROMENADE
PRS	PRINCESS
PRT	PORT
PT	POINT
PTH	PATH
PZ	PIAZZA
QD	QUADRANT
QU	QUEEN
QY	QUAY
R.	RIVER
RBT	ROUNDABOUT
RD	ROAD
RDG	RIDGE
REP	REPUBLIC
RES	RESERVOIR
RFC	RUGBY FOOTBALL CLUB
RI	RISE
RP	RAMP
RW	ROW
S	SOUTH
SCH	SCHOOL
SE	SOUTH EAST
SER	SERVICE AREA
SH	SHORE
SHOP	SHOPPING
SKWY	SKYWAY
SMT	SUMMIT
SOC	SOCIETY
SP	SPUR
SPR	SPRING
SQ	SQUARE
ST	STREET
STN	STATION
STR	STREAM
STRD	STRAND
SW	SOUTH WEST
TDG	TRADING
TER	TERRACE
THWY	THROUGHWAY
TNL	TUNNEL
TOLL	TOLLWAY
TPK	TURNPIKE
TR	TRACK
TRL	TRAIL
TWR	TOWER
U/P	UNDERPASS
UNI	UNIVERSITY
UPR	UPPER
V	VALE
VA	VALLEY
VIAD	VIADUCT
VIL	VILLA
VIS	VISTA
VLG	VILLAGE
VLS	VILLAS
VW	VIEW
W	WEST
WD	WOOD
WHF	WHARF
WK	WALK
WKS	WALKS
WLS	WELLS
WY	WAY
YD	YARD
YHA	YOUTH HOSTEL

POSTCODE TOWNS AND AREA ABBREVIATIONS

ALMDB	Almondsbury
AVONM	Avonmouth
BMSTR	Bedminster
BMSTRD/HC/WWD	Bedminster Down/Hartcliffe/Withywood
BRSG/KWL/STAPK	Brislington/Knowle/St Anne's Park
BRSTK/PCHW	Bradley Stoke/Patchway
CBRIS/FH	Central Bristol/Floating Harbour
CBRISNE	Central Bristol north and east
CFTN/FAIL	Clifton/Failand
EVILLE/WHL	Eastville/Whitehall
FRCTL/WBN	Frampton Cotterell/Winterbourne
HGRV/WHIT	Hengrove/Whitchurch
HNBRY/STHM	Henbury/Southmead
HNLZ/SM/SNYPK/WT	Henleaze/Sea Mills/Sneyd Park/Westbury-on-Trym
HORF/LLZ	Horfield/Lockleaze
KEYN	Keynsham
KGWD/HNM	Kingswood/Hanham
LGASH	Long Ashton
MANG/FISH	Mangotsfield/Fishponds
OLD/WMLY/WICK	Oldland/Warmley/Wick
PTSHD/EG	Portishead/Easton-in-Gordano
RDLND/MONT	Redland/Montpelier
THNB/SVB	Thornbury/Severn Beach

A

Abbey Ct *BRSG/KWL/STAPK* BS4 .... **90** A2 🔟
Abbeydale *FRCTL/WBN* BS36 .... **56** B1
Abbey Pk *KEYN* BS31 .... **113** C1
Abbey Rd *HNLZ/SM/SNYPK/WT* BS9 .... **2** A1
Abbeywood Dr
  HNLZ/SM/SNYPK/WT BS9 .... **76** B2 🔟
Abbots Av *KGWD/HNM* BS15 .... **91** D3
Abbots Cl *HGRV/WHIT* BS14 .... **107** D4
Abbotsford Rd *RDLND/MONT* BS6...... **19** F2
Abbots Leigh Rd *CFTN/FAIL* BS8 ...... **82** A4

Abbots Rd *KGWD/HNM* BS15 .... 101 D1
Abbots Wy *HNLZ/SM/SNYPK/WT* BS9 ... 5 D1
Abbotswood *KGWD/HNM* BS15 ...... 86 A4🔟
Aberdeen Rd *RDLND/MONT* BS6 ...... 19 F3
Abingdon Rd *MANG/FISH* BS16 .... 78 B4
Ableton Wk
  HNLZ/SM/SNYPK/WT BS9 .... 76 B2🔟
Abraham Cl *EVILLE/WHL* BS5 .... 23 E3
Acacia Av *MANG/FISH* BS16 .... 79 D3
Acacia Cl *MANG/FISH* BS16 .... 79 D4🔟
Acacia Ct *KEYN* BS31 .... 111 D3🔟
Acacia Rd *MANG/FISH* BS16 .... 80 A4
Acraman's Rd *BMSTR* BS3 .... 36 B1
Acresbush Cl
  BMSTRD/HC/WWD BS13 .... 104 B2
Acton Rd *MANG/FISH* BS16 .... 78 A4🔟
Adams Hay
  BRSG/KWL/STAPK BS4 .... 99 C2🔟
Addiscombe Rd *HGRV/WHIT* BS14 .... 108 A2
Addison Rd *BMSTR* BS3 .... 37 E4
Adelaide Pl *EVILLE/WHL* BS5 .... 23 F3
  MANG/FISH BS16 .... 78 A3🔟
Agate St *BMSTR* BS3 .... 35 F3
Aiken St *EVILLE/WHL* BS5 .... 31 F2
Aintree Dr *MANG/FISH* BS16 .... 73 C2
Air Balloon Rd *EVILLE/WHL* BS5 ...... 84 B4
Airport Rd *HGRV/WHIT* BS14 .... 97 D3
Akeman Wy *AVONM* BS11 .... 59 D3
Alard Rd *BRSG/KWL/STAPK* BS4 ...... 97 C4
Albany Ga *BRSTK/PCHW* BS34 .... 53 D2
Albany Rd *RDLND/MONT* BS6 .... 22 A1
Albany St *KGWD/HNM* BS15 .... 85 D3
Albemarle Rw *CFTN/FAIL* BS8 .... 26 B3🔟
Albert Crs *CBRISNE* BS2 .... 31 D5
Albert Gv *EVILLE/WHL* BS5 .... 84 A3🔟
Alberton Rd *MANG/FISH* BS16 .... 78 A1
Albert Pde *EVILLE/WHL* BS5 .... 24 B4
Albert Pk *RDLND/MONT* BS6 .... 22 A1
Albert Park Pl *RDLND/MONT* BS6 .... 21 F2
Albert Pl *HNLZ/SM/SNYPK/WT* BS9 .. 64 B4
Albert Rd *CBRISNE* BS2 .... 39 E1
  KEYN BS31 .... 112 B2🔟
  KGWD/HNM BS15 .... 92 A2
  MANG/FISH BS16 .... 80 B3
Albert St *EVILLE/WHL* BS5 .... 24 B5🔟
Albert Ter *MANG/FISH* BS16 .... 78 A3🔟
Albion Cl *MANG/FISH* BS16 .... 81 C2
Albion Rd *EVILLE/WHL* BS5 .... 23 F1
Albion St *EVILLE/WHL* BS5 .... 24 B5
Alcove Rd *MANG/FISH* BS16 .... 17 F3
Aldercombe Rd
  HNLZ/SM/SNYPK/WT BS9 .... 62 B3
Alderdown Cl *AVONM* BS11 .... 61 D3🔟
Alder Dr *EVILLE/WHL* BS5 .... 25 F2
Aldermoor Wy
  OLD/WMLY/WICK BS30 .... 92 B3
Aldernay Av *BRSG/KWL/STAPK* BS4 .. 90 A3
Alderton Rd *HORF/LLZ* BS7 .... 66 B3
Aldwick Av
  BMSTRD/HC/WWD BS13 .... 105 D4
Alexandra Cl *MANG/FISH* BS16 ...... 80 A3🔟
Alexandra Gdns *MANG/FISH* BS16 .. 80 A3
Alexandra Pk *MANG/FISH* BS16 ...... 78 A3🔟
  RDLND/MONT BS6 .... 12 A5
Alexandra Pl *MANG/FISH* BS16 ...... 80 A3🔟
Alexandra Rd
  BMSTRD/HC/WWD BS13 .... 94 A4
  CFTN/FAIL BS8 .... 19 E3
  HNBRY/STHM BS10 .... 65 D3🔟
  KGWD/HNM BS15 .... 92 A2🔟
Alford Rd *BRSG/KWL/STAPK* BS4 .... 40 B5
Alfred Hl *CBRISNE* BS2 .... 20 C4

Alfred Pde *CBRISNE* BS2 .... 20 C4
Alfred Pl *CBRISNE* BS2 .... 20 B3
Alfred Rd *BMSTR* BS3 .... 37 D3
  RDLND/MONT BS6 .... 11 D1
Alfred St *CBRISNE* BS2 .... 30 C2
  EVILLE/WHL BS5 .... 24 B4
Algiers St *BMSTR* BS3 .... 37 D3
Allanmead Rd *HGRV/WHIT* BS14 .... 98 A3🔟
Allerton Crs *HGRV/WHIT* BS14 ...... 108 A3
Allerton Gdns *HGRV/WHIT* BS14.... 108 A2
Allerton Rd *HGRV/WHIT* BS14........ 107 D3
Allfoxton Rd *HORF/LLZ* BS7 .... 15 D3
All Hallows Rd *EVILLE/WHL* BS5 ...... 23 F3
Allington Dr *OLD/WMLY/WICK* BS30 .. 93 C3
Allington Rd *BMSTR* BS3 .... 28 A5
Allison Av *BRSG/KWL/STAPK* BS4.... 41 F2
Allison Rd *BRSG/KWL/STAPK* BS4.... 41 D3
All Saints' La *CBRIS/FH* BS1 .... 29 D2🔟
All Saints' Rd *CFTN/FAIL* BS8 .... 19 D3
All Saints' St *CBRIS/FH* BS1 .... 29 D1
Alma Cl *KGWD/HNM* BS15 .... 86 B3
Alma Rd *CFTN/FAIL* BS8 .... 19 E3
  KGWD/HNM BS15 .... 86 B2
Alma Road Av *CFTN/FAIL* BS8 ...... 19 E3
Alma St *CFTN/FAIL* BS8 .... 19 E3
Alma Vale Rd *CFTN/FAIL* BS8 ...... 19 D3
Almeda Rd *EVILLE/WHL* BS5 .... 90 B1
Almond Wy *MANG/FISH* BS16 .... 81 C2
Almorah Rd *BMSTR* BS3 .... 37 E4
Alpha Rd *BMSTR* BS3 .... 36 C1
Alpine Rd *EVILLE/WHL* BS5 .... 24 A2
Alsop Rd *KGWD/HNM* BS15 .... 86 A3
Alton Rd *HORF/LLZ* BS7 .... 6 A2
Altringham Rd *EVILLE/WHL* BS5 .... 25 D2
Alverstoke *HGRV/WHIT* BS14 .... 97 C4
Alveston Wk
  HNLZ/SM/SNYPK/WT BS9 .... 62 A4
Alwins Ct *OLD/WMLY/WICK* BS30 .... 93 C3🔟
Amberley Cl *KEYN* BS31 .... 112 B3🔟
  MANG/FISH BS16 .... 72 A4
Amberley Rd *BRSTK/PCHW* BS34.... 44 A3🔟
  MANG/FISH BS16 .... 72 A4
Amble Cl *KGWD/HNM* BS15 .... 87 C4
Ambleside Av *HNBRY/STHM* BS10 .... 45 E2
Ambra V *CFTN/FAIL* BS8.............. 26 C3
Ambra V East *CFTN/FAIL* BS8 ...... 27 D3
Ambra V South *CFTN/FAIL* BS8 .... 26 C3🔟
Ambra V West *CFTN/FAIL* BS8 ...... 26 C3
Ambrose Rd *CFTN/FAIL* BS8 .... 27 D3
Amercombe Wk *HGRV/WHIT* BS14 .. 99 C4
Anchor Rd *CBRIS/FH* BS1 .... 27 F3
  KGWD/HNM BS15 .... 87 D2
Anchor Wy *PTSHD/EG* BS20 .... 74 A3
Andereach Cl *HGRV/WHIT* BS14 .... 98 A3🔟
Andover Rd *BRSG/KWL/STAPK* BS4 .. 97 C1
Angels Gnd
  BRSG/KWL/STAPK BS4 .... 90 A1🔟
Angers Rd *BRSG/KWL/STAPK* BS4.... 38 D2
Anglesea Pl *CFTN/FAIL* BS8 .... 11 D5
Anstey's Rd *KGWD/HNM* BS15 ...... 91 C2
Anstey St *EVILLE/WHL* BS5 .... 23 F1
Anthea Rd *EVILLE/WHL* BS5 .... 17 F5
Antona Cl *AVONM* BS11 .... 60 A4🔟
Antona Dr *AVONM* BS11 .... 60 A4🔟
Antrim Rd *HNLZ/SM/SNYPK/WT* BS9 .. 3 E2
Anvil St *CBRISNE* BS2 .... 30 D2
Appleby Wk
  BRSG/KWL/STAPK BS4 .... 96 A4🔟
Appledore Cl *HGRV/WHIT* BS14 ...... 98 A3
Applegate *HNBRY/STHM* BS10 ...... 49 C4
Apseleys Md *ALMDB* BS32 .... 44 B1
Apsley Rd *CFTN/FAIL* BS8 .... 18 C1

Apsley St *EVILLE/WHL* BS5 .... 16 A4
Arbutus Dr
  HNLZ/SM/SNYPK/WT BS9.......... 62 B4
Archer Ct *OLD/WMLY/WICK* BS30........ 93 C4
Archer Wk *HGRV/WHIT* BS14 .... 109 D1
Archfield Rd *RDLND/MONT* BS6 .... 20 B1
Arden Cl *ALMDB* BS32 .... 53 D1
Ardenton Wk *HNBRY/STHM* BS10 ... 48 B4 ❶
Ardern Cl *HNLZ/SM/SNYPK/WT* BS9 .. 62 A3
Argus Rd *BMSTR* BS3 .... 36 A4
Argyle Av *EVILLE/WHL* BS5 .... 16 A4
Argyle Pl *CFTN/FAIL* BS8 .... 27 D3
Argyle Rd *CBRISNE* BS2 .... 21 F5
  MANG/FISH BS16 .... 85 C1
Argyle St *BMSTR* BS3 .... 36 A2
  EVILLE/WHL BS5 .... 16 A4
Arley Cottages *RDLND/MONT* BS6...... 21 D1
Arley Hl *RDLND/MONT* BS6 .... 21 D1
Arley Pk *RDLND/MONT* BS6 .... 21 D1
Arley Ter *EVILLE/WHL* BS5 .... 25 E2
Arlingham Wy *BRSTK/PCHW* BS34...... 42 B3
Arlington Rd *BRSG/KWL/STAPK* BS4 ... 33 D4
Arlington Vls *CFTN/FAIL* BS8 .... 19 D5
Armada Pl *CBRIS/FH* BS1..................... 21 E3
Armidale Av *RDLND/MONT* BS6 ...... 21 E1 ❷
Armoury Sq *EVILLE/WHL* BS5 .... 23 D5
Arnall Dr *HNBRY/STHM* BS10 .... 64 A2
Arneside Rd *HNBRY/STHM* BS10 .... 65 D2
Arno's St *BRSG/KWL/STAPK* BS4........ 39 D3
Arthur Skemp Cl *EVILLE/WHL* BS5 ...... 31 E1
Arthur St *CBRISNE* BS2 .... 31 D4
  EVILLE/WHL BS5 .... 24 B4
Arthurswood Rd
  BMSTRD/HC/WWD BS13............ 104 B3
Arundel Cl *BMSTRD/HC/WWD* BS13... 105 C3
Arundel Rd *HORF/LLZ* BS7................. 13 D2
Ascot Cl *MANG/FISH* BS16 .... 73 C2
Ascot Rd *HNBRY/STHM* BS10 .... 66 A1
Ashburton Rd *HNBRY/STHM* BS10...... 65 D2
Ash Cl *BRSTK/PCHW* BS34 .... 45 C4
Ashcott *HGRV/WHIT* BS14 .... 107 C1
Ashcroft Av *KEYN* BS31 .... 112 A4
Ashcroft Rd
  HNLZ/SM/SNYPK/WT BS9 .... 62 B4
Ashdene Av *EVILLE/WHL* BS5 .... 17 D3
Asher La *CBRISNE* BS2 .... 22 A5
Ashfield Pl *RDLND/MONT* BS6 .... 22 A1
Ashfield Rd *BMSTR* BS3 .... 35 E3
Ashford Rd *BRSTK/PCHW* BS34 .... 43 D4
Ash Gv *MANG/FISH* BS16 .... 79 D4
Ashgrove Av *CFTN/FAIL* BS8 .... 82 A4
  HORF/LLZ BS7 .... 6 B5
Ashgrove Rd *BMSTR* BS3 .... 35 E4
  HORF/LLZ BS7 .... 6 B5
Ashland Rd
  BMSTRD/HC/WWD BS13............ 104 B3
Ashley Cl *KGWD/HNM* BS15 .... 87 C3
Ashley Cl *HORF/LLZ* BS7 .... 6 A5
Ashley Court Rd *RDLND/MONT* BS6 .. 14 A4
Ashley Down Rd *HORF/LLZ* BS7 .... 6 A5
Ashley Grove Rd *CBRISNE* BS2 ...... 14 B5 ❸
  CBRISNE BS2 .... 22 C1 ❹
Ashley Hl *RDLND/MONT* BS6............... 14 A4
Ashley Pde *CBRISNE* BS2 .... 14 B5
Ashley Pk *RDLND/MONT* BS6 .... 14 A3
Ashley Rd *RDLND/MONT* BS6 .... 21 F2
Ashley St *CBRISNE* BS2 .... 22 C1
Ashman Cl *EVILLE/WHL* BS5 .... 23 D4
Ashmead Wy *CBRIS/FH* BS1 .... 26 B5
Ash Rd *HORF/LLZ* BS7 .... 5 E3
Ashton Av *CBRIS/FH* BS1 .... 26 C5
Ashton Gate Rd *BMSTR* BS3 .... 35 D1

Ashton Gate Ter *BMSTR* BS3 .... 35 D1
Ashton Rd *BMSTR* BS3....................... 34 B3
  LGASH BS41 .... 88 B4
Ashton Vale Rd *BMSTR* BS3 .... 89 D4
Ashton Wy *KEYN* BS31..................... 112 B1
Ashville Rd *BMSTR* BS3 .... 35 D2
Ash Wk *HNBRY/STHM* BS10 .... 49 C4
Ashwell Cl *HGRV/WHIT* BS14 .... 109 D1
Ashwicke *HGRV/WHIT* BS14 .... 107 C1
Assembly Rooms La
  CBRIS/FH BS1 .... 28 C3 ❶
Astry Cl *AVONM* BS11 .... 61 D2
Atchley St *EVILLE/WHL* BS5 .... 31 E1 ❷
Athlone Wk *BRSG/KWL/STAPK* BS4 ... 96 B2
Atkins Cl *HGRV/WHIT* BS14 .... 109 D1
Atlantic Rd *AVONM* BS11 .... 59 D3
Atlas Cl *EVILLE/WHL* BS5 .... 84 B1
Atlas St *CBRISNE* BS2 .... 31 E4
Atwell Dr *ALMDB* BS32 .... 44 A2
Atwood Dr *AVONM* BS11 .... 62 A1
Aubrey Rd *BMSTR* BS3....................... 35 E4
Auburn Rd *RDLND/MONT* BS6 .... 11 F5
Austen Gv *HORF/LLZ* BS7 .... 67 D3 ❸
Avalon Rd *EVILLE/WHL* BS5 .... 91 C1
Avening Rd *KGWD/HNM* BS15 .... 84 B3
The Avenue *BRSTK/PCHW* BS34......... 44 A1
  BRSTK/PCHW BS34 .... 52 B1
  CFTN/FAIL BS8 .... 18 B2
  EVILLE/WHL BS5 .... 84 A4
  HNLZ/SM/SNYPK/WT BS9 .... 83 C1
  HORF/LLZ BS7 .... 13 F2
  KEYN BS31 .... 102 B4
  MANG/FISH BS16 .... 69 D2
Averay Rd *MANG/FISH* BS16 .... 16 B1
Avon Cl *BRSG/KWL/STAPK* BS4 .... 90 A1
  KEYN BS31 .... 113 C1
Avon Crs *CBRIS/FH* BS1 .... 26 C5
Avondown Cl *HNBRY/STHM* BS10 ... 66 A1 ❺
Avon Gv *HNLZ/SM/SNYPK/WT* BS9 ... 83 C3
Avonlea Rd *KGWD/HNM* BS15 .... 91 D2 ❻
Avonleaze
  HNLZ/SM/SNYPK/WT BS9 .... 76 A2
Avonleigh Rd *BMSTR* BS3 .... 35 E5
Avon Mill La *KEYN* BS31 .... 113 C1
Avonmouth Rd *AVONM* BS11 .... 59 C2
Avonmouth Wy *AVONM* BS11 .... 59 D2
Avonmouth Wy West *AVONM* BS11 ... 59 C1
Avon Pk *EVILLE/WHL* BS5 .... 32 C1
Avon Rd *BMSTRD/HC/WWD* BS13 .... 104 B3
  KEYN BS31 .... 113 C2
Avonside Rd *CBRISNE* BS2 .... 32 B3
Avonside Wy
  BRSG/KWL/STAPK BS4............. 90 A1 ❼
Avon St *CBRISNE* BS2 .... 30 A2
Avon V *HNLZ/SM/SNYPK/WT* BS9 ...... 77 C3
Avonvale Rd *EVILLE/WHL* BS5 .... 32 A1
Avon Vw *KGWD/HNM* BS15 .... 91 C4
Avon Walkway *PTSHD/EG* BS20........ 74 A3
Avon Wy *HNBRY/STHM* BS10 .... 66 A3
  HNLZ/SM/SNYPK/WT BS9 .... 76 B2
Avonwood Cl *AVONM* BS11 .... 74 B1
Awdelett Cl *AVONM* BS11 .... 62 A2
Axbridge Rd *BRSG/KWL/STAPK* BS4 ... 97 C1
Aylesbury Crs *BMSTR* BS3 .... 95 C2
Aylesbury Rd *BMSTR* BS3 .... 95 C2
Aylmer Crs *HGRV/WHIT* BS14 .... 108 A1
Aylminton Wk *AVONM* BS11 .... 62 A1

B

Backfields *CBRISNE* BS2 .... **21** E4
Backfields La *CBRISNE* BS2 .... **21** E3
Back of Kingsdown Pde
  RDLND/MONT BS6 .... **20** C3
Back Rd *BMSTR* BS3 .... **35** D1
Back Stoke La
  HNLZ/SM/SNYPK/WT BS9 .... **2** B1 🔒
Backwell Wk
  BMSTRD/HC/WWD BS13 .... **94** A3 🔒
Badenham Gv *AVONM* BS11 .... **61** C3
Baden Rd *EVILLE/WHL* BS5 .... **32** B1
  KGWD/HNM BS15 .... **87** D4
Badgers Wk
  BRSG/KWL/STAPK BS4 .... **41** D5 🔒
Badmington Rd *MANG/FISH* BS16 ... **73** C3
Badminton Rd *CBRISNE* BS2 .... **22** B1
  FRCTL/WBN BS36 .... **57** D4
  MANG/FISH BS16 .... **72** B4
Baglyn Av *KGWD/HNM* BS15 .... **81** C4
Bagnell Cl *HGRV/WHIT* BS14 .... **109** D2 🔒
Bagnell Rd *HGRV/WHIT* BS14 .... **109** D2
Bagworth Dr
  OLD/WMLY/WICK BS30 .... **93** C4 🔒
Baileys Court Rd *ALMDB* BS32 .... **53** D1
Baileys Mead Rd *MANG/FISH* BS16 .. **8** B4
Bakersfield
  OLD/WMLY/WICK BS30 .... **93** D4 🔒
Bakers Gnd *BRSTK/PCHW* BS34 ..... **54** A2 🔒
Balaclava Rd *MANG/FISH* BS16 ...... **78** A4 🔒
Baldwin St *CBRIS/FH* BS1 .... **29** D2
Balfour Rd *BMSTR* BS3 .... **35** E3
Balmain St *BRSG/KWL/STAPK* BS4 ... **39** D2
Balmoral Cl *BRSTK/PCHW* BS34 ..... **53** C3
Balmoral Ct *MANG/FISH* BS16 .... **81** D2 🔒
Balmoral Rd *KEYN* BS31 .... **112** B3
  OLD/WMLY/WICK BS30 .... **103** C1
  RDLND/MONT BS6 .... **14** A4
Baltic Pl *PTSHD/EG* BS20 .... **74** A3 🔒
Bamfield *HGRV/WHIT* BS14 .... **107** D1
Bampton Cl
  BMSTRD/HC/WWD BS13 .... **95** C4 🔒
Bampton Dr *MANG/FISH* BS16 .... **72** A2 🔒
Banfield Cl *AVONM* BS11 .... **61** D3
Bangor Gv *BRSG/KWL/STAPK* BS4 .. **90** A2
Bangrove Wk *AVONM* BS11 .... **60** B3 🔒
Bank Pl *PTSHD/EG* BS20 .... **74** A3 🔒
Bank Rd *KGWD/HNM* BS15 .... **86** A3 🔒
Bankside *MANG/FISH* BS16 .... **81** C3 🔒
Bankside Rd *BRSG/KWL/STAPK* BS4 .. **41** D4
Bannerleigh La *CFTN/FAIL* BS8 ...... **89** D1 🔒
Bannerleigh Rd *CFTN/FAIL* BS8 ..... **83** D4
Bannerman Rd *EVILLE/WHL* BS5 .... **23** F3
Banner Rd *RDLND/MONT* BS6 .... **21** F2
Bantry Rd *BRSG/KWL/STAPK* BS4 .. **96** B3
Banwell Cl *BMSTRD/HC/WWD* BS13 .. **94** B3
Banwell Rd *BMSTR* BS3 .... **34** C2
Baptist St *EVILLE/WHL* BS5 .... **23** D1 🔒
Barbour Gdns
  BMSTRD/HC/WWD BS13 .... **106** A4
Barbour Rd
  BMSTRD/HC/WWD BS13 .... **106** A4 🔒
Barcroft Cl *KGWD/HNM* BS15 .... **85** D3 🔒
Barker Wk *EVILLE/WHL* BS5 .... **22** C3
Barkleys Hl *MANG/FISH* BS16 .... **8** B4
Barley Cl *MANG/FISH* BS16 .... **81** C1
Barley Cft *HNLZ/SM/SNYPK/WT* BS9 ... **2** A3

Barnabas St *CBRISNE* BS2 .... **21** F2
Barnard Wk *KEYN* BS31 .... **112** A3
Barnes St *EVILLE/WHL* BS5 .... **24** C4 🔒
Barn Owl Wy *BRSTK/PCHW* BS34 ... **54** A2
Barnstaple Rd
  BRSG/KWL/STAPK BS4 .... **96** B3
Barnstaple Wk
  BRSG/KWL/STAPK BS4 .... **97** C3 🔒
Barossa Pl *CBRIS/FH* BS1 .... **29** D4
Barrack's La *AVONM* BS11 .... **60** A3
Barratt St *EVILLE/WHL* BS5 .... **23** F2
Barrington Cl *KGWD/HNM* BS15 ..... **87** C1
Barrington Ct *KGWD/HNM* BS15 ..... **86** B2
Barrow Hill Crs *AVONM* BS11 .... **59** D4
Barrowmead Dr *AVONM* BS11 .... **61** C3
Barrow Rd *EVILLE/WHL* BS5 .... **31** E2
Barrs Court Av
  OLD/WMLY/WICK BS30 .... **93** D2
Barrs Court Rd
  OLD/WMLY/WICK BS30 .... **93** D2
Bartlett's Rd *BMSTR* BS3 .... **36** A5
Bartley St *BMSTR* BS3 .... **36** C2
Barton Cl *BRSG/KWL/STAPK* BS4 ... **90** A1 🔒
  FRCTL/WBN BS36 .... **56** B2
Barton Ct *EVILLE/WHL* BS5 .... **32** A2
Barton Hill Rd *EVILLE/WHL* BS5 ..... **31** E2
Bartonia Gv
  BRSG/KWL/STAPK BS4 .... **99** C2 🔒
Barton Mnr *CBRISNE* BS2 .... **30** C2
Barton Rd *CBRISNE* BS2 .... **30** B2
Barton St *CBRIS/FH* BS1 .... **21** D4 🔒
The Barton *KGWD/HNM* BS15 .... **91** C3
Barton V *CBRISNE* BS2 .... **30** C2 🔒
Barwood Cl *KGWD/HNM* BS15 .... **87** C3 🔒
Bates Cl *EVILLE/WHL* BS5 .... **22** C3
Bath Br *BRSG/KWL/STAPK* BS4 ...... **30** A5
Bath Buildings *RDLND/MONT* BS6 ... **21** E1
Bath Hl *KEYN* BS31 .... **113** C2
Bath Rd *BRSG/KWL/STAPK* BS4 ..... **30** B5
  BRSG/KWL/STAPK BS4 .... **38** C2
  BRSG/KWL/STAPK BS4 .... **40** A3
  BRSG/KWL/STAPK BS4 .... **100** A2
  KEYN BS31 .... **101** C3
  KEYN BS31 .... **113** D2
  OLD/WMLY/WICK BS30 .... **93** C4
Bath Road Brislington Hl
  BRSG/KWL/STAPK BS4 .... **99** D1
Bath St *BMSTR* BS3 .... **34** C2
  CBRIS/FH BS1 .... **29** E2
  MANG/FISH BS16 .... **80** B3
Bathurst Pde *CBRIS/FH* BS1 .... **28** C5
Bathwell Rd *BRSG/KWL/STAPK* BS4 .. **38** C3
Battenburg Rd *EVILLE/WHL* BS5 .... **84** B3
Batten's La *EVILLE/WHL* BS5 .... **90** B1
Battens Rd *EVILLE/WHL* BS5 .... **90** B1
Battersby Wy *HNBRY/STHM* BS10 .. **63** D1
Battersea Rd *EVILLE/WHL* BS5 ...... **24** A3
Battson Rd *HGRV/WHIT* BS14 .... **109** D3
Baugh Gdns *MANG/FISH* BS16 ...... **72** B2
Baxter Cl *KGWD/HNM* BS15 .... **87** C3 🔒
Bay Gdns *EVILLE/WHL* BS5 .... **16** A5
Bayham Rd *BRSG/KWL/STAPK* BS4 .. **38** B3
Bayleys Dr *KGWD/HNM* BS15 .... **91** D1
Baynton Rd *BMSTR* BS3 .... **34** C2
Bayswater Av *RDLND/MONT* BS6 ... **11** E1
Bayswater Rd *HORF/LLZ* BS7 .... **47** C4
Bay Tree Cl *BRSTK/PCHW* BS34 ..... **43** C4
Beachgrove Gdns *MANG/FISH* BS16 .. **79** D3
Beachgrove Rd *MANG/FISH* BS16 .. **79** C3
Beachley Wk *AVONM* BS11 .... **60** A4
Beacon La *MANG/FISH* BS16 .... **55** C3
Beaconlea *KGWD/HNM* BS15 .... **92** A1

Beaconsfield Rd
BRSG/KWL/STAPK BS4 .... **39** D4
CFTN/FAIL BS8 .... **10** C5
EVILLE/WHL BS5 .... **25** F4
Beaconsfield St *EVILLE/WHL* BS5 ... **31** F3 🆔
Beale Cl *HGRV/WHIT* BS14 .... **109** D1 🆔
Beam St *EVILLE/WHL* BS5 .... **32** A1
The Bean Acre *AVONM* BS11 .... **60** A3
Bean St *EVILLE/WHL* BS5 .... **23** D2
Bearbridge Rd
BMSTRD/HC/WWD BS13............ **104** A3
Beauchamp Rd *HORF/LLZ* BS7 .... **4** C5
Beaufort Cl *EVILLE/WHL* BS5 .... **25** D5
Beaufort Crs *BRSTK/PCHW* BS34 ..... **53** D3
Beaufort Hts *EVILLE/WHL* BS5 .... **25** F5
Beaufort Pl *EVILLE/WHL* BS5 .... **22** C4
MANG/FISH BS16 .... **71** C2 🆔
Beaufort Rd *CFTN/FAIL* BS8 .... **18** C2
EVILLE/WHL BS5 .... **25** D5
HORF/LLZ BS7 .... **6** A2
KGWD/HNM BS15 .... **85** C2 🆔
MANG/FISH BS16 .... **73** D4
MANG/FISH BS16 .... **80** B3
Beaufort St *BMSTR* BS3 .... **36** A5 🆔
EVILLE/WHL BS5 .... **22** C4 🆔
Beaufort Ter *EVILLE/WHL* BS5 .... **22** C4 🆔
Beaufort Wy *HNBRY/STHM* BS10 ..... **66** A3
Beauley Rd *BMSTR* BS3 .... **35** F1
Beaumont Cl
OLD/WMLY/WICK BS30 .... **93** D4 🆔
Beaumont St *EVILLE/WHL* BS5 .... **23** D3
Beaumont Ter *EVILLE/WHL* BS5 ...... **23** D3
Beazer Cl *MANG/FISH* BS16 .... **80** A4 🆔
Beckford Gdns
HGRV/WHIT BS14 .... **107** D4 🆔
Beckington Rd *BMSTR* BS3 .... **38** A5
Beckington Wk *BMSTR* BS3 .... **38** A5
Beckspool Rd *MANG/FISH* BS16 ...... **71** D5 🆔
Bedford Crs *HORF/LLZ* BS7 .... **6** B3
Bedminster Br *BMSTR* BS3 .... **37** E1
Bedminster Down Rd *BMSTR* BS3 ... **95** C1 🆔
BMSTRD/HC/WWD BS13............ **94** B3
Bedminster Pde *BMSTR* BS3 .... **37** D1
Bedminster Pl *BMSTR* BS3 .... **37** D1 🆔
Bedminster St *BMSTR* BS3.......... **95** D1
Beech Cl *OLD/WMLY/WICK* BS30 ..... **93** D2
Beechcroft Wk *HORF/LLZ* BS7 .... **67** D3
Beechen Dr *MANG/FISH* BS16 .... **85** C1
Beeches Gv
BRSG/KWL/STAPK BS4 .... **99** C1 🆔
The Beeches *ALMDB* BS32........... **45** C3
BRSG/KWL/STAPK BS4 .... **33** E5 🆔
Beechmount Gv *HGRV/WHIT* BS14 .... **98** A3
Beech Rd *HORF/LLZ* BS7 .... **5** E4
Beechwood Av *KGWD/HNM* BS15 ..... **92** A2
Beechwood Cl *HGRV/WHIT* BS14 ..... **98** B3
Beechwood Rd *MANG/FISH* BS16 ..... **78** B3
Begbrook Dr *MANG/FISH* BS16 .... **78** A1
Begbrook La *MANG/FISH* BS16 .... **78** A1
Begbrook Pk *MANG/FISH* BS16 .... **70** B4
Beggarswell Cl *CBRISNE* BS2 .... **22** A3
Belfast Wk *BRSG/KWL/STAPK* BS4 ... **96** B3 🆔
Belgrave Hl *CFTN/FAIL* BS8 .... **10** C5
Belgrave Pl *CFTN/FAIL* BS8 .... **19** D5 🆔
Belgrave Rd *CFTN/FAIL* BS8 .... **19** F3
Bellamy Av
BMSTRD/HC/WWD BS13............ **105** D3
Bellamy Cl *KGWD/HNM* BS15 .... **90** B2
Belland Dr *HGRV/WHIT* BS14........ **107** C3
Bell Barn Rd
HNLZ/SM/SNYPK/WT BS9.......... **77** C1
Bell Cl *HNBRY/STHM* BS10 .... **66** B4
Bellevue *CFTN/FAIL* BS8............. **27** E2

Bellevue Cl *KGWD/HNM* BS15 .... **86** B4 🆔
Bellevue Crs *CFTN/FAIL* BS8 .... **27** E2
Bellevue Pk *BRSG/KWL/STAPK* BS4 ... **41** D5
Belle Vue Rd *EVILLE/WHL* BS5 .... **16** A5
Bellevue Rd *BRSG/KWL/STAPK* BS4 ... **38** B1
EVILLE/WHL BS5 .... **84** B3
KGWD/HNM BS15 .... **87** C4
Bellevue Ter *BMSTR* BS3 .... **38** B1
BRSG/KWL/STAPK BS4 .... **41** D5
Bell Hl *MANG/FISH* BS16............. **16** A1
Bell Hill Rd *EVILLE/WHL* BS5 .... **84** A3
Bellhouse Wk *AVONM* BS11 .... **62** A2 🆔
Bell La *CBRIS/FH* BS1 .... **29** D1
Belluton Rd *BRSG/KWL/STAPK* BS4 ... **38** C4
Belmont Dr *BRSTK/PCHW* BS34 ...... **53** D2
Belmont Rd *BRSG/KWL/STAPK* BS4 ... **40** B2
RDLND/MONT BS6................... **13** E4
Belmont St *EVILLE/WHL* BS5 .... **23** E1
Beloe Rd *HORF/LLZ* BS7 .... **5** D3
Belroyal Av *BRSG/KWL/STAPK* BS4 ... **90** A4
Belsher Dr *KGWD/HNM* BS15 .... **93** D1
Belstone Wk *BRSG/KWL/STAPK* BS4 .. **95** D4
Belton Rd *EVILLE/WHL* BS5 .... **23** E2
Belvedere Rd *RDLND/MONT* BS6 ..... **11** D2
Belvoir Rd *RDLND/MONT* BS6........ **13** E4
Bence Ct *KGWD/HNM* BS15 .... **91** C2 🆔
Benford Cl *MANG/FISH* BS16........ **79** D1
Bennett Rd *EVILLE/WHL* BS5 .... **25** F5
Bensaunt Gv *HNBRY/STHM* BS10..... **50** A3
Bentley Cl *HGRV/WHIT* BS14 .... **107** C4 🆔
Benville Rd
HNLZ/SM/SNYPK/WT BS9.......... **62** B3
Berkeley Av *CFTN/FAIL* BS8 .... **28** A1
HORF/LLZ BS7 .... **12** C2
Berkeley Cl *MANG/FISH* BS16 .... **73** C3
Berkeley Gdns *KEYN* BS31........... **112** A3
Berkeley Gn *EVILLE/WHL* BS5 .... **16** B4
MANG/FISH BS16 .... **71** C2 🆔
Berkeley Gv *EVILLE/WHL* BS5 .... **16** B4
Berkeley Md *ALMDB* BS32........... **54** A1
Berkeley Rd *HORF/LLZ* BS7 .... **12** C2
KGWD/HNM BS15 .... **86** B3 🆔
MANG/FISH BS16 .... **80** A3
MANG/FISH BS16 .... **84** B1
RDLND/MONT BS6................... **11** D1
Berkeley Sq *CFTN/FAIL* BS8 .... **27** F1
Berkeley St *EVILLE/WHL* BS5 .... **16** B3
Berkshire Rd *HORF/LLZ* BS7 .... **12** C2
Berrow Wk *BMSTR* BS3 .... **37** F5
Berry La *HORF/LLZ* BS7 .... **6** B1
Berwick Rd *EVILLE/WHL* BS5 .... **15** F5
Beryl Gv *HGRV/WHIT* BS14 .... **98** B3
Beryl Rd *BMSTR* BS3 .... **35** E4
Bethel Rd *EVILLE/WHL* BS5 .... **84** A3
Betjeman Ct
OLD/WMLY/WICK BS30 .... **93** D2 🆔
Bevan Ct *BRSTK/PCHW* BS34 .... **67** C1
Beverley Av *MANG/FISH* BS16 .... **73** C2
Beverley Cl *EVILLE/WHL* BS5 .... **91** C1 🆔
Beverley Gdns
HNLZ/SM/SNYPK/WT BS9.......... **61** C3
Beverstone *KGWD/HNM* BS15 .... **85** D3 🆔
Beverston Gdns *AVONM* BS11 .... **62** A1 🆔
Bevington Cl *BRSTK/PCHW* BS34..... **42** B2
Bevington Wk *BRSTK/PCHW* BS34.... **42** B2
Bexley Rd *MANG/FISH* BS16 .... **79** C4
Bibstone *KGWD/HNM* BS15........... **87** D3
Bibury Av *BRSTK/PCHW* BS34........ **44** A3
Bibury Cl *HNLZ/SM/SNYPK/WT* BS9... **66** A4
Bibury Crs *HNLZ/SM/SNYPK/WT* BS9.. **66** A4
KGWD/HNM BS15 .... **91** D2
Bickerton Cl *HNBRY/STHM* BS10 ..... **48** A4

Bickford Cl *OLD/WMLY/WICK* BS30 .... **93** D1
Bickley Cl *KGWD/HNM* BS15 .... **101** D1 🔲
Biddestone Rd *HORF/LLZ* BS7 .... **66** B3
Bideford Crs *BRSG/KWL/STAPK* BS4 .. **97** C3
Bidwell Cl *HNBRY/STHM* BS10 .... **49** C4
Bifield Cl *HGRV/WHIT* BS14 .... **110** A3
Bifield Gdns *HGRV/WHIT* BS14 .... **109** D2
Bifield Rd *HGRV/WHIT* BS14 .... **110** A3
Bigwood La *CBRIS/FH* BS1 .... **28** A2
Bilberry Cl
   HNLZ/SM/SNYPK/WT BS9 .... **62** B3 🔲
Bilbie Cl *HNBRY/STHM* BS10 .... **5** D1
Bindon Dr *HNBRY/STHM* BS10 .... **50** A3
Binley Gv *HGRV/WHIT* BS14............ **109** C2
Binmead Gdns
   BMSTRD/HC/WWD BS13 .... **105** C3 🔲
Birbeck Rd
   HNLZ/SM/SNYPK/WT BS9.............. **77** D2
Birchall Rd *RDLND/MONT* BS6 .... **12** A1
Birch Cl *BRSTK/PCHW* BS34............. **42** B4
Birch Ct *KEYN* BS31 .... **111** D3
Birch Cft *HGRV/WHIT* BS14 .... **108** A4 🔲
Birchdale Rd *HGRV/WHIT* BS14 .... **97** C3
Birch Rd *BMSTR* BS3 .... **35** E1
   KGWD/HNM BS15........................ **80** B4
Birchwood Rd
   BRSG/KWL/STAPK BS4 .... **41** F2
Birdwood *KGWD/HNM* BS15............. **92** A1
Birkin St *CBRISNE* BS2 .... **30** B2
Bishop Manor Rd
   HNBRY/STHM BS10 .... **66** A4
Bishop Rd *HORF/LLZ* BS7 .... **4** A5
Bishops Cl *HNLZ/SM/SNYPK/WT* BS9.. **77** D4
Bishops Cove
   BMSTRD/HC/WWD BS13 .... **104** A2 🔲
Bishops Knoll
   HNLZ/SM/SNYPK/WT BS9.............. **76** B4
Bishop St *CBRISNE* BS2 .... **21** F3
Bishopsworth Rd
   BMSTRD/HC/WWD BS13 .... **94** B2
Bishopthorpe Rd
   HNBRY/STHM BS10 .... **66** A4
Bishport Av
   BMSTRD/HC/WWD BS13 .... **104** B3
Bishport Cl
   BMSTRD/HC/WWD BS13 .... **105** C3
Blackacre *HGRV/WHIT* BS14 .... **108** B4
Blackberry Av *MANG/FISH* BS16 .... **9** E4
Blackberry Hl *MANG/FISH* BS16 .... **9** E4
Blackdown Cl *HGRV/WHIT* BS14 .. **108** A2 🔲
Blackfriars *CBRIS/FH* BS1 .... **21** D5 🔲
Blackhorse La *MANG/FISH* BS16........ **73** D3
Blackhorse Pl *MANG/FISH* BS16 .... **81** D1 🔲
Blackhorse Rd *KGWD/HNM* BS15....... **86** A3
   MANG/FISH BS16 .... **81** D1
Blackmoors La *BMSTR* BS3 .... **89** D4
Blacksworth Rd *EVILLE/WHL* BS5 ...... **33** D1
Blackthorn Cl
   BMSTRD/HC/WWD BS13 .... **106** A2
Blackthorn Dr *ALMDB* BS32 .... **45** C4 🔲
Blackthorn Rd
   BMSTRD/HC/WWD BS13 .... **106** A2
Blackthorn Wk *KGWD/HNM* BS15 .. **86** B1 🔲
Blagrove Cl
   BMSTRD/HC/WWD BS13 .... **105** D4
Blagrove Crs
   BMSTRD/HC/WWD BS13 .... **105** D4
Blaisdon Cl *HNBRY/STHM* BS10 .... **64** A2
Blaise Wk *HNLZ/SM/SNYPK/WT* BS9 .. **76** B1
Blakeney Rd *BRSTK/PCHW* BS34 .... **42** B2
   HORF/LLZ BS7 .... **67** D4
Blake Rd *HORF/LLZ* BS7 .... **7** E2

Blandford Cl
   HNLZ/SM/SNYPK/WT BS9 .... **3** F1 🔲
Blenheim Dr *BRSTK/PCHW* BS34 .... **52** A3
Blenheim Rd *RDLND/MONT* BS6 .... **11** E2
Blenheim St *EVILLE/WHL* BS5 .... **23** D2
Blenman Cl *MANG/FISH* BS16 .... **70** B4 🔲
Blethwin Cl *HNBRY/STHM* BS10 .... **64** A2
Bloomfield Rd
   BRSG/KWL/STAPK BS4 .... **40** A2 🔲
Bloomfield Road Link
   BRSG/KWL/STAPK BS4 .... **40** A2
Bloy St *EVILLE/WHL* BS5 .... **24** A2
The Bluebells *ALMDB* BS32 .... **45** D4 🔲
   ALMDB BS32 .... **46** A4 🔲
Bodey Cl *OLD/WMLY/WICK* BS30 ...... **93** D2
Bodmin Wk *BRSG/KWL/STAPK* BS4 ... **97** C3
Boiling Wells La *CBRISNE* BS2.......... **14** C3
Bolton Rd *HORF/LLZ* BS7................. **13** E2
Bond St *CBRIS/FH* BS1 .... **21** F4
Bonnington Wk *HORF/LLZ* BS7 .... **68** A4
Bonville Rd *BRSG/KWL/STAPK* BS4 ... **99** D2
Booth Rd *BMSTR* BS3 .... **36** B2 🔲
Boot La *BMSTR* BS3 .... **37** D1
Bordesley Rd *HGRV/WHIT* BS14 ...... **107** D4
Borleyton Wk
   BMSTRD/HC/WWD BS13 .... **104** A3 🔲
Borver Gv *BMSTRD/HC/WWD* BS13.. **105** C3
Boscombe Crs *MANG/FISH* BS16 ...... **73** C4 🔲
Boswell St *EVILLE/WHL* BS5 .... **16** A4
Botham Dr *BRSG/KWL/STAPK* BS4 .. **99** D2 🔲
Bottom Cl *HGRV/WHIT* BS14........... **107** D1
Boucher Pl *CBRISNE* BS2 .... **14** C4 🔲
Boulters Rd
   BMSTRD/HC/WWD BS13 .... **105** D3 🔲
Boulton's Rd *KGWD/HNM* BS15 .... **86** A3
Bourchier Gdns
   BMSTRD/HC/WWD BS13.............. **105** C4
Bourne Cl *KGWD/HNM* BS15 .... **85** C3
Bourne La *EVILLE/WHL* BS5.............. **15** F4
Bourne Rd *KGWD/HNM* BS15 .... **84** B3
Bourneville Rd *EVILLE/WHL* BS5 .... **24** A2
Boursland Cl *ALMDB* BS32 .... **45** C1 🔲
Bourton Av *BRSTK/PCHW* BS34 .... **44** B3
Bourton Cl *BRSTK/PCHW* BS34 .... **44** B3
Bourton Wk
   BMSTRD/HC/WWD BS13 .... **94** B3 🔲
Bouverie St *EVILLE/WHL* BS5 .... **23** E3
Boverton Rd *BRSTK/PCHW* BS34 .... **52** A4
Bowden Cl
   HNLZ/SM/SNYPK/WT BS9.............. **62** B3
Bowden Pl *MANG/FISH* BS16 .... **73** C4 🔲
Bowden Rd *EVILLE/WHL* BS5 .... **25** E2
Bowerleaze
   HNLZ/SM/SNYPK/WT BS9.............. **76** A2
Bower Rd *BMSTR* BS3 .... **34** C4
Bower Wk *BMSTR* BS3 .... **37** F4
Bowring Cl
   BMSTRD/HC/WWD BS13 .... **105** D4
Bowsland Wy *ALMDB* BS32............. **45** C1
Boyce Dr *CBRISNE* BS2................... **14** C4
Boyce's Av *CFTN/FAIL* BS8.............. **26** C1
Brabazon Rd *BRSTK/PCHW* BS34 ...... **68** A1
Bracewell Gdns *HNBRY/STHM* BS10 .. **49** D3
Bracey Dr *MANG/FISH* BS16 .... **79** D3
Brackenbury Dr *BRSTK/PCHW* BS34 .. **53** D2
Brackendene *ALMDB* BS32 .... **44** B2 🔲
Bracton Dr *HGRV/WHIT* BS14 .... **107** D3
Bradestone Gv *MANG/FISH* BS16 ...... **70** B4
Bradhurst St *EVILLE/WHL* BS5 .... **31** F3
Bradley Av *AVONM* BS11 .... **74** B1
   FRCTL/WBN BS36........................ **56** B2
Bradley Crs *AVONM* BS11 .... **74** B1

Bradley Rd *BRSTK/PCHW* BS34........... **43** C3
Bradley Stoke Wy *ALMDB* BS32........ **44** B1
  ALMDB BS32
Bradstone Rd *FRCTL/WBN* BS36 ...... **56** A2 🔢
Bradwell Gv *HNBRY/STHM* BS10 ...... **65** D3
Braemar Av *HORF/LLZ* BS7 .... **67** C2
Braemar Crs *HORF/LLZ* BS7 .... **67** C2
Bragg's La *CBRISNE* BS2 .... **22** B5
Braikenridge Rd
  BRSG/KWL/STAPK BS4 .... **41** D1
Brainsfield *HNLZ/SM/SNYPK/WT* BS9 .. **2** A1
Brake Cl *ALMDB* BS32 .... **53** D1
  KGWD/HNM BS15 .... **87** C4 🔢
Bramble Dr
  HNLZ/SM/SNYPK/WT BS9............. **76** B4
Bramble La
  HNLZ/SM/SNYPK/WT BS9............. **76** B4
The Brambles *KEYN* BS31 .... **112** A4
Brambling Wk *MANG/FISH* BS16 ...... **78** A1
Bramley Ct
  OLD/WMLY/WICK BS30 .... **93** C3 🔢
Branche Gv
  BMSTRD/HC/WWD BS13.............. **106** A4
Brandon Steep *CBRIS/FH* BS1 .... **28** A2 🔢
Brandon St *CBRIS/FH* BS1 .... **28** A3
Brangwyn Gv *HORF/LLZ* BS7 .... **7** E2
Branksome Crs
  BRSTK/PCHW BS34 .... **52** A4 🔢
Branksome Dr *BRSTK/PCHW* BS34 ... **52** A4
  FRCTL/WBN BS36 .... **56** B1
Branksome Rd *RDLND/MONT* BS6..... **11** F2
Branscombe Rd
  HNLZ/SM/SNYPK/WT BS9............. **76** B3
Branwhite Cl *HORF/LLZ* BS7 .... **68** A4 🔢
Bratton Rd *BRSG/KWL/STAPK* BS4 ... **96** A4 🔢
Braunton Av *BMSTR* BS3 .... **36** A3
Braydon Av *BRSTK/PCHW* BS34 .... **45** C3
Brayne Ct *OLD/WMLY/WICK* BS30 .... **93** C4
Breaches Ga *ALMDB* BS32 .... **54** A1
Breach Rd *BMSTR* BS3 .... **35** D4
Brean Down Av
  HNLZ/SM/SNYPK/WT BS9............. **3** E5
Brecknock Rd
  BRSG/KWL/STAPK BS4 .... **38** C4
Brecon Rd *HNLZ/SM/SNYPK/WT* BS9 .. **3** D2
Bredon Cl *KGWD/HNM* BS15 .... **87** C4 🔢
Bredon Nook Rd
  HNBRY/STHM BS10 .... **65** D4 🔢
Brendon Rd *BMSTR* BS3 .... **37** D4
Brenner St *EVILLE/WHL* BS5 .... **15** F5
Brent Rd *HORF/LLZ* BS7 .... **6** A3
Brentry Av *EVILLE/WHL* BS5 .... **23** E5
Brentry La *HNBRY/STHM* BS10.......... **64** B1
Brentry Rd *MANG/FISH* BS16 .... **17** F2
Brewerton Cl *HNBRY/STHM* BS10 ..... **49** D4
Briarfield *KGWD/HNM* BS15 .... **91** D2 🔢
Briarside Rd *HNBRY/STHM* BS10 ...... **49** D4
Briar Wk *MANG/FISH* BS16 .... **79** C4
Briar Wy *MANG/FISH* BS16 .... **79** C3
Briarwood *HNLZ/SM/SNYPK/WT* BS9 .. **2** J2
Briavels Gv *RDLND/MONT* BS6 .... **14** B4
Brick St *CBRISNE* BS2 .... **22** B5
Bridewell St *CBRIS/FH* BS1 .... **21** D5 🔢
Bridge Cl *HGRV/WHIT* BS14 .... **108** B3 🔢
Bridge Farm Cl
  HGRV/WHIT BS14 .... **107** D4 🔢
Bridgeleap Rd *MANG/FISH* BS16 ...... **73** C3
Bridge Rd *CFTN/FAIL* BS8 .... **89** C1
  EVILLE/WHL BS5 .... **15** E3
  KGWD/HNM BS15 .... **81** C1 🔢
Bridges Ct *MANG/FISH* BS16 .... **79** C3 🔢
Bridges Dr *MANG/FISH* BS16 .... **79** D1 🔢

Bridge St *CBRIS/FH* BS1 .... **29** D2
  EVILLE/WHL BS5 .... **16** C4
Bridge Valley Rd *CFTN/FAIL* BS8 ...... **83** D3
Bridge Wk *HORF/LLZ* BS7 .... **67** D3
Bridgman Gv *BRSTK/PCHW* BS34..... **52** A4
Bridgwater Rd
  BMSTRD/HC/WWD BS13.............. **94** A3
Briercliffe Rd
  HNLZ/SM/SNYPK/WT BS9............. **63** C4
Brierly Furlong *BRSTK/PCHW* BS34.... **53** C4
Briery Leaze Rd *HGRV/WHIT* BS14.... **107** D2 🔢
Brighton Crs *BMSTR* BS3 .... **35** F5
  BMSTR BS3 .... **95** C1
Brighton Pk *EVILLE/WHL* BS5 .... **23** F3 🔢
Brighton Pl *KGWD/HNM* BS15 .... **86** A2 🔢
Brighton Rd *BRSTK/PCHW* BS34 ...... **43** C3
  RDLND/MONT BS6.......................... **20** A1
Brighton St *CBRISNE* BS2 .... **21** F2
Brighton Ter *BMSTR* BS3 .... **35** F5
Bright St *EVILLE/WHL* BS5 .... **23** F5
  KGWD/HNM BS15 .... **86** A3
Brigstocke Rd *CBRISNE* BS2 .... **21** E2
Brimbles *HORF/LLZ* BS7 .... **68** A1
Brinkworthy Rd *MANG/FISH* BS16....... **9** D2
Brinmead Wk
  BMSTRD/HC/WWD BS13............. **104** A3 🔢
Brins Cl *BRSTK/PCHW* BS34 .... **54** A3
Briscoes Av
  BMSTRD/HC/WWD BS13............. **105** D3
Bristol Br *CBRIS/FH* BS1 .... **29** E2
Bristol Hl *BRSG/KWL/STAPK* BS4 ..... **99** C1
Bristol Rd *HGRV/WHIT* BS14 .... **108** B4
  KEYN BS31 .... **112** A1
  MANG/FISH BS16 .... **56** A4
  MANG/FISH BS16 .... **71** C3
Bristow Broadway *AVONM* BS11....... **59** D2
Britannia Crs *BRSTK/PCHW* BS34..... **53** C2
Britannia Rd *BRSTK/PCHW* BS34 ..... **42** C4
  EVILLE/WHL BS5 .... **23** F2
  KGWD/HNM BS15 .... **85** D3
British Rd *BMSTR* BS3 .... **36** A4
Britten Ct *OLD/WMLY/WICK* BS30 ... **93** C3 🔢
Brixham Rd *BMSTR* BS3 .... **95** D1
Brixton Rd *EVILLE/WHL* BS5 .... **23** F4
Broadbury Rd
  BRSG/KWL/STAPK BS4 .... **96** B3
Broad Cft *ALMDB* BS32 .... **44** B1 🔢
Broadfield Av *KGWD/HNM* BS15 .... **85** D2
Broadfield Rd
  BRSG/KWL/STAPK BS4 .... **97** C2
Broadlands Av *KEYN* BS31 .... **112** A1
Broadlands Dr *AVONM* BS11............ **61** D2
Broadleas *BMSTRD/HC/WWD* BS13... **95** C4
Broadleaze *AVONM* BS11 .... **60** B4 🔢
Broadleys Av
  HNLZ/SM/SNYPK/WT BS9............. **65** C4
Broadmead *CBRIS/FH* BS1 .... **21** E5
Broadmead La *KEYN* BS31 .... **113** D1
Broad Oak Rd
  BMSTRD/HC/WWD BS13............. **104** A4
Broad Oaks *CFTN/FAIL* BS8 .... **89** D1 🔢
Broadoak Wk *MANG/FISH* BS16 .... **79** C3
Broad Quay *CBRIS/FH* BS1 .... **28** C2
Broad Rd *KGWD/HNM* BS15 .... **85** D2
Broadstone Wk
  BMSTRD/HC/WWD BS13............. **106** A2
Broad St *CBRIS/FH* BS1 .... **29** D1
  MANG/FISH BS16 .... **80** B3
Broad Wk *BRSG/KWL/STAPK* BS4 .... **97** C1
Broadstone Av
  BMSTRD/HC/WWD BS13............. **106** A2
Broadway Av
  HNLZ/SM/SNYPK/WT BS9............... **4** C1

Broadway Rd
BMSTRD/HC/WWD BS13 .... **104** A2 🖻
HORF/LLZ BS7 .... **13** D2
Broadways Dr *MANG/FISH* BS16 .... **70** A4 🖻
Broad Weir *CBRIS/FH* BS1 .... **29** F1
Brockhurst Gdns *KGWD/HNM* BS15 .. **84** B3
Brockhurst Rd *KGWD/HNM* BS15.... **84** B3
Brockley Cl *BRSTK/PCHW* BS34 ...... **44** B4 🖻
Brockley Wk
BMSTRD/HC/WWD BS13 .... **94** B3 🖻
Brocks Rd *BMSTRD/HC/WWD* BS13.. **105** D3
Brockworth Crs *MANG/FISH* BS16 .... **78** A1
Bromley Dr *MANG/FISH* BS16 .... **72** A3
Bromley Heath Av *MANG/FISH* BS16.. **72** A2
Bromley Heath Rd
MANG/FISH BS16 .... **72** A3 🖻
Bromley Rd *HORF/LLZ* BS7 .... **6** A4
Brompton Cl *KGWD/HNM* BS15 .... **87** C3
Broncksea Rd *HORF/LLZ* BS7 .... **67** C2
Brookcote Dr *BRSTK/PCHW* BS34 .... **53** C1
Brookdale Rd
BMSTRD/HC/WWD BS13 .... **105** C1
Brookfield Av *HORF/LLZ* BS7 .... **13** D3
Brookfield La *RDLND/MONT* BS6 ..... **13** D5
Brookfield Rd *BRSTK/PCHW* BS34 .... **44** A3
RDLND/MONT BS6 .... **13** D5 🖻
Brook Hl *RDLND/MONT* BS6 .... **21** F1
Brookland Cl *RDLND/MONT* BS6....... **4** C3
Brook La *MANG/FISH* BS16 .... **9** E2
RDLND/MONT BS6 .... **22** A1
Brookleaze
HNLZ/SM/SNYPK/WT BS9............ **76** B2
Brook Lintons
BRSG/KWL/STAPK BS4 .... **41** D3
Brooklyn Rd
BMSTRD/HC/WWD BS13 .... **95** C3
Brook Rd *BMSTR* BS3 .... **36** C1 🖻
EVILLE/WHL BS5 .... **25** F1
KGWD/HNM BS15 .... **87** D3 🖻
MANG/FISH BS16 .... **78** B3
MANG/FISH BS16 .... **81** C1
RDLND/MONT BS6 .... **22** A1
Brookside *PTSHD/EG* BS20 .... **74** A4
Brookside Rd *BRSG/KWL/STAPK* BS4.. **41** D5
Brook St *EVILLE/WHL* BS5 .... **24** A5
Brookthorpe Wk *AVONM* BS11 .... **61** D3
Brookview Wk
BMSTRD/HC/WWD BS13 .... **95** C4
Brook Wy *ALMDB* BS32 .... **44** B2
Broom Hl *MANG/FISH* BS16 .... **9** E3
Broomhill Rd *BRSG/KWL/STAPK* BS4.. **90** A4
The Brooms *MANG/FISH* BS16 .... **73** D3
Browning Ct *HORF/LLZ* BS7 .... **68** A3 🖻
Broxholme Wk *AVONM* BS11 .... **61** D3 🖻
Bruce Av *EVILLE/WHL* BS5............... **24** B1
Bruce Rd *EVILLE/WHL* BS5............... **24** B2
Brunel Lock Rd *CBRIS/FH* BS1 .... **26** B5
Brunel Rd *BMSTRD/HC/WWD* BS13... **94** A3
Brunel Wy *BMSTR* BS3.................... **26** B5
BMSTR BS3 .... **34** A3
BMSTR BS3 .... **89** D4
Brunswick Pl *CBRIS/FH* BS1 .... **26** B5 🖻
Brunswick Sq *CBRISNE* BS2 .... **21** E4
Brunswick St *CBRISNE* BS2 .... **21** E3
EVILLE/WHL BS5 .... **32** A1
Bruton Cl *EVILLE/WHL* BS5 .... **84** A3 🖻
Bryansons Cl *MANG/FISH* BS16 .... **9** D2
Bryants Cl *MANG/FISH* BS16 .... **71** D2 🖻
Bryant's Hl *EVILLE/WHL* BS5 .... **91** C1
Brynland Av *HORF/LLZ* BS7............... **5** F5
Buckingham Dr *BRSTK/PCHW* BS34 .. **53** C3
Buckingham Gdns *MANG/FISH* BS16.. **80** B1

Buckingham Pl *MANG/FISH* BS16 .. **80** B1 🖻
Buckingham Rd
BRSG/KWL/STAPK BS4 .... **33** D5
Buckingham St *BMSTR* BS3 .... **36** A5 🖻
Buckingham V *CFTN/FAIL* BS8 .... **19** D3
Bude Av *EVILLE/WHL* BS5 .... **84** B3
Bude Rd *BRSTK/PCHW* BS34 .... **52** A4
Buller Rd *BRSG/KWL/STAPK* BS4 ..... **40** A5
Bull La *EVILLE/WHL* BS5 .... **90** A1
Burbank Cl *OLD/WMLY/WICK* BS30 .. **93** D4
Burchells Green Cl
KGWD/HNM BS15 .... **85** C3
Burchells Green Rd
KGWD/HNM BS15 .... **85** C2
Burden Cl *ALMDB* BS32 .... **53** D1
Burfoote Gdns *HGRV/WHIT* BS14.... **109** D3
Burfoot Rd *HGRV/WHIT* BS14 .... **109** D3
Burford Gv *AVONM* BS11................. **75** C2
Burgess Green Cl
BRSG/KWL/STAPK BS4 .... **33** F1
Burghill Rd *HNBRY/STHM* BS10 .... **64** B2
Burghley Ct *FRCTL/WBN* BS36 .... **56** B2 🖻
Burghley Rd *RDLND/MONT* BS6 ...... **13** E4
Burgis Rd *HGRV/WHIT* BS14 .... **109** C1 🖻
Burley Av *MANG/FISH* BS16 .... **81** C2
Burley Crest *MANG/FISH* BS16 .... **81** C1
Burley Gv *MANG/FISH* BS16 .... **81** C1
Burlington Rd *RDLND/MONT* BS6 .... **11** E5
Burnbush Cl *HGRV/WHIT* BS14 .... **109** D1
Burnell Dr *CBRISNE* BS2.................. **22** A3
Burneside Cl *HNBRY/STHM* BS10 ..... **65** D1 🖻
Burney Wy *OLD/WMLY/WICK* BS30 .. **93** D4
Burnham Cl *KGWD/HNM* BS15 .... **87** C2 🖻
Burnham Dr *KGWD/HNM* BS15........ **87** C2
Burnham Rd *AVONM* BS11.............. **74** A1
Burrington Wk
BMSTRD/HC/WWD BS13 .... **94** B3 🖻
Burrough Wy *FRCTL/WBN* BS36....... **56** B2
Burton Cl *CBRIS/FH* BS1 .... **29** E5
Burton Ct *CFTN/FAIL* BS8 .... **27** E1 🖻
Burwalls Rd *CFTN/FAIL* BS8 .... **89** D1
Burycourt Cl *AVONM* BS11 .... **61** D2 🖻
Bury Hl *MANG/FISH* BS16 .... **56** B4
Bush Av *BRSTK/PCHW* BS34 .... **52** B2
Bushy Pk *BRSG/KWL/STAPK* BS4 .... **38** B3
Butcombe Wk *HGRV/WHIT* BS14 .... **108** A2
Butlers Cl *EVILLE/WHL* BS5 .... **84** A4
Butterfield Cl *HNBRY/STHM* BS10 .... **66** B4
Butterfield Rd *HNBRY/STHM* BS10.... **66** B4
Butterworth Ct
BRSG/KWL/STAPK BS4 .... **96** A4 🖻
Buxton Wk *HORF/LLZ* BS7............... **67** D3
Bye Md *MANG/FISH* BS16 .... **73** D3
Byron Pl *CFTN/FAIL* BS8 .... **27** F1 🖻
MANG/FISH BS16 .... **80** B3
Byron St *CBRISNE* BS2 .... **22** C1
EVILLE/WHL BS5 .... **24** B5

C

Cabot Wy *CFTN/FAIL* BS8 .... **26** A3
PTSHD/EG BS20 .... **74** A4
Caddick Cl *KGWD/HNM* BS15 .... **87** C1
Cade Cl *BRSTK/PCHW* BS34 .... **53** D2
KGWD/HNM BS15 .... **93** C1
Cadogan Rd *HGRV/WHIT* BS14 .... **97** D3
Caen Rd *BMSTR* BS3...................... **37** D4
Caernarvon Rd *KEYN* BS31............. **111** D3
Caine Rd *HORF/LLZ* BS7 .... **67** C4 🖻
Cains Cl *KGWD/HNM* BS15.............. **92** B1

Cairn Gdns *FRCTL/WBN* BS36 .... 56 B3 🔟
Cairns' Crs *CBRISNE* BS2 .... 22 B1
Cairns Rd *RDLND/MONT* BS6 .... 4 A5
Calcott Rd *BRSG/KWL/STAPK* BS4 ...... 38 C5
Caldbeck Cl *HNBRY/STHM* BS10 ...... 66 A1 🔟
Calder Cl *KEYN* BS31.......................... 113 D3
Caldicot Cl *AVONM* BS11 .... 62 B1 🔟
Caledonia Ms *CFTN/FAIL* BS8 .... 26 B2
Caledonia Pl *CFTN/FAIL* BS8 .... 26 A2
California Rd
    OLD/WMLY/WICK BS30 .... 93 D4
Callicroft Rd *BRSTK/PCHW* BS34 .... 43 D4
Callington Rd
    BRSG/KWL/STAPK BS4 .... 99 C2
    HGRV/WHIT BS14 .... 98 B2
Callowhill Ct *CBRIS/FH* BS1 .... 21 E5
Camberley Rd
    BRSG/KWL/STAPK BS4 .... 96 A3
Camborne Rd *HORF/LLZ* BS7 .... 67 D4
Cambridge Crs
    HNLZ/SM/SNYPK/WT BS9............. 64 B4
Cambridge Pk *RDLND/MONT* BS6 ...... 11 E3
Cambridge Rd *HORF/LLZ* BS7 .... 5 D5
Cambridge St *BMSTR* BS3 .... 38 A1
    EVILLE/WHL BS5 .... 32 B1
Camden Rd *BMSTR* BS3........................ 35 F1
Camden Ter *CFTN/FAIL* BS8 .... 26 C3 🔟
Camelford Rd *EVILLE/WHL* BS5 .... 16 C5
Cameron Wk *HORF/LLZ* BS7 .... 8 A1
Camerons Cl *KEYN* BS31 .... 112 B2
Camerton Rd *EVILLE/WHL* BS5 .... 24 C1
Campbell Farm Dr *AVONM* BS11 .... 61 D2
Campbell St *CBRISNE* BS2 .... 21 F2
Campion Dr *ALMDB* BS32 .... 45 C1 🔟
Camp Rd *CFTN/FAIL* BS8 .... 18 A5
Camwal Rd *CBRISNE* BS2 .... 31 D4
Canada Wy *CBRIS/FH* BS1 .... 27 D5
Canberra Gv *BRSTK/PCHW* BS34 .... 52 A3
Canford La
    HNLZ/SM/SNYPK/WT BS9............. 63 D4
Canford Rd
    HNLZ/SM/SNYPK/WT BS9............. 64 A4
Cannon St *BMSTR* BS3 .... 36 B2
    CBRIS/FH BS1 .... 21 D5
Canon's Rd *CBRIS/FH* BS1 .... 27 F4
    CBRIS/FH BS1 .... 28 B4
Canon St *EVILLE/WHL* BS5 .... 24 A4
Canon's Wk *KGWD/HNM* BS15 .... 86 B1
Canons Wy *CBRIS/FH* BS1 .... 28 A3
Canowie Rd *RDLND/MONT* BS6 .... 11 F3
Cantell Gv *HGRV/WHIT* BS14 .... 110 A2 🔟
Canterbury St *EVILLE/WHL* BS5 .... 31 F2
Canvey Cl *HNBRY/STHM* BS10 .... 66 B4 🔟
Canynge Rd *CFTN/FAIL* BS8 .... 18 A4
Canynge Sq *CFTN/FAIL* BS8 .... 18 A4
Canynge St *CBRIS/FH* BS1 .... 29 E3
Capel Rd *AVONM* BS11 .... 62 A2
Capgrave Cl *BRSG/KWL/STAPK* BS4 ... 90 B4
Capgrave Crs *BRSG/KWL/STAPK* BS4 .. 90 B4
Caraway Gdns *EVILLE/WHL* BS5 .... 16 B5
Cardigan La
    HNLZ/SM/SNYPK/WT BS9............... 3 E2
Cardill Cl *BMSTRD/HC/WWD* BS13 .... 94 B3
Carisbrooke Rd
    BRSG/KWL/STAPK BS4 .... 96 A3
Carlow Rd *BRSG/KWL/STAPK* BS4 ...... 96 B3
Carlton Pk *EVILLE/WHL* BS5 .... 24 A4
Carlyle Rd *EVILLE/WHL* BS5 .... 24 B1
Carmarthen Rd
    HNLZ/SM/SNYPK/WT BS9............... 3 D3 🔟
Carnarvon Rd *RDLND/MONT* BS6 ...... 12 B4

Caroline Cl *KEYN* BS31 .... 111 D3
Carpenters La *KEYN* BS31 .... 112 B2
Carrington Rd *BMSTR* BS3 .... 35 D2
Carter Wk *ALMDB* BS32 .... 45 C3 🔟
Cartledge Rd *EVILLE/WHL* BS5 .... 24 A1 🔟
Cassell Rd *MANG/FISH* BS16 .... 79 D2
Cassey Bottom La *EVILLE/WHL* BS5 84 B4 🔟
Castle Cl *HNBRY/STHM* BS10............. 63 D1
Castle Ct *BRSG/KWL/STAPK* BS4 .... 40 A1
Castle Farm Rd *KGWD/HNM* BS15 ... 101 C1
Castle Rd *KGWD/HNM* BS15 .... 85 D1
Castle St *CBRISNE* BS2 .... 29 F1
Catbrain HI *HNBRY/STHM* BS10 .... 49 C1
Catbrain La *HNBRY/STHM* BS10......... 49 C1
Cater Rd *BMSTRD/HC/WWD* BS13 .... 105 C1
Catherine Mead St *BMSTR* BS3 .... 36 B2
Catherine St *AVONM* BS11 .... 59 D4
Cato St *EVILLE/WHL* BS5 .... 23 F1 🔟
Cattistock Dr *EVILLE/WHL* BS5 .... 90 B1
Cattle Market Rd *CBRIS/FH* BS1......... 30 A4
Cattybrook St *EVILLE/WHL* BS5 .... 23 F4 🔟
    EVILLE/WHL BS5 .... 23 F5 🔟
Causley Dr *OLD/WMLY/WICK* BS30.... 93 C2
Cavan Wk *BRSG/KWL/STAPK* BS4....... 96 A2
Cave Dr *MANG/FISH* BS16 .... 80 A1
Cavendish Gdns
    HNLZ/SM/SNYPK/WT BS9............. 76 B3
Cavendish Rd *BRSTK/PCHW* BS34 ..... 43 C3
    HNLZ/SM/SNYPK/WT BS9............... 3 D3
Cave St *CBRISNE* BS2 .... 21 F3
Cecil Av *EVILLE/WHL* BS5 .... 84 A2
Cecil Rd *CFTN/FAIL* BS8 .... 18 A3
    KGWD/HNM BS15 .... 86 A3
Cedar Cl *BRSTK/PCHW* BS34 .... 43 C4
Cedar Dr *KEYN* BS31 .... 112 A3
Cedar Gv *HNLZ/SM/SNYPK/WT* BS9 ... 77 C2
Cedar Pk *HNLZ/SM/SNYPK/WT* BS9 ... 77 C2
Cedar Wy *FRCTL/WBN* BS36 .... 56 A2
Celia Ter *BRSG/KWL/STAPK* BS4 ...... 90 A1 🔟
Cemetery Rd *BRSG/KWL/STAPK* BS4 .. 39 D3
Cennick Av *KGWD/HNM* BS15 .... 86 B2
Central Av *KGWD/HNM* BS15 .... 91 D2
Ceres Cl *OLD/WMLY/WICK* BS30 ..... 103 C1
Cerimon Ga *BRSTK/PCHW* BS34 .... 53 D2 🔟
Cerney La *AVONM* BS11 .... 74 B2
Chadleigh Gv *BRSG/KWL/STAPK* BS4 . 95 D4
Chakeshill Cl *HNBRY/STHM* BS10 ...... 49 D4
Chakeshill Dr *HNBRY/STHM* BS10 ..... 49 D4
Chalcombe Cl *BRSTK/PCHW* BS34 ..... 44 B3
Chalks Rd *EVILLE/WHL* BS5 .... 24 C3
Challender Av *HNBRY/STHM* BS10...... 64 A1
Challoner Ct *CBRIS/FH* BS1 .... 28 C5
Champion Rd *KGWD/HNM* BS15 .... 87 D1
Champneys Av *HNBRY/STHM* BS10 48 A4 🔟
Chancel Cl *HNLZ/SM/SNYPK/WT* BS9.. 77 C4
Chancery St *EVILLE/WHL* BS5 .... 31 E1
Chandag Rd *KEYN* BS31 .... 113 D1
Chandos Rd *KEYN* BS31 .... 102 B4
    RDLND/MONT BS6........................ 19 F1
Channell's HI
    HNLZ/SM/SNYPK/WT BS9............. 64 B3
Channon's HI *MANG/FISH* BS16 .... 78 A3
Chantry Gv *AVONM* BS11 .... 62 B1 🔟
Chantry La *MANG/FISH* BS16 .... 73 C2 🔟
Chantry Rd *CFTN/FAIL* BS8 .... 19 E2
Chapel Gdns *HNBRY/STHM* BS10 ...... 64 B2
Chapel Green La *RDLND/MONT* BS6 ... 11 F4
Chapel La *AVONM* BS11 .... 62 A1
    EVILLE/WHL BS5 .... 17 F5
    MANG/FISH BS16 .... 71 D4
Chapel Rd *BMSTRD/HC/WWD* BS13.. 104 B1
    EVILLE/WHL BS5 .... 23 F1

KGWD/HNM BS15 .... **91** D2
Chapel St *CBRISNE* BS2 .... **30** C4
Chapel Wy *BRSG/KWL/STAPK* BS4 ...... **33** E2
Chaplin Rd *EVILLE/WHL* BS5 .... **23** E2
Chapter St *CBRISNE* BS2 .... **21** F3
Charbon Ga *BRSTK/PCHW* BS34 ...... **53** D2 🄳
Charborough Rd
    BRSTK/PCHW BS34 .... **67** C1
Chardstock Av
    HNLZ/SM/SNYPK/WT BS9 .... **62** B3
Charfield *KGWD/HNM* BS15 .... **87** D3 🄳
Charfield Rd *HNBRY/STHM* BS10 ...... **65** D2
Charis Av *HNBRY/STHM* BS10 .... **65** D4
Charlecombe Rd
    HNLZ/SM/SNYPK/WT BS9 .... **2** A1
Charles Av *BRSTK/PCHW* BS34 ...... **53** D3 🄳
Charles Pl *CFTN/FAIL* BS8 .... **26** C3
Charles Rd *BRSTK/PCHW* BS34 ...... **52** A4
Charles St *CBRISNE* BS2 .... **21** D4
Charlotte St *CBRIS/FH* BS1 .... **28** A2
    CBRISNE BS2 .... **22** A4 🄳
Charlotte St South *CBRIS/FH* BS1 ...... **28** A2
Charlton Av *BRSTK/PCHW* BS34 ...... **67** C1
Charlton Gdns *HNBRY/STHM* BS10 .... **50** A3
Charlton La *HNBRY/STHM* BS10 ...... **48** B4
Charlton Mead Dr
    HNBRY/STHM BS10 .... **50** A3
Charlton Pk *KEYN* BS31 .... **112** A2
Charlton Pl *HNBRY/STHM* BS10 ...... **50** A3 🄳
Charlton Rd *HNBRY/STHM* BS10 ...... **49** D4
    HNBRY/STHM BS10 .... **65** C2
    KGWD/HNM BS15 .... **85** C2
Charlton St *EVILLE/WHL* BS5 .... **31** E1
Charminster Rd *MANG/FISH* BS16 .... **79** C4
Charnell Rd *MANG/FISH* BS16 .... **80** B3
Charnhill Brow *MANG/FISH* BS16... **81** D3
Charnhill Crs *MANG/FISH* BS16 ...... **81** C3
Charnhill Dr *MANG/FISH* BS16 ...... **81** C3
Charnhill Rdg *MANG/FISH* BS16 ...... **81** C3
Charnhill V *MANG/FISH* BS16 .... **81** D3
Charnwood *MANG/FISH* BS16 .... **81** D3
Charnwood Rd *HGRV/WHIT* BS14 .... **108** A4
Charterhouse Rd
    EVILLE/WHL BS5 .... **25** D3 🄳
Chasefield La *MANG/FISH* BS16 ...... **79** C3 🄳
Chase Rd *KGWD/HNM* BS15 .... **86** A1
The Chase *MANG/FISH* BS16 .... **79** D4 🄳
Chatsworth Rd
    BRSG/KWL/STAPK BS4 .... **39** F2
    MANG/FISH BS16 .... **79** C4
Chatterton Gn *HGRV/WHIT* BS14 .... **107** C4 🄳
Chatterton Sq *CBRIS/FH* BS1 .... **29** F5
Chaundey Gv
    BMSTRD/HC/WWD BS13............ **105** C2
Cheapside *CBRISNE* BS2 .... **22** A3
Cheapside St *BMSTR* BS3 .... **38** B2
Cheddar Gv
    BMSTRD/HC/WWD BS13............ **94** B3
Chedworth *KGWD/HNM* BS15 ...... **80** B4
Chedworth Rd *HORF/LLZ* BS7 .... **6** C1
Cheese La *CBRISNE* BS2 .... **29** F2
Chelford Gv *BRSTK/PCHW* BS34 ...... **44** A3 🄳
Chelmer Gv *KEYN* BS31 .... **113** C3
Chelmsford Wk
    BRSG/KWL/STAPK BS4 .... **33** F4
    BRSG/KWL/STAPK BS4 .... **90** A2 🄳
Chelsea Cl *KEYN* BS31 .... **113** D2 🄳
Chelsea Pk *EVILLE/WHL* BS5 .... **24** A3
Chelsea Rd *EVILLE/WHL* BS5 .... **24** A3
Chelston Rd *BRSG/KWL/STAPK* BS4... **96** A4
Cheltenham La *RDLND/MONT* BS6 .... **13** E5
Cheltenham Rd *RDLND/MONT* BS6 .... **21** D1

Chelvy Cl *BMSTRD/HC/WWD* BS13.... **106** A4
Chelwood Rd *AVONM* BS11............ **60** A4
Chepstow Pk *MANG/FISH* BS16 ...... **73** C2 🄳
Chepstow Rd *BRSG/KWL/STAPK* BS4.. **96** A3
Cherington *KGWD/HNM* BS15 .... **91** C2
Cherington Rd *HNBRY/STHM* BS10 .... **65** D4
Cheriton Pl
    HNLZ/SM/SNYPK/WT BS9................ **65** C4
Cherry Gv *MANG/FISH* BS16 .... **81** D1
Cherry La *CBRIS/FH* BS1 .... **21** D4
Cherry Tree Cl *KEYN* BS31 .... **111** D3 🄳
Cherrytree Crs *MANG/FISH* BS16 .... **85** D1
Cherrytree Rd *KGWD/HNM* BS15 .... **85** D1
Chertsey Rd *RDLND/MONT* BS6 ...... **19** E1
Cherwell Rd *KEYN* BS31 .... **113** D3
Chesham Wy *KGWD/HNM* BS15 .... **86** A2 🄳
Chessel Cl *ALMDB* BS32 .... **44** B1
Chessel St *BMSTR* BS3 .... **35** E4
Chessington Av *HGRV/WHIT* BS14 .. **108** A2
Chesterfield Cl *RDLND/MONT* BS6 ... **13** E5
Chesterfield Rd *MANG/FISH* BS16 .... **80** B2
    RDLND/MONT BS6.................... **13** E5
Chester Pk *EVILLE/WHL* BS5 .... **25** E3
Chester Park Rd *MANG/FISH* BS16 .... **85** C1
Chester Rd *EVILLE/WHL* BS5 .... **25** E2
Chesters *OLD/WMLY/WICK* BS30 .... **93** D3 🄳
Chester St *EVILLE/WHL* BS5 .... **15** F5
Chestnut Cl *HGRV/WHIT* BS14....... **109** D2
Chestnut Ct *MANG/FISH* BS16 ...... **81** D2
Chestnut Rd *KGWD/HNM* BS15 .... **81** C4 🄳
    MANG/FISH BS16 .... **80** A1 🄳
Chestnut Wk
    BMSTRD/HC/WWD BS13............ **104** B1
Chestnut Wy *KGWD/HNM* BS15 .... **81** D4
Chetwode Cl *HNBRY/STHM* BS10 .... **50** A4
Chevening Cl *BRSTK/PCHW* BS34 .... **53** C3 🄳
Chewton Cl *MANG/FISH* BS16 ...... **79** C4
Cheyne Rd
    HNLZ/SM/SNYPK/WT BS9............ **77** C1
Chillington Ct *BRSTK/PCHW* BS34 .... **42** B2
Chiltern Cl *HGRV/WHIT* BS14 ...... **108** A3
Chilton Rd *BRSG/KWL/STAPK* BS4 .... **97** C3
The Chine *MANG/FISH* BS16 .... **8** C3
Chine Vw *MANG/FISH* BS16 .... **73** C3
Chiphouse Rd *KGWD/HNM* BS15 .... **86** B1
Chipperfield Dr *KGWD/HNM* BS15 .... **87** C2
The Chippings *MANG/FISH* BS16 .... **8** C3
Chisbury St *EVILLE/WHL* BS5 ...... **16** A3 🄳
Chock La *HNLZ/SM/SNYPK/WT* BS9.... **64** B4
Christchurch Av *MANG/FISH* BS16 .. **80** A2 🄳
Christchurch La *MANG/FISH* BS16 .. **80** A2 🄳
Christchurch Rd *CFTN/FAIL* BS8........ **18** C5
Christmas St *CBRIS/FH* BS1 .... **28** C3 🄳
Chubb Cl *OLD/WMLY/WICK* BS30 .... **93** C2
Church Av *EVILLE/WHL* BS5 .... **23** F1
    HNLZ/SM/SNYPK/WT BS9............ **77** C3
Church Dr *EVILLE/WHL* BS5.......... **25** F4
Church Hl *BRSG/KWL/STAPK* BS4 .... **41** E5
Churchill Cl
    OLD/WMLY/WICK BS30 .... **93** D2 🄳
Churchill Dr
    HNLZ/SM/SNYPK/WT BS9............ **63** C4
Churchill Rd *BRSG/KWL/STAPK* BS4.. **40** B2
Church La *BMSTR* BS3 .... **36** C3
    CBRIS/FH BS1............................ **29** F3
    CFTN/FAIL BS8 .... **27** E3
    FRCTL/WBN BS36...................... **55** D1
    HNBRY/STHM BS10 .... **63** D1
    MANG/FISH BS16 .... **72** B1
Church Leaze *AVONM* BS11 .... **74** A1
Church Pde
    BRSG/KWL/STAPK BS4 .... **99** D1 🄳

Church Rd *BMSTR* BS3.................... 36 B2
  BMSTRD/HC/WWD BS13............... 104 B2
  BRSTK/PCHW BS34 .... 51 D4
  BRSTK/PCHW BS34 .... 53 D4
  CFTN/FAIL BS8 .... 82 A2
  CFTN/FAIL BS8 .... 89 C1
  EVILLE/WHL BS5 .... 24 A5
  FRCTL/WBN BS36...................... 56 B3
  HGRV/WHIT BS14...................... 108 A4
  HNLZ/SM/SNYPK/WT BS9............. 64 B4
  HNLZ/SM/SNYPK/WT BS9............. 77 C4
  HORF/LLZ BS7 .... 5 E2
  KGWD/HNM BS15....................... 86 B3
  KGWD/HNM BS15....................... 91 C2
  MANG/FISH BS16 .... 71 C4
  MANG/FISH BS16 .... 86 A1
Churchside *MANG/FISH* BS16 .... 71 C4 🖪
Church St *CBRIS/FH* BS1 .... 29 F3
  EVILLE/WHL BS5 .... 23 F1
  EVILLE/WHL BS5 .... 31 F2
Churchward Cl *KGWD/HNM* BS15 .. 91 C2 🖪
Churchways *HGRV/WHIT* BS14...... 108 B3
Churchways Av *HORF/LLZ* BS7 ...... 5 E2
Churchways Crs *HORF/LLZ* BS7 ...... 5 F2
Churchlands Rd *BMSTR* BS3 .... 35 F5 🖪
Churston Cl *HGRV/WHIT* BS14 ..... 107 D4 🖪
Circular Rd
  HNLZ/SM/SNYPK/WT BS9............. 83 D1
City Rd *CBRISNE* BS2 .... 21 F3
Clanage Rd *BMSTR* BS3 .... 89 D3
Clapton Wk
  HNLZ/SM/SNYPK/WT BS9............. 76 A2
Clare Av *HORF/LLZ* BS7 .... 12 B2
Claremont Av *HORF/LLZ* BS7 .... 12 B2
Claremont Rd *HORF/LLZ* BS7 .... 12 C3
Claremont St *EVILLE/WHL* BS5 ...... 23 D4
Claremont Ter *EVILLE/WHL* BS5 ..... 24 C5 🖪
Clarence Av *MANG/FISH* BS16 .... 80 B3
Clarence Gdns *MANG/FISH* BS16 ... 80 B2 🖪
Clarence Pl *CBRISNE* BS2 .... 20 B4
Clarence Rd *CBRIS/FH* BS1 .... 37 E1
  CBRISNE BS2 .... 22 C5
  KGWD/HNM BS15....................... 85 C2
  MANG/FISH BS16 .... 80 A2
Clarendon Rd *RDLND/MONT* BS6..... 12 A4
Clare Rd *EVILLE/WHL* BS5 .... 15 F5
  KGWD/HNM BS15....................... 85 D1
  RDLND/MONT BS6..................... 20 C2
Clare St *EVILLE/WHL* BS5 .... 24 B4
Clark Dr *MANG/FISH* BS16 .... 78 A1
Clarke St *BMSTR* BS3 .... 37 D2
Clark St *EVILLE/WHL* BS5 .... 22 C3
Clatworthy Dr *HGRV/WHIT* BS14 ... 97 C4
Clavell Rd *HNBRY/STHM* BS10 .... 64 A1
Claverham Rd *MANG/FISH* BS16 .... 78 B2 🖪
Clay Bottom *EVILLE/WHL* BS5 .... 17 E4
Clayfield Rd *BRSG/KWL/STAPK* BS4 .. 41 E4
Clay Hi *EVILLE/WHL* BS5................. 17 F4
Clay La *BRSTK/PCHW* BS34 .... 44 B4
Claymore Crs *KGWD/HNM* BS15 ..... 85 C2 🖪
Claypiece Rd
  BMSTRD/HC/WWD BS13............. 104 A3
Clay Pit Rd
  HNLZ/SM/SNYPK/WT BS9............. 11 D2
Claypool Rd *KGWD/HNM* BS15 .... 86 A4
Clayton St *AVONM* BS11 .... 58 B2
  EVILLE/WHL BS5 .... 23 F4
Cleave St *CBRISNE* BS2 .... 14 C5
Cleeve Av *MANG/FISH* BS16 .... 72 A4
Cleeve Gdns *MANG/FISH* BS16 ...... 72 A4
Cleeve Gv *KEYN* BS31 .... 112 A2
Cleeve Hi *MANG/FISH* BS16 .... 72 A4

Cleeve Hill Extension
  MANG/FISH BS16 .... 80 B1
Cleeve Lawns *MANG/FISH* BS16 .... 72 A4
Cleeve Lodge Rd *MANG/FISH* BS16 .. 72 B4
Cleeve Park Rd *MANG/FISH* BS16 ... 72 A4
Cleeve Rd *BRSG/KWL/STAPK* BS4 ... 39 F5
  MANG/FISH BS16 .... 71 D3
  MANG/FISH BS16 .... 80 B1
Cleeve Wood Rd
  MANG/FISH BS16 .... 72 A4 🖪
Clement St *CBRISNE* BS2 .... 22 A4
Clevedale *MANG/FISH* BS16 .... 72 A4
Clevedon Rd *HORF/LLZ* BS7 .... 5 D5
Clevedon Ter *RDLND/MONT* BS6 ..... 20 C3
Cleve Rd *BRSTK/PCHW* BS34......... 51 D3
Clewson Ri *HGRV/WHIT* BS14 ...... 107 C4 🖪
Cliff Court Dr *MANG/FISH* BS16 ..... 71 C4
Clifford Gdns *AVONM* BS11 .... 74 B1
Clifford Rd *MANG/FISH* BS16 .... 79 D3
Cliff House Rd *BMSTR* BS3 .... 34 C1
Clifton Down *CFTN/FAIL* BS8 .... 18 A4
Clifton Down Rd *CFTN/FAIL* BS8 .... 18 B5
  CFTN/FAIL BS8 .... 26 C1
Clifton Gv
  HNLZ/SM/SNYPK/WT BS9 .... 77 D2 🖪
Clifton Hi *CFTN/FAIL* BS8 .... 27 D2
Clifton Pk *CFTN/FAIL* BS8 .... 18 C5
Clifton Park Rd *CFTN/FAIL* BS8....... 18 B4
Clifton Pl *EVILLE/WHL* BS5 .... 23 D4
Clifton Rd *CFTN/FAIL* BS8 .... 27 D2
Clifton St *BMSTR* BS3 .... 36 A4
Clifton V *CFTN/FAIL* BS8............... 26 C3
Clifton Vale Cl *CFTN/FAIL* BS8 .... 26 C3
Cliftonwood Crs *CFTN/FAIL* BS8..... 27 E3
Clifton Wood Rd *CFTN/FAIL* BS8 .... 27 E2
Cliftonwood Ter *CFTN/FAIL* BS8 ..... 27 D3
Clift *CBRIS/FH* BS1 .... 29 D4
Clift Rd *BMSTR* BS3 .... 34 C1
Clinton Rd *BMSTR* BS3................. 36 B5
Clive Rd *HGRV/WHIT* BS14 .... 98 B4
Cloisters Rd *FRCTL/WBN* BS36 ...... 56 B1
Clonmel Rd *BRSG/KWL/STAPK* BS4 .. 96 A2
The Close *BRSTK/PCHW* BS34 .... 44 B2
  HNBRY/STHM BS10 .... 48 A2
  MANG/FISH BS16 .... 80 A4
Clothier Rd
  BRSG/KWL/STAPK BS4 .... 100 A1 🖪
Clouds Hill Av *EVILLE/WHL* BS5...... 25 F3
Clouds Hill Rd *EVILLE/WHL* BS5 ..... 25 F4
  EVILLE/WHL BS5 .... 84 A3
Clovelly Cl *EVILLE/WHL* BS5........... 84 A3
Clovelly Rd *EVILLE/WHL* BS5 .... 84 A3
Cloverdale Dr
  OLD/WMLY/WICK BS30............... 93 D4
Clover Gnd
  HNLZ/SM/SNYPK/WT BS9............. 65 C3
Clover Leaze *BRSTK/PCHW* BS34 ... 53 C1
Clyde Av *KEYN* BS31 .... 113 C3
Clyde Gdns *EVILLE/WHL* BS5 .... 91 C1 🖪
Clyde Gv *BRSTK/PCHW* BS34......... 67 C1
Clyde La *RDLND/MONT* BS6 .... 11 F5
Clyde Rd *BRSG/KWL/STAPK* BS4 .... 39 D4
  RDLND/MONT BS6..................... 11 F5
Clydesdale Cl *HGRV/WHIT* BS14 .... 97 C4
  HGRV/WHIT BS14.................... 107 C1
Clyde Ter *BMSTR* BS3 .... 36 A3
  BRSG/KWL/STAPK BS4 .... 39 D3
Coaley Rd *AVONM* BS11 .... 74 A2
Coape Rd *HGRV/WHIT* BS14 .... 110 A2
Cobblestone Ms *CFTN/FAIL* BS8 .... 18 C5
Cobden St *EVILLE/WHL* BS5 .... 23 F5
Coberley *KGWD/HNM* BS15............ 91 D1

Cobhorn Dr
BMSTRD/HC/WWD BS13................ **104** A3
Cobourg Rd *RDLND/MONT BS6* **22** A1
Cock Rd *KGWD/HNM BS15*................ **92** B1
Codrington Pl *CFTN/FAIL BS8* .... **19** D5 ⑤
Codrington Rd *HORF/LLZ BS7* **13** D2
Cogan Rd *MANG/FISH BS16*.............. **80** B4
Cogsall Rd *HGRV/WHIT BS14* .... **110** A1 ①
Colchester Crs
BRSG/KWL/STAPK BS4 .... **96** A4
Coldharbour La *BRSTK/PCHW BS34* .. **69** D2
MANG/FISH BS16........................ **69** D3
Coldharbour Rd *RDLND/MONT BS6*... **11** E2
Coldrick Cl *HGRV/WHIT BS14* **107** C4
Coleford Rd *HNBRY/STHM BS10* **66** A3
Colemead *BMSTRD/HC/WWD BS13*... **105** C2
Coleridge Rd *EVILLE/WHL BS5* **116** A1
Cole Rd *CBRISNE BS2* **31** F3
Coleshill Dr
BMSTRD/HC/WWD BS13............... **105** C2
College Av *MANG/FISH BS16* .... **78** B2 ②
College Ct *MANG/FISH BS16* **78** B2
College Flds *CFTN/FAIL BS8* **18** B3
College Gn *CBRIS/FH BS1* **28** B3
College Park Dr *HNBRY/STHM BS10* .. **64** A4
College Rd *CFTN/FAIL BS8* **18** B3
HNLZ/SM/SNYPK/WT BS9 .... **64** B4
MANG/FISH BS16........................ **78** B2
College Sq *CBRIS/FH BS1* **28** A3
College St *CBRIS/FH BS1* **28** A2
Collett Cl *KGWD/HNM BS15* .... **91** C2 ③
Collingwood Av
KGWD/HNM BS15 .... **86** B2 ①
Collingwood Rd *RDLND/MONT BS6*... **19** F1
Collin Rd *BRSG/KWL/STAPK BS4* **41** D1
Collins Av *BRSTK/PCHW BS34* **52** B1
Collinson Rd
BMSTRD/HC/WWD BS13............... **105** C2
Collins St *AVONM BS11* **59** C3
Colliter Crs *BMSTR BS3* **35** D5
Colston Av *CBRIS/FH BS1* **28** C2
Colston Cl *FRCTL/WBN BS36* **56** B3
MANG/FISH BS16........................ **80** A4 ④
Colston Dl *MANG/FISH BS16* **9** E5
Colston Hl *MANG/FISH BS16* **8** C5
Colston Pde *CBRIS/FH BS1* **29** E4
Colston Rd *EVILLE/WHL BS5* **24** A2
Colston St *CBRIS/FH BS1* **28** C1
MANG/FISH BS16........................ **80** A4
Colthurst Dr *KGWD/HNM BS15*......... **92** A1
Colwyn Rd *EVILLE/WHL BS5* **24** A2
Combe Cross Wk
BMSTRD/HC/WWD BS13 .... **105** C4 ①
Combfactory La *EVILLE/WHL BS5* .. **23** E3 ①
Comb Paddock
HNLZ/SM/SNYPK/WT BS9 .... **65** C4
Commercial Rd *CBRIS/FH BS1* **28** C5
The Common (East) *ALMDB BS32* **44** B2
Commonfield Rd *AVONM BS11* **62** A2
Common Mead La *MANG/FISH BS16*.. **70** B2
Common Rd *KGWD/HNM BS15* **91** C4
The Common *BRSTK/PCHW BS34* **44** A2
MANG/FISH BS16........................ **71** C4
Compton Gn *KEYN BS31* **112** B3
Compton St *EVILLE/WHL BS5* **32** B1
Comyn Wk *MANG/FISH BS16* **78** B2
Concorde Dr *HNBRY/STHM BS10* ...... **65** C1 ①
Condover Rd *BRSG/KWL/STAPK BS4*.. **90** A4
Conduit Pl *CBRISNE BS2* .... **22** C1 ②
Conduit Rd *CBRISNE BS2* **22** C1
Congleton Rd *EVILLE/WHL BS5* **25** D2

Conham Hl *KGWD/HNM BS15*........... **90** B2
Conham Rd *KGWD/HNM BS15* **90** A2
Conham V *KGWD/HNM BS15* **90** A2
Conifer Cl *MANG/FISH BS16* .... **80** A1 ②
Coniston Av
HNLZ/SM/SNYPK/WT BS9 .... **77** D1
Coniston Rd *BRSTK/PCHW BS34* **42** B3
Connaught Rd
BRSG/KWL/STAPK BS4 .... **96** B3
Constable Cl *KEYN BS31* .... **113** C1 ①
Constable Rd *HORF/LLZ BS7* **7** E1
Constantine Av *BRSTK/PCHW BS34*... **53** D2
Constitution Hl *CFTN/FAIL BS8* **27** E2
Conway Gn *KEYN BS31* **113** D4
Conway Rd *BRSG/KWL/STAPK BS4* **40** B1
Conygre Gv *BRSTK/PCHW BS34* .... **52** B4 ①
Conygre Rd *BRSTK/PCHW BS34* **52** A4
Cook's Folly Rd
HNLZ/SM/SNYPK/WT BS9 .... **77** C4 ①
Cooksley Rd *EVILLE/WHL BS5*.......... **24** B4
Cook St *AVONM BS11* **59** C3
Cookworthy Cl *EVILLE/WHL BS5* **31** F2
Coombe Bridge Av
HNLZ/SM/SNYPK/WT BS9 .... **77** C1
Coombe Dl
HNLZ/SM/SNYPK/WT BS9 .... **76** B1
Coombe Gdns
HNLZ/SM/SNYPK/WT BS9 .... **77** D1
Coombe La
HNLZ/SM/SNYPK/WT BS9 .... **77** C1
Coombe Rd *EVILLE/WHL BS5* **16** B3
Coombe Wy *HNBRY/STHM BS10* **64** A2
Cooperage La *BMSTR BS3*................ **27** E5
Cooperage Rd *EVILLE/WHL BS5* **32** B1
Co-operation Rd *EVILLE/WHL BS5*.... **24** B1
Cooper Rd
HNLZ/SM/SNYPK/WT BS9 .... **64** A4
The Coots *HGRV/WHIT BS14* **109** D1
Copeland Dr *HGRV/WHIT BS14* .... **108** A2 ②
Copley Ct *KGWD/HNM BS15* .... **92** B2 ①
Copley Gdns *HORF/LLZ BS7* **7** F1
The Coppice *ALMDB BS32* **45** D4
Copse Rd *BRSG/KWL/STAPK BS4* **39** E4
Copthorne Cl *HGRV/WHIT BS14* ...... **108** A2 ①
Corbet Cl *AVONM BS11* **62** A1
Cordwell Wk *HNBRY/STHM BS10* ..... **66** A4 ①
Corey Cl *CBRISNE BS2* **22** A2
Corfe Crs *KEYN BS31* **112** B2
Corfe Rd *BRSG/KWL/STAPK BS4* ...... **96** A1 ②
Coriander Dr *ALMDB BS32* **46** B4
Coriander Wk *EVILLE/WHL BS5* **16** A5
Cornfield Cl *ALMDB BS32* **44** B2
Cornhill Dr *HGRV/WHIT BS14* **97** D4
Cornish Gv *HGRV/WHIT BS14* .... **109** D1 ②
Cornish Rd *HGRV/WHIT BS14* **109** D1
Cornish Wk *HGRV/WHIT BS14*........ **109** D1
Cornleaze
BMSTRD/HC/WWD BS13 .... **104** D2 ①
Corn St *CBRIS/FH BS1* **29** D2
Cornwallis Av *CFTN/FAIL BS8* .... **26** B3 ②
Cornwallis Crs *CFTN/FAIL BS8*.......... **26** B2
Cornwall Rd *HORF/LLZ BS7* **4** C5
Coronation Av *KEYN BS31* **112** A3
MANG/FISH BS16........................ **78** B3
Coronation Cl
OLD/WMLY/WICK BS30 .... **93** D2 ③
Coronation Pl *CBRIS/FH BS1* .... **29** D2 ①
Coronation Rd *BMSTR BS3* **27** F5
BMSTR BS3............................... **34** C1
BMSTR BS3............................... **36** C1
KGWD/HNM BS15 .... **87** C4
MANG/FISH BS16........................ **80** B2

Corsley Wk *BRSG/KWL/STAPK* BS4 .. **97** C3 🔢
Corston Wk *AVONM* BS11 .... **60** A4
Cossham Rd *EVILLE/WHL* BS5 .... **25** D5
Cossham Wk *EVILLE/WHL* BS5 .... **84** B2
Cossington Rd
  BRSG/KWL/STAPK BS4 .... **97** C3
Cossins Rd *RDLND/MONT* BS6 .... **11** F2
Costiland Dr
  BMSTRD/HC/WWD BS13 .... **104** A1 🔢
Cote Dr *HNLZ/SM/SNYPK/WT* BS9 ..... **2** C5
Cote House La
  HNLZ/SM/SNYPK/WT BS9 .... **2** B4
Cote La *HNLZ/SM/SNYPK/WT* BS9 ..... **2** C3
Cote Lea Pk
  HNLZ/SM/SNYPK/WT BS9 .... **64** B4 🔢
Cote Paddock
  HNLZ/SM/SNYPK/WT BS9 .... **2** B5
Cote Pk *HNLZ/SM/SNYPK/WT* BS9 .... **77** D1
Cote Rd *HNLZ/SM/SNYPK/WT* BS9 ..... **2** C5
Cotham Brow *RDLND/MONT* BS6 ..... **13** D5
Cotham Gdns *RDLND/MONT* BS6 ..... **19** F2 🔢
Cotham Gv *RDLND/MONT* BS6 .... **20** C2
Cotham Hl *RDLND/MONT* BS6 .... **19** F2 🔢
Cotham Lawn Rd
  RDLND/MONT BS6 .... **20** A3
Cotham Pk *RDLND/MONT* BS6 .... **20** B2
Cotham Pk North
  RDLND/MONT BS6 .... **20** B1
Cotham Rd *RDLND/MONT* BS6 .... **20** B3
Cotham Rd South
  RDLND/MONT BS6 .... **20** C3
Cotham Side *RDLND/MONT* BS6 .... **20** C2
Cotham V *RDLND/MONT* BS6 .... **20** A2
Cotman Rd *HORF/LLZ* BS7 .... **7** E2
Cotswold Rd *BMSTR* BS3 .... **36** C4
Cotswold Vw *KGWD/HNM* BS15 ...... **86** A1
Cottage Pl *CBRISNE* BS2 .... **20** C4
Cottington Ct *KGWD/HNM* BS15 ...... **92** B2 🔢
Cottisford Rd *EVILLE/WHL* BS5 .... **15** F1 🔢
Cottle Gdns *HGRV/WHIT* BS14 .... **110** A1
Cottle Rd *HGRV/WHIT* BS14............ **110** A1
Cottonwood Dr
  OLD/WMLY/WICK BS30 .... **93** D4
Cottrell Av *KGWD/HNM* BS15 .... **85** C1
Cottrell Rd *EVILLE/WHL* BS5 .... **16** A2
Coulson's Cl *HGRV/WHIT* BS14 ...... **107** D4
Coulson's Rd *HGRV/WHIT* BS14 ..... **107** D4
Coulson Wk *KGWD/HNM* BS15 .... **85** D1 🔢
Counterpool Rd *KGWD/HNM* BS15 ... **85** B4
Countership *CBRIS/FH* BS1 .... **29** E2
Countership Gdns
  HGRV/WHIT BS14 .... **108** B1
Countess Wk *MANG/FISH* BS16 .... **9** D2
County St *BRSG/KWL/STAPK* BS4 ..... **38** B2
Court Av *BRSTK/PCHW* BS34 .... **54** A2 🔢
Court Cl *HORF/LLZ* BS7 .... **66** B4
Courteney Crs
  BRSG/KWL/STAPK BS4 .... **96** A4 🔢
Court Farm Rd *HGRV/WHIT* BS14 .... **107** C4
  OLD/WMLY/WICK BS30 .... **102** A2
Courtfield Gv *MANG/FISH* BS16 .... **78** B3
Courtlands *ALMDB* BS32 .... **44** B3
  KEYN BS31 .... **112** B2
Courtlands La *BMSTR* BS3 .... **89** D3
Courtney Rd *KGWD/HNM* BS15 .... **86** B4
Courtney Wy *KGWD/HNM* BS15 ...... **87** D4
Court Rd *KGWD/HNM* BS15 .... **86** B4
Courtside Ms *RDLND/MONT* BS6 ..... **20** B1
Cousins Ms *BRSG/KWL/STAPK* BS4 .. **90** A4 🔢
Cousins Wy *MANG/FISH* BS16 .... **73** D3
Couzens Pl *BRSTK/PCHW* BS34 ...... **54** A2 🔢

Coventry Wk
  BRSG/KWL/STAPK BS4 .... **90** A1 🔢
Cowdray Rd
  BRSG/KWL/STAPK BS4 .... **96** A4 🔢
Cowler Wk
  BMSTRD/HC/WWD BS13 .... **104** A3 🔢
Cowling Dr *HGRV/WHIT* BS14 .... **108** B2
Cowling Rd *HGRV/WHIT* BS14.......... **108** B2
Cowper Rd *RDLND/MONT* BS6 .... **19** F1
Cowper St *EVILLE/WHL* BS5 .... **24** A5
Cox Ct *OLD/WMLY/WICK* BS30 .... **93** C3
Crabtree Wk *EVILLE/WHL* BS5 .... **17** D5
Cranberry Wk
  HNLZ/SM/SNYPK/WT BS9 .... **62** B3 🔢
Cranbourne Rd *BRSTK/PCHW* BS34 ... **43** C4
Cranbrook Rd *RDLND/MONT* BS6 ..... **12** B2
Crandell Cl *HNBRY/STHM* BS10 .... **48** A3
Cranham Cl *KGWD/HNM* BS15 .... **33** C1 🔢
Cranham Dr *BRSTK/PCHW* BS34 ...... **44** B2
Cranham Rd *HNBRY/STHM* BS10 ..... **65** D3
Cranleigh Gdns
  HNLZ/SM/SNYPK/WT BS9 .... **77** D3
Cranleigh Rd *HGRV/WHIT* BS14 ..... **108** A2 🔢
Cranmore Av *KEYN* BS31 .... **112** B1
Cranmore Crs *HNBRY/STHM* BS10 ... **66** A2
Cranside Av *RDLND/MONT* BS6 .... **12** A2
Cransley Crs
  HNLZ/SM/SNYPK/WT BS9 .... **65** D4
Crantock Av
  BMSTRD/HC/WWD BS13 .... **95** C3
Cranwell Gv *HGRV/WHIT* BS14 ...... **107** D2
Craven Cl *OLD/WMLY/WICK* BS30 ... **93** C2
Craven Wy *OLD/WMLY/WICK* BS30 ... **93** C2
Craydon Gv *HGRV/WHIT* BS14 .... **109** C3
Craydon Rd *HGRV/WHIT* BS14 .... **109** C2
Craydon Wk *HGRV/WHIT* BS14 ...... **109** C2 🔢
Crediton Crs *BRSG/KWL/STAPK* BS4 .. **97** C2
Crescent Rd *MANG/FISH* BS16 .... **79** D1
The Crescent
  HNLZ/SM/SNYPK/WT BS9 .... **4** A1
  HNLZ/SM/SNYPK/WT BS9 .... **76** B1
  MANG/FISH BS16 .... **70** A2
  MANG/FISH BS16 .... **80** A4
The Crest *BRSG/KWL/STAPK* BS4 ..... **40** A5
Creswicke Av *KGWD/HNM* BS15 ...... **91** D2 🔢
Creswicke Rd
  BRSG/KWL/STAPK BS4 .... **96** B4
Crew's Hole Rd *EVILLE/WHL* BS5 ..... **33** D1
  EVILLE/WHL BS5 .... **90** A1 🔢
Cribbs Cswy *HNBRY/STHM* BS10 ..... **48** B2
Cricklade Rd *HORF/LLZ* BS7 .... **13** E1
Cripps Rd *BMSTR* BS3 .... **36** A4
Crispin Wy *KGWD/HNM* BS15 .... **87** C1
Croft Av *MANG/FISH* BS16.............. **66** B2
Crofters Wk *ALMDB* BS32 .... **45** C3
Crofton Av *HORF/LLZ* BS7 .... **5** F1
Crofts End Rd *EVILLE/WHL* BS5 .... **25** F1
The Croft *EVILLE/WHL* BS5 .... **81** C2
Crokeswood Wk *AVONM* BS11 .... **61** D2 🔢
Crome Rd *HORF/LLZ* BS7 .... **68** D4
Cromer Rd *EVILLE/WHL* BS5 .... **16** A5
Cromwell Ct *KGWD/HNM* BS15 .... **92** B2 🔢
Cromwell Rd *EVILLE/WHL* BS5 .... **84** B3
  RDLND/MONT BS6........................ **13** E5
Cromwells Hide *MANG/FISH* BS16 ..... **9** E4
Cromwell St *BMSTR* BS3 .... **36** A4
Croomes Hl *MANG/FISH* BS16 .... **80** A1
Cropthorne Rd *HORF/LLZ* BS7 .... **67** D2 🔢
Cropthorne Rd South
  HORF/LLZ BS7 .... **67** D3 🔢
Crosby Rw *CFTN/FAIL* BS8 .... **27** D3 🔢

Crosscombe Dr
  BMSTRD/HC/WWD BS13.............. **105** C4
Cross Elms La
  HNLZ/SM/SNYPK/WT BS9........... **77** D2
Crossfield Rd *MANG/FISH BS16* **80** B4
Crossleaze Rd *KGWD/HNM BS15* ... **91** D4
Crossman Av *FRCTL/WBN BS36*....... **56** B2
Cross St *KEYN BS31* **103** C4
  KGWD/HNM BS15 .... **85** D2
Cross Tree Gv *ALMDB BS32*.............. **45** C3
Crossways Rd
  BRSG/KWL/STAPK BS4 .... **97** C2
Crow La *CBRIS/FH BS1*................... **29** D2
  HNBRY/STHM BS10.................... **64** A1
Crowley Wy *AVONM BS11*................ **59** C2
Crowndale Rd
  BRSG/KWL/STAPK BS4 .... **38** C4
Crown Hl *EVILLE/WHL BS5* **84** A3
Crown Hill Wk *EVILLE/WHL BS5* **84** A3
Crownleaze *MANG/FISH BS16* **80** A4
Crown Rd *KGWD/HNM BS15* **86** A1
Crowther Pk *HORF/LLZ BS7* **7** D5
Crowther Rd *HORF/LLZ BS7* **7** D5
Crowther St *BMSTR BS3* .... **35** F3 ⬚
Croydon St *EVILLE/WHL BS5* **23** E4
The Crunnis *ALMDB BS32*............... **53** D1
Cuckoo La *FRCTL/WBN BS36*............. **57** C4
Cuffington Av
  BRSG/KWL/STAPK BS4 .... **40** C1
Culvers Rd *KEYN BS31* **112** B1
Culver St *CBRIS/FH BS1*................... **28** B2
The Culvert *ALMDB BS32*............... **45** C3 ⬚
Culverwell Rd
  BMSTRD/HC/WWD BS13............. **104** B3
Cumberland Basin Rd
  CFTN/FAIL BS8 .... **26** A4
Cumberland Cl *CBRIS/FH BS1*........... **27** D5
Cumberland Gv
  RDLND/MONT BS6 .... **14** B5 ⬚
Cumberland Pl *CFTN/FAIL BS8* **26** B3
Cumberland Rd *CBRIS/FH BS1* **26** C5
Cumberland St *CBRISNE BS2* **21** E4
Cunningham Gdns
  MANG/FISH BS16 .... **79** C2 ⬚
Curland Gv *HGRV/WHIT BS14* .... **108** A2 ⬚
Curlew Cl *MANG/FISH BS16* .... **78** A1 ⬚
Curtis La *BRSTK/PCHW BS34*............. **54** B4
Custom Cl *HGRV/WHIT BS14* **97** D4
Cutler Rd *BMSTRD/HC/WWD BS13* .. **104** A1
Cylde Pk *RDLND/MONT BS6* **11** F5
Cynder Wy *MANG/FISH BS16* **73** C2
Cypress Gdns *CFTN/FAIL BS8* **89** D1
Cypress Gv *HNLZ/SM/SNYPK/WT BS9* .. **4** B1

D

Daisy Rd *EVILLE/WHL BS5* **16** A5
Dakota Dr *HGRV/WHIT BS14*............ **107** D3
Dalby Av *BMSTR BS3* **36** C3
Dale St *CBRISNE BS2* **22** A4
  EVILLE/WHL BS5 .... **84** A3
Dalkeith Av *KGWD/HNM BS15* .... **85** D2 ⬚
Dalrymple Rd *RDLND/MONT BS6*....... **21** D2
Dalston Rd *BMSTR BS3* .... **35** F1 ⬚
Dalton Sq *CBRISNE BS2* **21** E3
Dampier Rd *BMSTR BS3* **35** D3
Danbury Crs *HNBRY/STHM BS10*........ **65** D2
Danbury Wk *HNBRY/STHM BS10* ... **65** D2 ⬚
Dapps Hl *KEYN BS31*...................... **113** C2
Darnley Av *HORF/LLZ BS7* **6** A1

Dartmoor St *BMSTR BS3*................... **35** F2
Daubeny Cl *MANG/FISH BS16* **79** C2
Daventry Rd *BRSG/KWL/STAPK BS4* ... **97** C2
Davey St *CBRISNE BS2* **22** B2
David's Rd *HGRV/WHIT BS14* **108** B1
David St *CBRISNE BS2* **30** A1
Davies Dr *BRSG/KWL/STAPK BS4* ...... **90** A2 ⬚
Davis Cl *OLD/WMLY/WICK BS30* .... **93** C2 ⬚
Davis St *AVONM BS11* **59** C3
Dawlish Rd *BMSTR BS3* **96** A1
Dawn Ri *KGWD/HNM BS15* **87** D2
Daws Ct *MANG/FISH BS16* .... **79** C3 ⬚
Day's Rd *CBRISNE BS2* **31** D2
Deacon Cl *FRCTL/WBN BS36*............. **56** B2
Dean Cl *KGWD/HNM BS15* **90** B3
Dean Crs *BMSTR BS3* .... **36** C1 ⬚
Deanery Rd *CBRIS/FH BS1* **28** A3
Dean La *BMSTR BS3* **36** B2
Dean's Dr *EVILLE/WHL BS5* .... **84** B1 ⬚
Deans Md *AVONM BS11* **61** D3
Dean St *BMSTR BS3* **36** B2
  CBRISNE BS2 .... **21** F3
De Clifford Rd *AVONM BS11* **62** B1
Deep Coombe Rd *BMSTR BS3* .... **35** D5 ⬚
Deep Pit Rd *EVILLE/WHL BS5* **25** F1
Deerhurst *KGWD/HNM BS15* .... **86** B3 ⬚
Deering Cl *AVONM BS11* **62** A2
Deerswood *KGWD/HNM BS15* **87** D1
Delabere Av *MANG/FISH BS16* **79** C3
Delius Gv *BRSG/KWL/STAPK BS4* ...... **96** A4 ⬚
The Dell *ALMDB BS32*..................... **45** D4
  HNLZ/SM/SNYPK/WT BS9............. **2** B3
Delvin Rd *HNBRY/STHM BS10*........... **65** D3
Denbigh St *CBRISNE BS2* **21** F2
Dene Cl *KEYN BS31* **113** C4
Dene Rd *HGRV/WHIT BS14* **108** B3
Denleigh Cl *HGRV/WHIT BS14* **107** D3
Denmark Pl *HORF/LLZ BS7* **13** E2
Denmark St *CBRIS/FH BS1* **28** B2
Dennor Pk *HGRV/WHIT BS14* **98** A4
Denston Wk
  BMSTRD/HC/WWD BS13............. **94** B4
Dentwood Gv
  HNLZ/SM/SNYPK/WT BS9........... **62** A4
Derby Rd *HORF/LLZ BS7* **13** F3
Derby St *EVILLE/WHL BS5* **24** C5
Derham Rd
  BMSTRD/HC/WWD BS13............. **104** D2
Dermot St *CBRISNE BS2* **22** B2
Derricke Rd *HGRV/WHIT BS14* **110** A1
Derrick Rd *KGWD/HNM BS15* **86** A3
Derry Rd *BMSTR BS3* **35** E5
Derwent Cl *BRSTK/PCHW BS34* **43** D3
Derwent Gv *KEYN BS31* **113** D2
Derwent Rd *EVILLE/WHL BS5* **84** A2
De Verose Ct *KGWD/HNM BS15* **92** B3
Devon Gv *EVILLE/WHL BS5* **24** B3
Devon Rd *EVILLE/WHL BS5* **24** A1
Devonshire Rd *RDLND/MONT BS6*..... **11** E1
Dewfalls Dr *ALMDB BS32*................. **45** C2
Dial La *MANG/FISH BS16* **80** A1
Diamond Rd *EVILLE/WHL BS5*............ **84** A4
Diamond St *BMSTR BS3* **36** C3
Diana Gdns *ALMDB BS32*................. **45** D3
Dibden Cl *MANG/FISH BS16*.............. **73** D3
Dibden La *MANG/FISH BS16* **73** D4
Dibden Rd *MANG/FISH BS16*............. **73** D3
Dickens Cl *HORF/LLZ BS7* **67** D3
Didsbury Cl *HNBRY/STHM BS10*......... **64** A1
Dighton Ga *BRSTK/PCHW BS34* ...... **53** D2 ⬚
Dighton St *CBRISNE BS2* **21** D4
Dingle Cl *HNLZ/SM/SNYPK/WT BS9* ... **76** B1

Dingle Rd *HNLZ/SM/SNYPK/WT* BS9 .... **62** B4
The Dingle *FRCTL/WBN* BS36 .... **56** B4
  HNLZ/SM/SNYPK/WT BS9.................. **62** B4
Dingle Vw *HNLZ/SM/SNYPK/WT* BS9.. **62** B4
Dinglewood Cl
  HNLZ/SM/SNYPK/WT BS9 .... **63** C4 🗓
Dings Wk *CBRISNE* BS2 .... **30** C2 🗓
Dixon Rd *BRSG/KWL/STAPK* BS4 .... **100** A1
Dock Gate La *CFTN/FAIL* BS8 .... **27** D4 🗓
Dodisham Wk *MANG/FISH* BS16.......... **79** C1
Dolman Cl *HNBRY/STHM* BS10 .... **48** A4 🗓
Dominion Rd *BMSTRD/HC/WWD* BS13.. **94** A4
Donald Rd *BMSTRD/HC/WWD* BS13 .... **94** A4
Doncaster Rd *HNBRY/STHM* BS10...... **65** C2
Donegal Rd *BRSG/KWL/STAPK* BS4 .... **96** A2
Dongola Av *HORF/LLZ* BS7 .... **5** F5
Dongola Rd *HORF/LLZ* BS7 .... **5** F5
Doone Rd *HORF/LLZ* BS7 .... **67** C3
Dorcas Av *BRSTK/PCHW* BS34 .... **54** A2
Dorchester Rd *HORF/LLZ* BS7 .... **67** D4
Dorester Cl *HNBRY/STHM* BS10 .... **49** D3
Dorian Cl *HORF/LLZ* BS7 .... **66** B4
Dorian Rd *HORF/LLZ* BS7 .... **66** B4
Dorian Wy *HNBRY/STHM* BS10........... **66** B3
Dormer Rd *EVILLE/WHL* BS5 .... **15** E3
Dorset Gv *CBRISNE* BS2 .... **14** C5 🗓
Dorset Rd *HNLZ/SM/SNYPK/WT* BS9 ... **3** F1
  KGWD/HNM BS15 .... **86** A2
Dorset St *BMSTR* BS3 .... **35** F3
Douglas Rd *HORF/LLZ* BS7 .... **67** C3
  KGWD/HNM BS15 .... **86** A4
Doulton Wy *HGRV/WHIT* BS14 .... **107** D2
Dove La *CBRISNE* BS2 .... **22** A3
Dovercourt Rd *HORF/LLZ* BS7 .... **6** C3
Dove St *CBRISNE* BS2 .... **21** D3
Dove St South *CBRISNE* BS2 .... **21** D4
Dowdeswell Cl
  HNBRY/STHM BS10 .... **48** A4 🗓
Dowling Rd
  BMSTRD/HC/WWD BS13 .... **106** A4
Downend Pk *HORF/LLZ* BS7 .... **6** B3
Downend Park Rd
  MANG/FISH BS16 .... **80** A2 🗓
Downend Rd *HORF/LLZ* BS7 .... **6** A3
  KGWD/HNM BS15 .... **86** A3
  MANG/FISH BS16 .... **79** D2
Downfield Rd *CFTN/FAIL* BS8 .... **18** C1
Downleaze
  HNLZ/SM/SNYPK/WT BS9 .... **10** A3
  MANG/FISH BS16 .... **72** A3
Downman Rd *HORF/LLZ* BS7 .... **7** D4
Down Rd *FRCTL/WBN* BS36................. **56** B3
Downs Cote Av
  HNLZ/SM/SNYPK/WT BS9............. **2** B1
Downs Cote Dr
  HNLZ/SM/SNYPK/WT BS9............. **2** B1
Downs Cote Gdns
  HNLZ/SM/SNYPK/WT BS9............. **2** C2
Downs Cote Pk
  HNLZ/SM/SNYPK/WT BS9............. **2** C1
Downs Cote Vw
  HNLZ/SM/SNYPK/WT BS9............. **2** C2
Downside Cl
  OLD/WMLY/WICK BS30 .... **93** C2 🗓
Downside Rd *CFTN/FAIL* BS8 .... **18** C1
Downs Pk East *RDLND/MONT* BS6 ..... **3** D4
Downs Pk West *RDLND/MONT* BS6 ..... **3** D4
Downs Rd *HNLZ/SM/SNYPK/WT* BS9 .. **3** D4
Downton Rd *BRSG/KWL/STAPK* BS4 ... **96** A2
Dowry Rd *CFTN/FAIL* BS8 .... **26** C3 🗓
Dowry Sq *CFTN/FAIL* BS8 .... **26** B3 🗓
Dragon Rd *FRCTL/WBN* BS36.............. **56** A2

Dragons Hill Cl *KEYN* BS31 .... **113** C2
Dragons Hill Ct *KEYN* BS31 .... **113** C2
Dragons Hill Gdns *KEYN* BS31 .... **113** C2 🗓
Dragonswell Rd *HNBRY/STHM* BS10... **64** B1
Dragon Wk *EVILLE/WHL* BS5 .... **84** A2 🗓
Drake Rd *BMSTR* BS3 .... **35** D3
Draycot Pl *CBRIS/FH* BS1 .... **28** C5
Draycott Rd *HORF/LLZ* BS7 .... **6** B4 🗓
Draydon Rd *BRSG/KWL/STAPK* BS4 .... **95** D4
Drayton Cl *HGRV/WHIT* BS14 .... **98** A3 🗓
Drayton Rd
  HNLZ/SM/SNYPK/WT BS9 .... **62** B3 🗓
The Drive *HGRV/WHIT* BS14 .... **108** B2
  HNLZ/SM/SNYPK/WT BS9............. **3** F2
Druetts Cl *HNBRY/STHM* BS10 .... **5** E1
Druid Cl *HNLZ/SM/SNYPK/WT* BS9 .... **77** D2
Druid Hl *HNLZ/SM/SNYPK/WT* BS9..... **77** D2
Druid Rd *HNLZ/SM/SNYPK/WT* BS9 .... **77** C3
Druid Stoke Av
  HNLZ/SM/SNYPK/WT BS9 .... **76** B2
Druid Woods
  HNLZ/SM/SNYPK/WT BS9 .... **76** B2 🗓
Drummond Ct
  OLD/WMLY/WICK BS30 .... **93** C3 🗓
Drummond Rd *MANG/FISH* BS16 .... **78** A4 🗓
  RDLND/MONT BS6....................... **21** F2
Dryleaze *KEYN* BS31 .... **102** B4
Dryleaze Rd *MANG/FISH* BS16 .... **78** A1
Dubbers La *EVILLE/WHL* BS5............. **17** E4
Dublin Crs *HNLZ/SM/SNYPK/WT* BS9... **3** E2
Duchess Rd *CFTN/FAIL* BS8 .... **19** D2
Duchess Wy *MANG/FISH* BS16 .... **9** D3
Ducie Rd *EVILLE/WHL* BS5 .... **23** F5
  MANG/FISH BS16 .... **80** B3
Duckmoor Rd *BMSTR* BS3 .... **34** C3
Dudley Cl *KEYN* BS31 .... **112** B3
Dudley Ct *OLD/WMLY/WICK* BS30 ..... **93** C3 🗓
Dudley Gv *HORF/LLZ* BS7 .... **67** C3
Dugar Wk *RDLND/MONT* BS6.............. **12** A2
Dulverton Rd *HORF/LLZ* BS7.............. **12** C1
Dumaine Av *BRSTK/PCHW* BS34 .... **53** D2
Duncombe La *KGWD/HNM* BS15 .... **84** B1
Duncombe Rd *KGWD/HNM* BS15 .... **85** C2 🗓
Dundas Cl *HNBRY/STHM* BS10 .... **63** D1 🗓
Dundonald Rd *RDLND/MONT* BS6 ...... **11** F2
Dundridge Gdns *EVILLE/WHL* BS5 ..... **90** B1 🗓
Dundridge La *EVILLE/WHL* BS5........... **90** A1
Dundry Cl *KGWD/HNM* BS15 .... **92** A1 🗓
Dundry Vw *BRSG/KWL/STAPK* BS4 .... **97** D2
Dunford Rd *BMSTR* BS3 .... **37** D4
Dunkeld Av *BRSTK/PCHW* BS34 .... **67** C1
Dunkerry Rd *BMSTR* BS3 .... **36** C4
Dunkirk Rd *MANG/FISH* BS16 .... **78** A4
Dunmail Rd *HNBRY/STHM* BS10......... **65** D1
Dunmore St *BMSTR* BS3 .... **38** B1 🗓
Dunster Rd
  BRSG/KWL/STAPK BS4 .... **97** C3 🗓
  KEYN BS31 .... **112** B3
Durban Rd *BRSTK/PCHW* BS34.......... **43** C3
Durbin Wk *EVILLE/WHL* BS5 .... **23** D4 🗓
Durdham Pk *RDLND/MONT* BS6.......... **11** D3
Durham Gv *KEYN* BS31 .... **112** A3
Durham Rd *CBRISNE* BS2 .... **14** C5 🗓
Durleigh Cl
  BMSTRD/HC/WWD BS13............... **104** B1
Durley Hl *KEYN* BS31 .... **101** C3
Durley La *KEYN* BS31 .... **102** A4
Durnford Av *BMSTR* BS3 .... **35** D2
Durnford St *BMSTR* BS3 .... **34** C2
Dursley Rd *AVONM* BS11 .... **74** B2
Durville Rd
  BMSTRD/HC/WWD BS13.................. **105** C1

Durweston Wk HGRV/WHIT BS14 ...... 98 B3
Dutton Cl HGRV/WHIT BS14 .... 109 C1 🖪
Dutton Rd HGRV/WHIT BS14........... 109 C2
Dutton Wk HGRV/WHIT BS14 .... 109 C1 🖪
Dyers Cl BMSTRD/HC/WWD BS13.... 106 A3
Dylan Thomas Ct
     OLD/WMLY/WICK BS30 .... 93 D2 🖪
     KGWD/HNM BS15 .... 87 C3 🖪
Dyrham Pde BRSTK/PCHW BS34 .... 44 B3
Dyrham Rd KGWD/HNM BS15 .... 87 C3

Ebenezer La
     HNLZ/SM/SNYPK/WT BS9 .... 77 D2 🖪
     HNLZ/SM/SNYPK/WT BS9 .... 77 C1 🖪
Ebenezer St EVILLE/WHL BS5 .... 25 D5
Eden Gv HORF/LLZ BS7 .... 67 D2
Edgecumbe Rd RDLND/MONT BS6 .... 12 C5
Edgefield Cl HGRV/WHIT BS14 .... 107 C4
Edgefield Rd HGRV/WHIT BS14 .... 107 C4
Edgeware Rd BMSTR BS3 .... 36 A1
     MANG/FISH BS16 .... 79 D3 🖪
Edgewood Cl HGRV/WHIT BS14 ..... 98 A3 🖪
     OLD/WMLY/WICK BS30 .... 93 D4
Edinburgh Rd KEYN BS31 .... 112 B3
Edington Gv HNBRY/STHM BS10 ...... 64 B1
Edmund Cl MANG/FISH BS16 .... 80 A1 🖪
Edna Av BRSG/KWL/STAPK BS4 .... 41 E4
Edward Rd BRSG/KWL/STAPK BS4..... 39 F2
     KGWD/HNM BS15 .... 86 B3
Edward St EVILLE/WHL BS5 .... 16 C4
     EVILLE/WHL BS5 .... 24 B4
Effingham Rd RDLND/MONT BS6 ..... 13 E4
Egerton Brow HORF/LLZ BS7 .... 13 D1 🖪
Egerton Rd HORF/LLZ BS7 .... 12 C1
Eighth Av HORF/LLZ BS7 .... 68 A3
Eirene Ter PTSHD/EG BS20 .... 74 A3
Elberton Rd KGWD/HNM BS15 ...... 87 D3 🖪
Elberton Rd
     HNLZ/SM/SNYPK/WT BS9 .... 62 A4
Elbury Av KGWD/HNM BS15 .... 85 D1
Elderberry Wk HNBRY/STHM BS10 ... 65 D1
Elderwood Dr
     OLD/WMLY/WICK BS30 .... 93 D4
Elderwood Rd HGRV/WHIT BS14 ... 98 A4 🖪
Eldon Ter BMSTR BS3........................ 36 C4
Eldon Wy BRSG/KWL/STAPK BS4 ...... 32 B5
Eldred Cl HNLZ/SM/SNYPK/WT BS9 .... 76 B2
Eleventh Av HORF/LLZ BS7 .... 68 A2 🖪
Elfin Rd MANG/FISH BS16 .... 78 B2
Elgar Cl BRSG/KWL/STAPK BS4 ...... 106 A1 🖪
Elgin Av HORF/LLZ BS7 .... 67 C2
Elgin Pk RDLND/MONT BS6............... 11 E4
Elgin Rd MANG/FISH BS16 .... 85 C1
Eliot Cl HORF/LLZ BS7 .... 67 D3
Elizabeth Crs BRSTK/PCHW BS34..... 53 D3
Elizabeths Ms
     BRSG/KWL/STAPK BS4 .... 90 A1 🖪
Ellacombe Rd
     OLD/WMLY/WICK BS30 .... 102 B1
Ellan Hay Rd ALMDB BS32................ 54 B1
Ellbridge Cl
     HNLZ/SM/SNYPK/WT BS9 .... 77 C2 🖪
Ellesmere Rd
     BRSG/KWL/STAPK BS4 .... 99 C2 🖪
     KGWD/HNM BS15 .... 86 A3 🖪
Ellfield Cl BMSTRD/HC/WWD BS13.... 104 A1
Ellicks Cl ALMDB BS32 .... 45 D1
Ellicott Rd HORF/LLZ BS7 .... 6 A2
Ellinghurst Cl HNBRY/STHM BS10 .. 64 B1 🖪
Elliott Av MANG/FISH BS16 .... 71 D2
Ellis Av BMSTRD/HC/WWD BS13...... 94 B3
Elliston La RDLND/MONT BS6............ 12 A5
Elliston Rd RDLND/MONT BS6............ 12 A5
Ellsworth Rd HNBRY/STHM BS10...... 64 A1
Elm Cl BRSTK/PCHW BS34 .... 45 C4
Elmcroft Crs HORF/LLZ BS7 .... 15 D1
Elmdale Rd BMSTR BS3 .... 35 E5
     CFTN/FAIL BS8 .... 19 F4
Elmfield KGWD/HNM BS15 .... 92 B1
Elmfield Cl KGWD/HNM BS15 .... 92 B1 🖪
Elmfield Rd
     HNLZ/SM/SNYPK/WT BS9 .... 64 B3 🖪
Elmgrove Av EVILLE/WHL BS5 .... 23 F3 🖪

Eagle Dr BRSTK/PCHW BS34 .... 42 B3
Eagle Rd BRSG/KWL/STAPK BS4 ...... 40 C5
Earl Russell Wy EVILLE/WHL BS5 ...... 23 E5
Earlsmead MANG/FISH BS16.............. 9 D3
Earlstone Cl OLD/WMLY/WICK BS30 .. 93 D3
Earlstone Crs
     OLD/WMLY/WICK BS30 .... 93 D2 🖪
Earl St CBRIS/FH BS1 .... 21 D4
Early Wy HNBRY/STHM BS10 .... 66 B3
Easedale Cl HNBRY/STHM BS10 .... 66 A1 🖪
Eastbourne Rd EVILLE/WHL BS5 .... 23 F3
Eastbury Rd MANG/FISH BS16 .... 78 B3
Eastcote Pk HGRV/WHIT BS14 .... 108 A2
East Cft HNLZ/SM/SNYPK/WT BS9.... 65 D2
Eastfield HNLZ/SM/SNYPK/WT BS9 .. 65 C4
Eastfield Rd
     HNLZ/SM/SNYPK/WT BS9............ 64 B4
     RDLND/MONT BS6 .... 13 D5
Eastfield Ter
     HNLZ/SM/SNYPK/WT BS9 .... 3 F1
East Gv RDLND/MONT BS6 .... 22 A1
East Hill Eastfield Rd
     HNLZ/SM/SNYPK/WT BS9 .... 64 B4 🖪
Eastlake Cl HORF/LLZ BS7 .... 68 A4
Eastleigh Cl MANG/FISH BS16 .... 80 B3 🖪
Eastleigh Rd HNBRY/STHM BS10 ...... 64 B3
     MANG/FISH BS16 .... 80 B3
Eastlyn Rd BMSTRD/HC/WWD BS13 .. 95 C3
Eastmead La
     HNLZ/SM/SNYPK/WT BS9............ 77 D3
Eastnor Rd HGRV/WHIT BS14 .... 107 D4
Easton Rd CBRISNE BS2..................... 22 C5
     EVILLE/WHL BS5 .... 23 F3
Easton Wy EVILLE/WHL BS5 .... 23 D2
Eastover Cl
     HNLZ/SM/SNYPK/WT BS9............ 64 B3
East Pde HNLZ/SM/SNYPK/WT BS9 .. 76 B1
East Pk EVILLE/WHL BS5 .... 16 A5
East Park Dr EVILLE/WHL BS5 .... 16 B4
East Priory Cl
     HNLZ/SM/SNYPK/WT BS9............ 64 B4
East Ridge Dr
     BMSTRD/HC/WWD BS13............ 104 A2
East Shrubbery
     RDLND/MONT BS6 .... 11 E4 🖪
East St AVONM BS11 .... 58 B2 🖪
     BMSTR BS3 .... 36 B3
     CBRISNE BS2 .... 22 A4
East Vw MANG/FISH BS16 .... 81 C1
Eastwood Crs
     BRSG/KWL/STAPK BS4 .... 90 A3
Eastwood Rd BRSG/KWL/STAPK BS4.. 90 A3
Eaton Cl HGRV/WHIT BS14 .... 109 D2 🖪
     MANG/FISH BS16 .... 79 C3
Eaton Crs CFTN/FAIL BS8.................. 19 D4
Eaton St BMSTR BS3 .... 36 B3 🖪

Elmgrove Pk *RDLND/MONT* BS6 .... 20 C1
Elmgrove Rd *MANG/FISH* BS16 .... 17 F2
　RDLND/MONT BS6 .... 20 C1
Elm Hayes
　BMSTRD/HC/WWD BS13 .... 104 A1
Elmhurst Rd *EVILLE/WHL* BS5 .... 17 D3
Elming Down Cl *ALMDB* BS32 .... 53 C1 🔟
Elm La *RDLND/MONT* BS6 .... 11 E4
Elmlea Av *HNLZ/SM/SNYPK/WT* BS9 .... 2 B4
Elmleigh Cl *MANG/FISH* BS16 .... 81 D2 🔟
Elmleigh Rd *MANG/FISH* BS16 .... 81 D2
Elmore *KGWD/HNM* BS15 .... 87 C1 🔟
Elmore Rd *BRSTK/PCHW* BS34 .... 43 C3
　HORF/LLZ BS7 .... 6 C1
Elm Pk *BRSTK/PCHW* BS34 .... 67 D1
Elm Rd *HORF/LLZ* BS7 .... 5 E3
　KGWD/HNM BS15 .... 92 B1
Elms Gv *BRSTK/PCHW* BS34 .... 44 A2
Elm Tree Av *MANG/FISH* BS16.......... 73 D4
Elmtree Cl *KGWD/HNM* BS15 .... 86 A2
Elmtree Dr
　BMSTRD/HC/WWD BS13.............. 104 A2
Elstree Rd *EVILLE/WHL* BS5.............. 25 E1
Elton La *HORF/LLZ* BS7 .... 13 D4
Elton Rd *CFTN/FAIL* BS8...................... 19 F5
　HORF/LLZ BS7 .... 12 C3
　KGWD/HNM BS15 .... 85 C2
Elton St *CBRISNE* BS2........................ 22 B4
Elvard Cl *BMSTRD/HC/WWD* BS13 .. 104 B3
Elvard Rd *BMSTRD/HC/WWD* BS13 .. 104 B2
Elvaston Rd *BMSTR* BS3 .... 37 E4
Ely Gv *HNLZ/SM/SNYPK/WT* BS9 ...... 62 A1
Embassy Rd *EVILLE/WHL* BS5 .... 25 E2
Embassy Wk *EVILLE/WHL* BS5 .... 25 E2
Embleton Rd *HNBRY/STHM* BS10 ...... 65 C1
Emerson Sq *HORF/LLZ* BS7................ 67 D3
Emery Rd *BRSG/KWL/STAPK* BS4 .... 100 A2 🔟
Emlyn Rd *EVILLE/WHL* BS5 .... 16 A5
Emma-chris Wy *BRSTK/PCHW* BS34 .. 68 B1
Emmett Wd *HGRV/WHIT* BS14 .... 108 A4
Emra Cl *EVILLE/WHL* BS5 .... 84 A2 🔟
Enfield Rd *MANG/FISH* BS16 .... 78 B4
Englishcombe Rd
　BMSTRD/HC/WWD BS13................ 105 D4
Ennerdale Rd *HNBRY/STHM* BS10 ...... 66 A1
Epney Cl *BRSTK/PCHW* BS34.............. 43 C2
Epsom Cl *MANG/FISH* BS16................ 73 C2
Epworth Rd *HNBRY/STHM* BS10 ...... 64 B1
Erin Wk *BRSG/KWL/STAPK* BS4.......... 96 A3
Ermine Wy *AVONM* BS11 .... 59 D4
Ermleet Rd *RDLND/MONT* BS6.......... 12 A4
Ernest Barker Cl *EVILLE/WHL* BS5 .... 31 E1 🔟
Ernestville Rd *MANG/FISH* BS16........ 78 A4
Ervine Ter *CBRISNE* BS2.................... 22 A3
Essery Rd *EVILLE/WHL* BS5 .... 16 B5
Esson Rd *KGWD/HNM* BS15 .... 85 C2
Etloe Rd *RDLND/MONT* BS6 .... 11 D1
Eton Rd *BRSG/KWL/STAPK* BS4 .... 40 C4
Ettricke Dr *MANG/FISH* BS16 .... 79 C1
Eugene St *CBRISNE* BS2...................... 20 C4
　EVILLE/WHL BS5.............................. 22 B4
Evans Cl *BRSG/KWL/STAPK* BS4 .... 90 A2
Evans Rd *RDLND/MONT* BS6 .... 11 E5
Evelyn Rd *HNBRY/STHM* BS10 .... 65 D4 🔟
Evenlode Gdns *AVONM* BS11 .... 75 C2
Evenlode Wy *KEYN* BS31 .... 113 D4
Evercreech Rd *HGRV/WHIT* BS14...... 107 D3
Everest Av *MANG/FISH* BS16 .... 17 F1
Everest Rd *MANG/FISH* BS16 .... 17 F1
Eve Rd *EVILLE/WHL* BS5.................... 23 E2
Exeter Buildings *RDLND/MONT* BS6 .. 11 E5
Exeter Rd *BMSTR* BS3........................ 35 E2

Exmoor St *BMSTR* BS3........................ 35 F2
Exmouth Rd *BRSG/KWL/STAPK* BS4 .. 97 C2
Eyer's La *CBRISNE* BS2........................ 22 A5

F

Faber Gv
　BMSTRD/HC/WWD BS13.............. 105 D3 🔟
Fabian Dr *BRSTK/PCHW* BS34............ 53 D2
Failand Crs
　HNLZ/SM/SNYPK/WT BS9............ 76 B2
Failand Wk
　HNLZ/SM/SNYPK/WT BS9 .... 76 B1 🔟
Fairacre Cl *HORF/LLZ* BS7 .... 7 F3
Fairacres Cl *KEYN* BS31 .... 112 B3
Fairfax St *CBRIS/FH* BS1 .... 29 E1
Fairfield Pl *BMSTR* BS3...................... 35 F2
Fairfield Rd *BMSTR* BS3...................... 35 F2
　RDLND/MONT BS6 .... 14 A5
Fairfoot Rd *BRSG/KWL/STAPK* BS4 .... 38 C3
Fairford Cl *KGWD/HNM* BS15 .... 87 C1 🔟
Fairford Crs *BRSTK/PCHW* BS34........ 44 A3
Fairford Rd *AVONM* BS11 .... 59 D4
Fair Furlong
　BMSTRD/HC/WWD BS13.............. 104 B3
Fairhaven Rd *RDLND/MONT* BS6 .... 4 A5
Fair Lawn *OLD/WMLY/WICK* BS30 .... 93 D3
Fairlawn Rd *RDLND/MONT* BS6 .... 14 A5
Fairlyn Dr *KGWD/HNM* BS15.............. 81 C4
Fairoaks *OLD/WMLY/WICK* BS30 .... 93 D3 🔟
Fair View Dr *RDLND/MONT* BS6 .... 12 A5
Fairview Rd *KGWD/HNM* BS15 .... 87 C3
Fairway *BRSG/KWL/STAPK* BS4 .... 99 C2
Falcon Cl *BRSTK/PCHW* BS34 .... 42 B3
　HNLZ/SM/SNYPK/WT BS9............ 64 A3
Falcondale Rd
　HNLZ/SM/SNYPK/WT BS9............ 64 A3
Falcondale Wk
　HNLZ/SM/SNYPK/WT BS9............ 64 B3
Falcon Dr *BRSTK/PCHW* BS34 .... 42 B3
Falcon Wk *BRSTK/PCHW* BS34 .... 42 B3
Falfield Rd *BRSG/KWL/STAPK* BS4 .... 40 A4
Falfield Wk *HNBRY/STHM* BS10 .... 65 D3 🔟
Falkland Rd *RDLND/MONT* BS6 .... 14 A5
Fallodon Ct
　HNLZ/SM/SNYPK/WT BS9 .... 3 E4 🔟
Fallodon Wy
　HNLZ/SM/SNYPK/WT BS9 .... 3 E4
Falmouth Rd *HORF/LLZ* BS7 .... 13 D1
Fane Cl *HNBRY/STHM* BS10 .... 48 B4 🔟
Fanshawe Rd *HGRV/WHIT* BS14........ 97 D4
Faraday Rd *CFTN/FAIL* BS8 .... 26 B4
Far Handstones
　OLD/WMLY/WICK BS30 .... 93 D3
Farington Rd
　HNLZ/SM/SNYPK/WT BS9............ 66 A4
Farleigh Rd *KEYN* BS31 .... 112 A3
Farleigh Wk
　BMSTRD/HC/WWD BS13................ 94 B3
Farley Cl *BRSTK/PCHW* BS34 .... 44 B4
Farm Ct *MANG/FISH* BS16 .... 72 B4
Farm Rd *MANG/FISH* BS16 .... 72 B4
Farmwell Cl
　BMSTRD/HC/WWD BS13.............. 105 C2 🔟
Farndale *EVILLE/WHL* BS5.................. 90 B1
Farne Cl *HNLZ/SM/SNYPK/WT* BS9 ...... 3 F4
Farrant Cl *BRSG/KWL/STAPK* BS4.... 106 A1
Farr's La *CBRIS/FH* BS1 .... 28 C3
Farr St *AVONM* BS11.......................... 59 C3
Featherstone Rd *MANG/FISH* BS16.... 17 F1

MANG/FISH BS16 .... 78 A3 1
Feeder Rd CBRISNE BS2 .... 30 C4
CBRISNE BS2 .... 32 A3
Felix Rd EVILLE/WHL BS5 .... 23 D3
Felstead Rd HNBRY/STHM BS10 .... 66 B2
Felton Gv BMSTRD/HC/WWD BS13 .... 94 A3
Fennel Dr ALMDB BS32 .... 46 B4
Fennell Gv HNBRY/STHM BS10 .... 64 B1 2
Fenton Rd HORF/LLZ BS7 .... 4 C5
Fermaine Av BRSG/KWL/STAPK BS4 .. 90 A4
Fernbank Rd RDLND/MONT BS6 .... 12 A5
Fernbrook Cl MANG/FISH BS16 .... 71 C2
Ferndale Av OLD/WMLY/WICK BS30 .. 93 C4
Ferndale Rd HORF/LLZ BS7 .... 67 D1
Ferndene ALMDB BS32 .... 44 B1
Ferndown Cl AVONM BS11 .... 61 D4 1
Fern Gv BRSTK/PCHW BS34 .... 45 C4
Fernhill La AVONM BS11 .... 62 A2
Fernhurst Rd EVILLE/WHL BS5 .... 84 A2 2
Fern Rd MANG/FISH BS16 .... 80 B1
Fernsteed Rd
    BMSTRD/HC/WWD BS13 .... 104 A1
Fern St CBRISNE BS2 .... 22 B2
Ferry Rd KGWD/HNM BS15 .... 102 A2
Ferry St CBRIS/FH BS1 .... 29 E3 1
Fiddes Rd RDLND/MONT BS6 .... 12 A1
Field Farm Cl BRSTK/PCHW BS34 ...... 54 A3
Field La OLD/WMLY/WICK BS30 .... 92 B4
Field Rd KGWD/HNM BS15 .... 85 D2
Field View Dr MANG/FISH BS16 .... 79 D1
Fiennes Cl MANG/FISH BS16 .... 80 B3 3
Fifth Av HORF/LLZ BS7 .... 67 D2
Filby Dr BRSTK/PCHW BS34 .... 44 B3 1
Filton Av BRSTK/PCHW BS34 .... 52 A4
    HORF/LLZ BS7 .... 6 A2
    HORF/LLZ BS7 .... 67 D4
Filton Gv HORF/LLZ BS7 .... 6 A1
Filton La BRSTK/PCHW BS34 .... 69 C1
Filton Rd BRSTK/PCHW BS34 .... 69 C1
    HORF/LLZ BS7 .... 67 C4
    MANG/FISH BS16 .... 70 A2
Filwood Broadway
    BRSG/KWL/STAPK BS4 .... 96 B3
Filwood Ct MANG/FISH BS16 .... 79 C4 1
Filwood Dr KGWD/HNM BS15 .... 87 C3
Filwood Rd MANG/FISH BS16 .... 78 B4
Firfield St BRSG/KWL/STAPK BS4 ...... 38 C2
First Av BRSG/KWL/STAPK BS4 .... 33 F5
First Wy AVONM BS11 .... 59 D2
Fir Tree Cl BRSTK/PCHW BS34 .... 42 B4
Fir Tree La EVILLE/WHL BS5 .... 90 B1
Fisher Av KGWD/HNM BS15 .... 87 D2
Fisher Rd KGWD/HNM BS15 .... 87 D2
Fishponds Rd EVILLE/WHL BS5 .... 16 A4
Fishpool Hl HNBRY/STHM BS10 .... 49 C3
Fitchett Wk HNBRY/STHM BS10 .... 48 A4
Fitzgerald Rd BMSTR BS3 .... 38 A4
Fitzroy Rd MANG/FISH BS16 .... 85 C1
Fitzroy St BRSG/KWL/STAPK BS4 ...... 39 D2
Five Acre Dr MANG/FISH BS16 .... 70 A4
Flaxman Ct HORF/LLZ BS7 .... 7 E1
Flaxpits La FRCTL/WBN BS36 .... 56 A1
Florence Pk RDLND/MONT BS6 .... 11 E1
Florence Rd MANG/FISH BS16 .... 80 B4
Flowers Hl BRSG/KWL/STAPK BS4 .... 99 D2
Flowers Hill Cl
    BRSG/KWL/STAPK BS4 .... 99 D2 1
Flowerwell Rd
    BMSTRD/HC/WWD BS13 .... 105 C2 1
Folliot Cl MANG/FISH BS16 .... 70 B3
Folly Brook Rd MANG/FISH BS16 ...... 73 D1
Folly La CBRISNE BS2 .... 31 D1
The Folly MANG/FISH BS16 .... 73 D4
Fonthill Rd HNBRY/STHM BS10 .... 66 A1
Fontmell Ct HGRV/WHIT BS14 .... 99 C4 1
Fontwell Dr MANG/FISH BS16 .... 73 C2
Footshill Cl KGWD/HNM BS15 .... 91 D1
Footshill Dr KGWD/HNM BS15 .... 85 D4
Footshill Rd KGWD/HNM BS15 .... 91 D1
Forde Cl OLD/WMLY/WICK BS30 ...... 93 C2 1
Fordell Pl BRSG/KWL/STAPK BS4 .... 39 D3 1
Ford St EVILLE/WHL BS5 .... 32 A2
Forest Av MANG/FISH BS16 .... 79 D4
Forest Dr HNBRY/STHM BS10 .... 49 D4
Forest Edge KGWD/HNM BS15 .... 91 D3
Forest Rd KGWD/HNM BS15 .... 86 A4
    MANG/FISH BS16 .... 79 C4
Forest Wk KGWD/HNM BS15 .... 85 D4
    MANG/FISH BS16 .... 85 C1 1
Fortfield Rd HGRV/WHIT BS14 .... 108 A3
Fossedale Av HGRV/WHIT BS14 ...... 108 A1
The Fosseway CFTN/FAIL BS8 .... 27 D1
Foster St EVILLE/WHL BS5 .... 15 F5
Foundry La EVILLE/WHL BS5 .... 84 A1
Fountaine Ct EVILLE/WHL BS5 .... 16 A4
Fountains Dr
    OLD/WMLY/WICK BS30 .... 93 C1
Four Acre Av MANG/FISH BS16 .... 72 B3
Four Acre Crs MANG/FISH BS16 .... 72 B2
Four Acre Rd MANG/FISH BS16 .... 72 B2
Four Acres Cl
    BMSTRD/HC/WWD BS13 .... 104 A3
Fourth Av HORF/LLZ BS7 .... 67 D1
Fox & Hounds La KEYN BS31 .... 113 C2 3
Foxborough Gdns ALMDB BS32 .... 45 C1 3
Foxcombe Rd HGRV/WHIT BS14 .... 108 A3 1
Foxcote KGWD/HNM BS15 .... 87 C3
Foxcote Rd BMSTR BS3 .... 35 D4
Fox Ct OLD/WMLY/WICK BS30 .... 93 C4
Foxcroft Cl ALMDB BS32 .... 54 A1
Foxcroft Rd EVILLE/WHL BS5 .... 24 C3
Fox Den Rd BRSTK/PCHW BS34 .... 53 C4
Foxglove Cl MANG/FISH BS16 .... 9 F4 1
Fox Rd EVILLE/WHL BS5 .... 23 E1
Fraley Rd HNLZ/SM/SNYPK/WT BS9 .. 64 B4
Frampton Ct
    OLD/WMLY/WICK BS30 .... 93 C3 1
Frampton Crs MANG/FISH BS16 .... 79 D3
Francis Pl OLD/WMLY/WICK BS30 .... 93 C3
Francis Rd BMSTR BS3 .... 36 B5
    HNBRY/STHM BS10 .... 65 D3 1
Francombe Gv HNBRY/STHM BS10 .... 5 E1
Franklyn La CBRISNE BS2 .... 22 B2 1
Franklyn St CBRISNE BS2 .... 22 A2
Fraser St BMSTR BS3 .... 37 D3
Frayne Rd BMSTR BS3 .... 34 C1
Frederick Pl CFTN/FAIL BS8 .... 19 E5
Fredrick St BRSG/KWL/STAPK BS4 .. 38 C2 1
Freeland Buildings
    EVILLE/WHL BS5 .... 16 B4 1
Freeland Pl CFTN/FAIL BS8 .... 26 A3
Freemantle Gdns EVILLE/WHL BS5 .. 16 B3 1
Freemantle Rd EVILLE/WHL BS5 .... 16 A3
Freestone Rd CBRISNE BS2 .... 30 C3
Free Tank CBRISNE BS2 .... 30 B3
Fremantle La RDLND/MONT BS6 ...... 20 C2
Fremantle Rd RDLND/MONT BS6 .. 20 C1 1
Frenchay Hl MANG/FISH BS16 .... 71 C4
Frenchay Park Rd MANG/FISH BS16 .. 9 F1
Frenchay Rd MANG/FISH BS16 .... 71 D4
Freshland Wy KGWD/HNM BS15 ...... 85 D3
Friary Grange Pk FRCTL/WBN BS36 .. 56 B1
Friary Rd HORF/LLZ BS7 .... 12 C2

Friendship Rd
  BRSG/KWL/STAPK BS4 .... **97** C1
Friezewood Rd *BMSTR* BS3 .... **35** D2
Fripp Cl *EVILLE/WHL* BS5 .... **31** E2
Frobisher Rd *BMSTR* BS3 .... **35** D3
Frog La *CBRIS/FH* BS1 .... **28** A2
Frogmore St *CBRIS/FH* BS1 .... **28** B2 **2**
Frome Pl *MANG/FISH* BS16 .... **9** E3
Frome St *CBRISNE* BS2 .... **22** A4 **2**
Frome Valley Rd *MANG/FISH* BS16 .. **78** A1
Frome Valley Walkway
  FRCTL/WBN BS36 .... **56** B4
  MANG/FISH BS16 .... **71** D4
Frome Wy *FRCTL/WBN* BS36 .... **56** B3
Froomshaw Rd *MANG/FISH* BS16 .... **70** B4
Fry's Cl *MANG/FISH* BS16 .... **8** C5 **1**
Frys Hl *KGWD/HNM* BS15 .... **86** B1 **3**
  KGWD/HNM BS15 .... **86** B2 **2**
Fulford Rd
  BMSTRD/HC/WWD BS13 .... **105** C2 **3**
Fulford Wk
  BMSTRD/HC/WWD BS13 .... **105** C2 **4**
Furber Ct *EVILLE/WHL* BS5 .... **91** C1
Furber Rdg *EVILLE/WHL* BS5 .... **91** C1
Furber Rd *EVILLE/WHL* BS5 .... **91** C1
Furber V *EVILLE/WHL* BS5 .... **91** C1
The Furlong
  HNLZ/SM/SNYPK/WT BS9 .... **4** B3
Furnwood *EVILLE/WHL* BS5 .... **90** B1
Furze Rd *MANG/FISH* BS16 .... **79** D4
Furzewood Rd *KGWD/HNM* BS15 .... **87** C3
Fylton Cft *HGRV/WHIT* BS14 .... **108** A4

G

Gable Rd *EVILLE/WHL* BS5 .... **23** D1 **2**
Gadshill Dr *BRSTK/PCHW* BS34 ...... **53** D2
Gadshill Rd *EVILLE/WHL* BS5 .... **16** B3
Gages Cl *KGWD/HNM* BS15 .... **87** C4
Gages Rd *KGWD/HNM* BS15 .... **87** C4
Gainsborough Dr *KEYN* BS31 .... **113** C2
Gainsborough Sq *HORF/LLZ* BS7 ...... **7** F1
Gallivan Cl *BRSTK/PCHW* BS34 ...... **44** A4
Galway Rd *BRSG/KWL/STAPK* BS4 .. **96** B2
Gander Cl
  BMSTRD/HC/WWD BS13 .... **105** C2 **5**
Garden Cl *HNLZ/SM/SNYPK/WT* BS9 .. **76** B2
The Gardens *MANG/FISH* BS16 .... **70** A2
Gardner Av *BMSTRD/HC/WWD* BS13.. **94** A4
Garfield Rd *EVILLE/WHL* BS5 .... **84** B3
Garnet St *BMSTR* BS3 .... **35** E4
Garnett Pl *MANG/FISH* BS16 .... **73** C4
Garrett Dr *ALMDB* BS32 .... **45** C4 **2**
Garth Rd *BMSTRD/HC/WWD* BS13 .... **84** A5
Gasferry Rd *CBRIS/FH* BS1 .... **27** F5
The Gaskins *HORF/LLZ* BS7 .... **7** D3
Gas La *CBRISNE* BS2 .... **30** C3
Gaston Av *KEYN* BS31 .... **113** C2
The Gastons *AVONM* BS11 .... **61** D3
Gatcombe Dr *BRSTK/PCHW* BS34 .... **53** D3
Gatcombe Rd
  BMSTRD/HC/WWD BS13 .... **105** C2
Gatehouse Av
  BMSTRD/HC/WWD BS13 .... **104** B2
Gatehouse Cl
  BMSTRD/HC/WWD BS13 .... **104** B2 **6**
Gatehouse Ct
  BMSTRD/HC/WWD BS13 .... **105** C2 **5**

Gatehouse Wy
  BMSTRD/HC/WWD BS13.............. **104** B2
Gatesby Md *BRSTK/PCHW* BS34...... **53** D2
Gathorne Rd *BMSTR* BS3................ **35** E2
Gatton Rd *CBRISNE* BS2................ **23** D1
Gaunt's La *CBRIS/FH* BS1 .... **28** B2 **2**
Gay Elms Rd
  BMSTRD/HC/WWD BS13.............. **104** B3
Gayner Rd *HORF/LLZ* BS7 .... **67** D2
Gays Rd *KGWD/HNM* BS15 .... **91** C3
Gee Moors *KGWD/HNM* BS15 .... **87** C4 **3**
Gefle Cl *CBRIS/FH* BS1 .... **27** E5
George St *EVILLE/WHL* BS5 .... **24** B4
George Whitefield Ct
  CBRIS/FH BS1 .... **21** F5 **1**
Gerald Rd *BMSTR* BS3 .... **34** C3
Gerrard Cl *BRSG/KWL/STAPK* BS4.... **96** A4
Gerrish Av *EVILLE/WHL* BS5 .... **24** A4
  MANG/FISH BS16 .... **81** C2
Gibbsfold Rd
  BMSTRD/HC/WWD BS13.............. **105** D4
Gibson Rd *RDLND/MONT* BS6 .... **21** D1
Gifford Rd *HNBRY/STHM* BS10 ...... **48** A3
Giffords Pl *BMSTRD/HC/WWD* BS13 .. **94** B4
Gilbert Rd *EVILLE/WHL* BS5 .... **24** B4
  KGWD/HNM BS15 .... **86** A2
Gilda Cl *HGRV/WHIT* BS14 .... **108** A2
Gilda Crs *HGRV/WHIT* BS14 .... **108** A1
Gilda Sq West *HGRV/WHIT* BS14...... **108** A2
Gillard Cl *KGWD/HNM* BS15 .... **85** C3
Gillard Rd *KGWD/HNM* BS15 .... **85** C3
Gill Av *MANG/FISH* BS16 .... **79** C1
Gillebank Cl *HGRV/WHIT* BS14 ...... **109** C2 **2**
Gillingham Hl *EVILLE/WHL* BS5 .... **91** C2 **6**
Gillray Cl *HORF/LLZ* BS7 .... **7** F2
Gilpin Cl *KGWD/HNM* BS15 .... **87** C2 **3**
Gilslake Av *HNBRY/STHM* BS10 ...... **49** C4
Gipsy Patch La *BRSTK/PCHW* BS34 .. **52** B3
The Glades *EVILLE/WHL* BS5 .... **17** E4
Gladstone Dr *MANG/FISH* BS16 ...... **80** B4 **1**
Gladstone Rd *HGRV/WHIT* BS14 .... **108** A1
  KGWD/HNM BS15 .... **86** A2 **2**
Gladstone St *BMSTR* BS3................ **35** F3
  EVILLE/WHL BS5 .... **24** C5 **3**
  MANG/FISH BS16 .... **80** A4
Glaisdale Rd *MANG/FISH* BS16 ...... **78** B2
Glanville Gdns *KGWD/HNM* BS15 .... **86** B4
Glass House La *CBRISNE* BS2 .... **31** E4
Glastonbury Cl
  OLD/WMLY/WICK BS30 .... **93** C2 **4**
Glebelands Rd
  BRSTK/PCHW BS34 .... **51** D4 **3**
Glebe Rd *EVILLE/WHL* BS5 .... **25** F4
Glena Av *BRSG/KWL/STAPK* BS4 .... **39** F5
Glenarm Rd *BRSG/KWL/STAPK* BS4.. **99** D1
Glenarm Wk *BRSG/KWL/STAPK* BS4.. **99** D1
Glenavon Pk
  HNLZ/SM/SNYPK/WT BS9 .... **76** B3 **1**
Glen Brook
  HNLZ/SM/SNYPK/WT BS9............ **77** C3
Glenburn Rd *KGWD/HNM* BS15 ...... **85** D2
Glencoyne Sq *HNBRY/STHM* BS10.... **65** D1
Glendale *CFTN/FAIL* BS8 .... **26** B3
  MANG/FISH BS16 .... **72** B3
  MANG/FISH BS16 .... **79** D4 **3**
Glendare St *EVILLE/WHL* BS5 .... **32** A2
Glendevon Rd *HGRV/WHIT* BS14 .... **107** D4 **3**
Glen Dr *HNLZ/SM/SNYPK/WT* BS9 .... **77** C3
Glenfrome Rd *CBRISNE* BS2 .... **15** E3
  EVILLE/WHL BS5 .... **15** F2
Glen La *BRSG/KWL/STAPK* BS4 .... **99** C1
Glen Pk *EVILLE/WHL* BS5 .... **16** A4

EVILLE/WHL BS5 .... **84** B3
Glen Park Gdns *EVILLE/WHL* BS5 ...... **84** B3
Glenroy Av *KGWD/HNM* BS15 .... **85** C2
Glenside Cl *MANG/FISH* BS16 .... **71** D4
Glenside Pk *MANG/FISH* BS16 ...... **9** E4 ②
The Glen *KGWD/HNM* BS15 .... **91** C3
   RDLND/MONT BS6 .... **11** E2
Glentworth Rd *CFTN/FAIL* BS8 ...... **27** E2 ⑥
   RDLND/MONT BS6 .... **12** B4
Glenwood *MANG/FISH* BS16 .... **79** D4 ④
Glenwood Rd *HNBRY/STHM* BS10 ...... **65** D4
Gloster Av *EVILLE/WHL* BS5 .... **16** C3
Gloucester Cl *BRSTK/PCHW* BS34.... **53** C2
Gloucester La *CBRISNE* BS2 .... **22** B5 ①
Gloucester Rd *AVONM* BS11 .... **58** D2
   BRSTK/PCHW BS34 .... **44** A2
   HORF/LLZ BS7 .... **13** E2
   MANG/FISH BS16 .... **80** B4 ⑦
Gloucester Rd North
   BRSTK/PCHW BS34 .... **51** D2
   HORF/LLZ BS7 .... **67** C2
Gloucester St *CBRISNE* BS2 .... **21** F4 ①
   CFTN/FAIL BS8 .... **26** B1
   EVILLE/WHL BS5 .... **16** C3
Glyn V *BMSTR* BS3 .... **96** A2
Godfrey Ct
   OLD/WMLY/WICK BS30 .... **93** C3 ⑦
Goffenton Dr *MANG/FISH* BS16 ...... **79** C1
Goldney Av *CFTN/FAIL* BS8 .... **26** C2
Goldney Rd *CFTN/FAIL* BS8 .... **27** D3
Goldsbury Wk *AVONM* BS11 .... **61** D2
Golf Course La *BRSTK/PCHW* BS34 .... **51** C4
Goodeve Rd
   HNLZ/SM/SNYPK/WT BS9.......... **83** C1
Goodhind St *EVILLE/WHL* BS5........ **16** C3
Goodneston Rd *MANG/FISH* BS16 .... **78** B4
Goodring Hl *AVONM* BS11 .... **61** D2
Good Shepherd Cl *HORF/LLZ* BS7 ...... **4** B5
Goodwood Gdns
   MANG/FISH BS16 .... **73** C2 ③
Goolden St *BRSG/KWL/STAPK* BS4 .... **38** C3
Goose Acre *ALMDB* BS32 .... **54** B1 ①
   ALMDB BS32 .... **54** A1 ①
Gooseland Cl *HGRV/WHIT* BS14 .... **107** C4 ①
Gordon Av *EVILLE/WHL* BS5 .... **25** D1
Gordon Cl *EVILLE/WHL* BS5 .... **25** F1
Gordon Rd *CBRISNE* BS2 .... **22** B1
   CFTN/FAIL BS8 .... **27** D1
   EVILLE/WHL BS5 .... **17** D5
Gore Rd *BMSTR* BS3 .... **35** D4
Gore's Marsh Rd *BMSTR* BS3 .... **35** D5
Gorham Cl *AVONM* BS11 .... **62** B1 ③
Gorlangton Cl *HGRV/WHIT* BS14 .... **97** D4
Gorse Hl *MANG/FISH* BS16............ **79** D4
Gorse La *CFTN/FAIL* BS8 .... **27** E2
Gosforth Rd *HNBRY/STHM* BS10 .... **65** C2
Goslet Rd *HGRV/WHIT* BS14 ...... **109** D2
Gotley Rd *BRSG/KWL/STAPK* BS4 ...... **99** C1
Gott Dr *BRSG/KWL/STAPK* BS4 ...... **32** C3
Grace Ct *MANG/FISH* BS16............ **80** A1
Grace Dr *KGWD/HNM* BS15 .... **87** D2
Grace Park Rd
   BRSG/KWL/STAPK BS4 .... **99** C2
Grace Rd *MANG/FISH* BS16 .... **79** D2

Graeme Cl *MANG/FISH* BS16 .... **78** B3
Graham Rd *BMSTR* BS3 .... **36** A3 ①
   EVILLE/WHL BS5 .... **23** F2
   MANG/FISH BS16 .... **81** C1
Grainger Ct *AVONM* BS11 ...... **60** B4 ②
Granby Hl *CFTN/FAIL* BS8 .... **26** B3
Grange Av *BRSTK/PCHW* BS34 ...... **52** B1
   KGWD/HNM BS15 .... **92** A2
Grange Cl *ALMDB* BS32 .... **44** B1
Grange Ct *KGWD/HNM* BS15 ...... **92** A2 ②
Grange Court Rd
   HNLZ/SM/SNYPK/WT BS9.......... **3** D1
Grange Dr *MANG/FISH* BS16 .... **79** D1
Grange Pk *HNLZ/SM/SNYPK/WT* BS9 .. **3** E1
   MANG/FISH BS16 .... **71** D3
Grange Rd
   BMSTR/HC/WWD BS13.............. **104** B2
   CFTN/FAIL BS8 .... **18** C5
The Grange
   HNLZ/SM/SNYPK/WT BS9.......... **63** C4
Grangewood Cl *MANG/FISH* BS16 .. **79** D1 ③
Granny's La *KGWD/HNM* BS15 ...... **92** B2
Grantham La *KGWD/HNM* BS15 .... **85** D3 ③
Grantham Rd *KGWD/HNM* BS15.... **85** D2
Grantson Cl *BRSG/KWL/STAPK* BS4 .. **41** E5
Granville Cl *KGWD/HNM* BS15 ...... **91** C4
Granville St *EVILLE/WHL* BS5 .... **32** A2
Grasmere Cl *HNBRY/STHM* BS10 .... **64** B3
Grass Meers Dr *HGRV/WHIT* BS14 .. **107** D3
Gratitude Rd *EVILLE/WHL* BS5 ...... **24** B1
Graveney Cl
   BRSG/KWL/STAPK BS4 .... **99** C2 ④
Grayle Rd *HNBRY/STHM* BS10 ...... **48** A4
Gray's Cl *HNBRY/STHM* BS10 ...... **63** D1 ③
Great Ann St *CBRISNE* BS2 .... **22** B5
Great Brockeridge
   HNLZ/SM/SNYPK/WT BS9............ **2** B2
Great Dowles
   OLD/WMLY/WICK BS30 .... **93** D3
Great George St *CBRIS/FH* BS1 ...... **27** F2
   CBRISNE BS2 .... **22** A5
Great Hayles Rd *HGRV/WHIT* BS14 .... **97** D4
Great Leaze *OLD/WMLY/WICK* BS30 .. **93** D3
Great Meadow Rd *ALMDB* BS32........ **46** A4
Great Stoke Wy *BRSTK/PCHW* BS34 .. **53** C4
Great Western La *EVILLE/WHL* BS5 .... **32** A2
Greenacre *HGRV/WHIT* BS14........ **107** C4
Greenbank Av *EVILLE/WHL* BS5 ...... **24** A1
Greenbank Av West
   EVILLE/WHL BS5 .... **23** F1
Greenbank Rd *BMSTR* BS3 .... **35** D1
   EVILLE/WHL BS5 .... **24** A1
   KGWD/HNM BS15 .... **92** A2
Greenbank Vw *EVILLE/WHL* BS5 .... **16** B4
Green Cft *EVILLE/WHL* BS5 .... **84** B2
Greendale Rd *BMSTR* BS3 .... **37** F4
   RDLND/MONT BS6 .... **11** F1
Greenditch Av
   BMSTR/HC/WWD BS13.............. **105** D2
Greendown *EVILLE/WHL* BS5 .... **84** B4
Green Dragon Rd *FRCTL/WBN* BS36 .. **56** A2
Greenfield Av *HNBRY/STHM* BS10 .. **66** A3 ①
Greenfield Rd *HNBRY/STHM* BS10 .. **66** A3 ①
Greenhill Gv *BMSTR* BS3 .... **34** C5
Greenhill La *AVONM* BS11 .... **62** B2 ①
Green La *AVONM* BS11 .... **59** C3
   FRCTL/WBN BS36........................ **47** D4
Greenleaze *BRSG/KWL/STAPK* BS4.... **98** A2
Greenleaze Av *MANG/FISH* BS16 .... **72** A2
Greenmore Rd
   BRSG/KWL/STAPK BS4 .... **39** E5
Greenore *KGWD/HNM* BS15 .... **85** D4

H

Harford Cl
  HNLZ/SM/SNYPK/WT BS9 .... 62 B4 🔢

Harford Dr *MANG/FISH* BS16 .... 71 D2

Harleston St *EVILLE/WHL* BS5.......... 22 B4

Harmer Cl *HNBRY/STHM* BS10 .... 48 A4

Harnhill Cl
  BMSTRD/HC/WWD BS13 .... 105 C3

Harolds Wy *KGWD/HNM* BS15 .... 91 D1

Harptree Ct
  OLD/WMLY/WICK BS30 .... 93 D3 🔢

Harptree Gv *BMSTR* BS3 .... 35 F5 🔢

Harrington Av *HGRV/WHIT* BS14 ... 109 D1

Harrington Gv *HGRV/WHIT* BS14 ... 109 D1 🔢

Harrington Rd *HGRV/WHIT* BS14 ..... 109 D1

Harrington Wk *HGRV/WHIT* BS14 .. 109 D1 🔢

Harris Ct *OLD/WMLY/WICK* BS30 .... 93 C5 🔢

Harrowdene Rd
  BRSG/KWL/STAPK BS4 .... 39 E4

Harrow Rd *BRSG/KWL/STAPK* BS4 .... 40 C3

Harry Stoke Rd *BRSTK/PCHW* BS34 ... 53 E4

Hartcliffe Rd *BRSG/KWL/STAPK* BS4 .. 96 B3

Hartcliffe Wk
  BMSTRD/HC/WWD BS13 .... 97 C3 🔢

Hartcliffe Wy *BMSTR* BS3 .... 95 D2
  BRSG/KWL/STAPK BS4 .... 95 D4

Hartfield Av *RDLND/MONT* BS6 .... 20 B3

Hartgill Cl *BMSTRD/HC/WWD* BS13 .. 105 C4

Hartington Pk *RDLND/MONT* BS6 ...... 11 F2

Harvest Cl *ALMDB* BS32 .... 45 C2

Haskins Ct *OLD/WMLY/WICK* BS30 ... 93 D3 🔢

Hassell Dr *CBRISNE* BS2 .... 22 C5

Hastings Cl *BMSTR* BS3 .... 95 D2 🔢

Hastings Rd *BMSTR* BS3 .... 95 D2

Hatchet La *BRSTK/PCHW* BS34....... 53 D3

Hatchet Rd *BRSTK/PCHW* BS34 .... 53 C2

Hatherley Rd *HORF/LLZ* BS7 .... 13 D1

Hathway Wk *EVILLE/WHL* BS5 .... 22 C3

The Haven *KGWD/HNM* BS15 .... 86 B2

Haverstock Rd
  BRSG/KWL/STAPK BS4 .... 38 C3

Hawburn Cl *BRSG/KWL/STAPK* BS4 .... 99 C1

Hawkesbury Rd *MANG/FISH* BS16 ..... 17 F2

Hawkesley Dr *BRSTK/PCHW* BS34 ..... 53 C1

Hawkfield Cl
  BMSTRD/HC/WWD BS13 .... 106 A2

Hawkfield Rd
  BMSTRD/HC/WWD BS13.............. 106 A2

Hawkfield Wy
  BMSTRD/HC/WWD BS13 .... 106 A2 🔢

Hawkins Crs *ALMDB* BS32 .... 45 C3

Hawkins St *CBRISNE* BS2............... 30 A1

Hawksmoor Cl *HGRV/WHIT* BS14 .... 107 D1

Hawksworth Dr *KGWD/HNM* BS15 .... 91 C3

Hawthorn Av *KGWD/HNM* BS15 ...... 91 C2 🔢

Hawthorn Cl *BRSTK/PCHW* BS34 ..... 42 A3

The Hawthornes *MANG/FISH* BS16 .... 81 C3

Hawthorne St
  BRSG/KWL/STAPK BS4 .... 39 D3

Hawthorns La *KEYN* BS31 .... 112 A3

Hawthorn Wy *BRSTK/PCHW* BS34..... 53 D2

Haycombe *HGRV/WHIT* BS14 .... 107 C1 🔢

Haydock Cl *MANG/FISH* BS16 .... 73 C2 🔢

Haydon Gdns *HORF/LLZ* BS7 .... 7 F3

Hayeley Dr *BRSTK/PCHW* BS34....... 53 D1

Hayes Cl *CBRISNE* BS2 .... 22 C5

The Haymarket *CBRIS/FH* BS1 .... 21 D5

Haynes La *MANG/FISH* BS16 .... 80 A2

Haythorn Ct *MANG/FISH* BS16 .... 81 C2

Haytor Pk *HNLZ/SM/SNYPK/WT* BS9.. 77 C1

Hayward Rd *EVILLE/WHL* BS5.......... 32 A1
  MANG/FISH BS16 .... 80 A4

Hazel Av *RDLND/MONT* BS6 .... 11 E4

Hazelbury Rd *HGRV/WHIT* BS14 .... 98 B3

Hazel Cote Rd *HGRV/WHIT* BS14 .... 108 A3

Hazeldene Rd *BRSTK/PCHW* BS34 ..... 43 D4

Hazelgrove *FRCTL/WBN* BS36 .... 56 A2 🔢

Hazel Gv *HORF/LLZ* BS7 .... 67 D3

Hazelton Rd *HORF/LLZ* BS7 .... 12 C3

Hazelwood Rd
  HNLZ/SM/SNYPK/WT BS9............ 77 C4

Headford Av *EVILLE/WHL* BS5 .... 85 C4

Headford Rd *BRSG/KWL/STAPK* BS4 .. 96 A2

Headington Cl *KGWD/HNM* BS15 .... 92 A3 🔢

Headley Ct
  BMSTRD/HC/WWD BS13............. 105 C1

Headley La
  BMSTRD/HC/WWD BS13............. 105 C1

Headley Park Av
  BMSTRD/HC/WWD BS13............... 95 C4

Headley Park Rd
  BMSTRD/HC/WWD BS13............... 94 B4

Headley Rd
  BMSTRD/HC/WWD BS13............. 104 B1

Headley Wk
  BMSTRD/HC/WWD BS13............... 95 C4

Heart Meers *HGRV/WHIT* BS14 ...... 108 A2 🔢

Heath Cl *FRCTL/WBN* BS36 .... 56 B1

Heathcote Rd *MANG/FISH* BS16 .... 80 B2 🔢
  MANG/FISH BS16 .... 85 C1

Heathcote Wk *KGWD/HNM* BS15....... 85 D1

Heath Ct *MANG/FISH* BS16 .... 72 A4 🔢

Heather Cl *KGWD/HNM* BS15 .... 85 C3

Heatherdene *HGRV/WHIT* BS14 .... 97 C4

Heathfield Cl *KEYN* BS31 .... 111 D2

Heathfield Crs *HGRV/WHIT* BS14 .... 107 D3

Heathfields *MANG/FISH* BS16.......... 72 A3

Heath Gdns *MANG/FISH* BS16.......... 72 A3

Heath House La *EVILLE/WHL* BS5 .... 7 F5
  MANG/FISH BS16 .... 8 B5

Heath Rd *EVILLE/WHL* BS5 .... 15 F2
  KGWD/HNM BS15 .... 91 C3
  MANG/FISH BS16 .... 72 A4

Heath St *EVILLE/WHL* BS5 .... 16 A3

Heath Wk *MANG/FISH* BS16 .... 72 A4

Heber St *EVILLE/WHL* BS5 .... 24 A5

Hebron Rd *BMSTR* BS3 .... 36 A3

Hedgemead Vw *MANG/FISH* BS16....... 9 D3

Hedwick Av *EVILLE/WHL* BS5 .... 25 E5 🔢

Hedwick St *EVILLE/WHL* BS5........... 25 E5

Heggard Cl
  BMSTRD/HC/WWD BS13............. 104 B2 🔢

Hellier Wk
  BMSTRD/HC/WWD BS13............. 105 D4 🔢

Hemplow Cl *HGRV/WHIT* BS14 .... 99 C4

Hempton La *ALMDB* BS32 .... 43 D1

Henacre Rd *AVONM* BS11 .... 61 C3

Henbury Rd *HNBRY/STHM* BS10 ...... 63 D1 🔢
  HNLZ/SM/SNYPK/WT BS9............ 64 B3
  KGWD/HNM BS15 .... 91 C2 🔢

Henbury Road Henbury Hl
  HNLZ/SM/SNYPK/WT BS9............ 64 A3

Hencliffe Rd *HGRV/WHIT* BS14 .... 109 C3

Hencliffe Wy *KGWD/HNM* BS15 .... 91 C4

Henderson Rd *KGWD/HNM* BS15........ 91 C2

Hendre Rd *BMSTR* BS3 .... 34 C5

Hengaston St *BMSTR* BS3 .... 35 F5

Hengrove Av *HGRV/WHIT* BS14 .... 98 A3

Hengrove La *HGRV/WHIT* BS14 .... 98 A3

Hengrove Rd *BRSG/KWL/STAPK* BS4... 39 D5

Hengrove Wy
  BMSTRD/HC/WWD BS13............. 105 C2
  BRSG/KWL/STAPK BS4 .... 106 B1

Henleaze Av
  HNLZ/SM/SNYPK/WT BS9.............. 3 D3

Henleaze Gdns
HNLZ/SM/SNYPK/WT BS9......................3 D4
Henleaze Pk
HNLZ/SM/SNYPK/WT BS9......................4 A3
Henleaze Park Dr
HNLZ/SM/SNYPK/WT BS9......................3 F2
Henleaze Rd
HNLZ/SM/SNYPK/WT BS9......................3 D4
Henleaze Ter
HNLZ/SM/SNYPK/WT BS9....................65 C4
Henley Gv *HNLZ/SM/SNYPK/WT* BS9....3 E3
Hennessy Cl *HGRV/WHIT* BS14 ....106 B4
Henrietta St *CBRISNE* BS2...................20 B3
EVILLE/WHL BS5.................................23 F1 ☑
Henry St *BMSTR* BS3............................38 B2
Henry Williamson Ct
OLD/WMLY/WICK BS30......................93 D2 ☒
Henshaw Cl *KGWD/HNM* BS15 ....85 D1 ☒
Henshaw Rd *KGWD/HNM* BS15.........85 D1
Henshaw Wk *KGWD/HNM* BS15......85 D1 ☒
Hensman's Hl *CFTN/FAIL* BS8 ....26 C2
Hepburn Rd *CBRISNE* BS2...................21 E3
Herald Cl *HNLZ/SM/SNYPK/WT* BS9....77 C2
Herapath St *EVILLE/WHL* BS5.............32 A3
Herbert Crs *EVILLE/WHL* BS5.............16 C3
Herbert St *BMSTR* BS3.........................36 B2
EVILLE/WHL BS5.................................24 B3
Hercules Cl *BRSTK/PCHW* BS34 ....53 C1
Hereford Rd *CBRISNE* BS2...................15 D5
Hereford St *BMSTR* BS3.......................36 C3
Herkomer Cl *HORF/LLZ* BS7...............68 A4
Hermitage Cl *AVONM* BS11..................60 B4
Hermitage Rd *MANG/FISH* BS16.........80 A2
Heron Rd *EVILLE/WHL* BS5..................23 E2
Herridge Cl
BMSTRD/HC/WWD BS13.................105 C3
Herridge Rd
BMSTRD/HC/WWD BS13.................105 C3
Hesding Cl *KGWD/HNM* BS15.........91 D4 ☑
Hestercombe Rd
BMSTRD/HC/WWD BS13.................105 C1 ☑
Hewland Ct *AVONM* BS11................62 B1 ☑
Heyford Av *EVILLE/WHL* BS5..............15 E2
Heyron Wk
BMSTRD/HC/WWD BS13.................105 C3
Hicks Common Rd
FRCTL/WBN BS36..............................56 B1
Hicks Ct *OLD/WMLY/WICK* BS30 ....93 C3 ☒
Higham St *BRSG/KWL/STAPK* BS4 ...38 C3 ☒
Highbury Rd *BMSTR* BS3......................95 D2
HORF/LLZ BS7....................................67 C4
Highbury Vls *CBRISNE* BS2.................20 A4
Highdale Rd *HGRV/WHIT* BS14.........108 A3
High Elm *KGWD/HNM* BS15 ....92 B1 ☒
Highett Dr *EVILLE/WHL* BS5...............23 D2
Highfield Av *KGWD/HNM* BS15..........92 A2
Highfield Gv *HORF/LLZ* BS7.................5 D3
Highfields Cl *BRSTK/PCHW* BS34 ....54 A4
High Gv *HNLZ/SM/SNYPK/WT* BS9....62 A4
Highgrove St *BRSG/KWL/STAPK* BS4 ...38 C2
Highland Crs *CFTN/FAIL* BS8 ....11 D5 ☑
Highmore Gdns *HORF/LLZ* BS7...........68 B4
Highnam Cl *BRSTK/PCHW* BS34 ....44 A2
High Pk *HGRV/WHIT* BS14...................98 A2
Highridge Crs
BMSTRD/HC/WWD BS13.................104 A2
Highridge Pk
BMSTRD/HC/WWD BS13............104 A2 ☒
High St *AVONM* BS11...........................60 A4
CBRIS/FH BS1....................................29 D1
CFTN/FAIL BS8..................................11 D5
EVILLE/WHL BS5.................................23 F1

FRCTL/WBN BS36................................56 A1
HNLZ/SM/SNYPK/WT BS9.................64 B3
KEYN BS31..112 B1
KGWD/HNM BS15..............................86 B3
KGWD/HNM BS15..............................91 D2
MANG/FISH BS16..............................79 D2
Highview Rd *KGWD/HNM* BS15.........86 B1
Highwood La *BRSTK/PCHW* BS34 ......42 B4
HNBRY/STHM BS10............................42 A4
Highwood Rd *BRSTK/PCHW* BS34 .....42 B4
Highworth Rd
BRSG/KWL/STAPK BS4......................33 D3
Hill Av *BMSTR* BS3...............................37 F4
Hill Burn *HNLZ/SM/SNYPK/WT* BS9 ...4 B1
Hillburn Rd *EVILLE/WHL* BS5..............84 B3
Hill Crest *BRSG/KWL/STAPK* BS4.......98 A2
Hillfields Av *MANG/FISH* BS16............79 D4
Hill Gv *HNLZ/SM/SNYPK/WT* BS9........4 A1
Hillgrove St *CBRISNE* BS2...............21 E3 ☑
Hill House Rd *MANG/FISH* BS16.........81 C2
Hill Lawn *BRSG/KWL/STAPK* BS4.......41 D3
Hillsborough Rd
BRSG/KWL/STAPK BS4......................40 B1
Hills Cl *KEYN* BS31.............................113 D2
Hillsdon Rd
HNLZ/SM/SNYPK/WT BS9.................64 A3
Hillside *MANG/FISH* BS16....................81 C2
RDLND/MONT BS6...............................20 A3
Hillside Av *KGWD/HNM* BS15.............85 D3
Hillside Rd *EVILLE/WHL* BS5...............84 B4
Hillside St *BRSG/KWL/STAPK* BS4......38 C2
Hill St *BMSTR* BS3................................38 A2
CBRIS/FH BS1.....................................28 A2
EVILLE/WHL BS5.................................84 A3
Hilltop Gdns *EVILLE/WHL* BS5............84 B4
Hilltop Rd *MANG/FISH* BS16...............86 A1
Hilltop Vw *EVILLE/WHL* BS5...............84 B4
Hill Vw *CFTN/FAIL* BS8........................27 E2
HNLZ/SM/SNYPK/WT BS9....................4 A2
MANG/FISH BS16...............................86 A1
Hill View Rd
BMSTRD/HC/WWD BS13...................94 B4
Hillyfield Rd
BMSTRD/HC/WWD BS13.................104 B1
Hinton Rd *EVILLE/WHL* BS5................24 B1
MANG/FISH BS16............................78 B3 ☑
Hobb's La *CBRIS/FH* BS1................28 B2 ☒
Hockey's La *MANG/FISH* BS16.......78 B3 ☒
Hogarth Wk *HORF/LLZ* BS7................68 A4
Hogues Wk
BMSTRD/HC/WWD BS13.................105 C3 ☒
Holbeach Wy *HGRV/WHIT* BS14 ....107 D4
Holbrook Crs
BMSTRD/HC/WWD BS13.................106 A3
Holcombe *HGRV/WHIT* BS14............107 C1 ☒
Holcombe Gv *KEYN* BS31.................112 A2
Holdenhurst Rd *KGWD/HNM* BS15 ... 85 D2
Holford Ct *HGRV/WHIT* BS14...........108 A2
Hollister's Dr
BMSTRD/HC/WWD BS13.................106 A4
Hollow Rd *KGWD/HNM* BS15.............86 B3
Hollway Cl *HGRV/WHIT* BS14 ....109 D2 ☒
Hollway Rd *HGRV/WHIT* BS14..........109 D2
Hollybush La
HNLZ/SM/SNYPK/WT BS9.................10 A1
Holly Cl *EVILLE/WHL* BS5...................84 B1
Holly Crs *KGWD/HNM* BS15...........86 B2 ☒
Holly Gn *KGWD/HNM* BS15................87 D2
Holly Gv *MANG/FISH* BS16.................79 D4
Hollyguest Rd *KGWD/HNM* BS15.......92 B1
Holly Hill Rd *KGWD/HNM* BS15.........87 C3
Hollyleigh Av *BRSTK/PCHW* BS34......67 C1

Holly Lodge Rd *EVILLE/WHL* BS5 .... 84 A1
Hollymead La
  HNLZ/SM/SNYPK/WT BS9............... 77 D3
Hollyridge *HGRV/WHIT* BS14............. 108 B1
Holly Wk *KEYN* BS31...................... 112 A4
Hollywood Rd
  BRSG/KWL/STAPK BS4 .... 41 D4
Holmdale Rd *BRSTK/PCHW* BS34....... 52 A4
Holmesdale Rd *BMSTR* BS3 .... 37 E4
Holmes Gv *HNLZ/SM/SNYPK/WT* BS9 .. 3 E3
Holmes Hill Rd *EVILLE/WHL* BS5.......... 84 A3
Holmes St *EVILLE/WHL* BS5.............. 31 F2
Holmoak Rd *KEYN* BS31................. 111 D3
Holmwood *KGWD/HNM* BS15............ 91 D2
Holmwood Cl *FRCTL/WBN* BS36 ...... 56 A1 🔲
Holmwood Gdns
  HNLZ/SM/SNYPK/WT BS9............... 64 B3
Holsom Cl *HGRV/WHIT* BS14............ 109 D1
Holsom Rd *HGRV/WHIT* BS14............ 110 A2 🔲
Holst Gdns *BRSG/KWL/STAPK* BS4 ...... 95 D4
Holton Rd *HORF/LLZ* BS7................... 6 C1
Holyrood Cl *BRSTK/PCHW* BS34 .... 53 C3 🔲
Holy Well Cl
  BRSG/KWL/STAPK BS4 .... 33 F2 🔲
Home Cl *HNBRY/STHM* BS10.............. 66 B1
Home Gnd *AVONM* BS11.................. 60 A4
  HNLZ/SM/SNYPK/WT BS9............... 65 C4
Homeleaze Rd *HNBRY/STHM* BS10 ..... 50 A4
Home Md *OLD/WMLY/WICK* BS30 ...... 93 D3
Homemead Dr
  BRSG/KWL/STAPK BS4 .... 99 C2 🔲
Homestead Gdns *MANG/FISH* BS16..... 71 C2
Homestead Rd *BRSTK/PCHW* BS34 .... 51 C4
Honey Garston Cl
  BMSTRD/HC/WWD BS13 .... 105 C3 🔲
Honey Garston Rd
  BMSTRD/HC/WWD BS13................ 105 C3
Honey Hill Rd *KGWD/HNM* BS15......... 87 C3
Honeymead *HGRV/WHIT* BS14.......... 108 B1 🔲
Honeysuckle Cl *ALMDB* BS32........... 45 D1 🔲
Honey Suckle La *MANG/FISH* BS16 ...... 9 E5
Honiton Rd *MANG/FISH* BS16.......... 78 B4
Hooper Rd *HGRV/WHIT* BS14........... 109 C2
Hopechapel Hl *CFTN/FAIL* BS8 .... 26 B3
Hope Rd *BMSTR* BS3 .... 36 A5
Hope Sq *CFTN/FAIL* BS8 .... 26 B3 🔲
Hopetoun *CBRISNE* BS2................... 14 B3
Hopewell Gdns *AVONM* BS11............ 61 C4
Hopp's Rd *KGWD/HNM* BS15............ 86 A4
Horesham Gv
  BMSTRD/HC/WWD BS13 .... 105 D2 🔲
Horfield Rd *CBRISNE* BS2................. 20 C5
Horley Rd *CBRISNE* BS2.................. 22 C1
Horsecroft Gdns
  OLD/WMLY/WICK BS30 .... 93 D1 🔲
The Horsefair *CBRIS/FH* BS1 .... 21 E5
Horseshoe Dr
  HNLZ/SM/SNYPK/WT BS9............... 76 B3
Horton St *CBRISNE* BS2.................. 30 B2
Horwood Ct
  OLD/WMLY/WICK BS30 .... 93 D3 🔲
Hosey Wk *BMSTRD/HC/WWD* BS13 ... 104 B2
Host St *CBRIS/FH* BS1 .... 28 C1
Hottom Gdns *HORF/LLZ* BS7.............. 67 D4
Hot Water La *KGWD/HNM* BS15......... 81 C4
Hotwell Rd *CFTN/FAIL* BS8 .... 26 B3 🔲
Houlton St *CBRISNE* BS2.................. 22 A4
Howard Av *EVILLE/WHL* BS5............. 25 E3
Howard Rd *BMSTR* BS3 .... 36 A1
  MANG/FISH BS16.......................... 80 A3
  RDLND/MONT BS6......................... 3 F5
Howard St *EVILLE/WHL* BS5............. 25 E2

Howecroft Gdns
  HNLZ/SM/SNYPK/WT BS9 .... 77 D3 🔲
Howes Cl *OLD/WMLY/WICK* BS30 ...... 93 D1
Howett Rd *EVILLE/WHL* BS5 .... 24 B5 🔲
Huckford La *FRCTL/WBN* BS36.......... 57 D3
Huckford Rd *FRCTL/WBN* BS36......... 56 B2
Huckley Wy *ALMDB* BS32................ 54 A1
Hudd's Hill Rd *EVILLE/WHL* BS5......... 84 A3
Hudd's Vale Rd *EVILLE/WHL* BS5....... 25 F3
Hughenden Rd *CFTN/FAIL* BS8.......... 10 C5
  HORF/LLZ BS7 .... 5 E3
Hulbert Cl *BRSG/KWL/STAPK* BS4 .. 100 B1 🔲
Hulse Rd *BRSG/KWL/STAPK* BS4....... 99 C2
Humberstan Wk *AVONM* BS11 .... 60 B3 🔲
Humphry Davy Wy
  CFTN/FAIL BS8 .... 26 B4 🔲
Humphrys Barton
  BRSG/KWL/STAPK BS4 .... 90 A2
Hungerford Cl
  BRSG/KWL/STAPK BS4 .... 99 D3
Hungerford Crs
  BRSG/KWL/STAPK BS4 .... 99 D3
Hungerford Gdns
  BRSG/KWL/STAPK BS4 .... 99 D3
Hungerford Rd
  BRSG/KWL/STAPK BS4 .... 99 D2
Hungerford Wk
  BRSG/KWL/STAPK BS4 .... 99 D2
Hung Rd *AVONM* BS11.................... 74 A3
Hunters Cl *KGWD/HNM* BS15 .... 91 D2 🔲
Hunters Dr *KGWD/HNM* BS15.......... 87 C2
Hunters Rd *KGWD/HNM* BS15.......... 91 D2
Hunters Rd East *KGWD/HNM* BS15.... 91 D2
Hunter's Wy *BRSTK/PCHW* BS34 ...... 52 A4
Hurle Crs *CFTN/FAIL* BS8 .... 19 D1
Hurle Rd *CFTN/FAIL* BS8................ 19 E1
Hurlingham Rd *RDLND/MONT* BS6 ..... 14 A4
Hurn La *KEYN* BS31...................... 113 C3
Hurston Rd *BRSG/KWL/STAPK* BS4 .... 96 A3
Hurst Rd *BRSG/KWL/STAPK* BS4....... 97 C3
Hurst Wk *BRSG/KWL/STAPK* BS4...... 96 B3
Hurstwood Rd *MANG/FISH* BS16....... 80 A2
Hutton Cl *HNLZ/SM/SNYPK/WT* BS9 .. 63 C4
Huyton Rd *EVILLE/WHL* BS5............. 17 E3
Hyland Gv *HNLZ/SM/SNYPK/WT* BS9.. 64 A3

I

Ida Rd *EVILLE/WHL* BS5................... 24 B3
Iddesleigh Rd *RDLND/MONT* BS6....... 11 E3
Idstone Rd *MANG/FISH* BS16 .... 79 C3
Ilchester Crs
  BMSTRD/HC/WWD BS13................ 95 C2
Ilchester Rd
  BMSTRD/HC/WWD BS13................ 95 C3
Iles Cl *KGWD/HNM* BS15................ 92 A3
Ilex Cl *BMSTRD/HC/WWD* BS13....... 104 A1
Ilminster Av *BRSG/KWL/STAPK* BS4.... 96 B2
Ilsyn Gv *HGRV/WHIT* BS14.............. 99 C4
Imber Court Cl *HGRV/WHIT* BS14...... 98 A3
Imperial Rd *CFTN/FAIL* BS8 .... 19 E2
  HGRV/WHIT BS14......................... 98 B3
Imperial Wk *HGRV/WHIT* BS14 .... 98 A3
Ingleside Rd *KGWD/HNM* BS15.......... 85 D2
Ingmire Rd *EVILLE/WHL* BS5............ 15 E3
Inkerman Cl *HORF/LLZ* BS7.............. 66 B4
Innox Gdns
  BMSTRD/HC/WWD BS13 .... 104 B2 🔲
Inns Court Av
  BRSG/KWL/STAPK BS4 .... 96 A4

Inns Court Dr
BRSG/KWL/STAPK BS4 .... **106** A1 🖫
Instow Rd *BRSG/KWL/STAPK* BS4 .... **96** B3
Instow Wk *BRSG/KWL/STAPK* BS4 .... **96** B3 🖫
Ipswich Dr *BRSG/KWL/STAPK* BS4 ..... **33** F3
Irby Rd *BMSTR* BS3 .... **34** C4
Irena Rd *MANG/FISH* BS16 .... **84** A1 🖫
Ireton Rd *BMSTR* BS3 .... **35** F4 🖫
Ironmould La
BRSG/KWL/STAPK BS4 .... **100** B2
Irving Cl *MANG/FISH* BS16 .... **80** B3 🖫
Island Gdns *MANG/FISH* BS16 .... **8** A5 🖫
Isleys Ct *OLD/WMLY/WICK* BS30 ..... **93** C4 🖫
Islington Rd *BMSTR* BS3 .... **35** F1
Ivor Rd *EVILLE/WHL* BS5 .... **24** B3
Ivy La *MANG/FISH* BS16 .... **78** B4 🖫
Ivywell Rd
HNLZ/SM/SNYPK/WT BS9............... **77** D4

J

Jacob St *CBRISNE* BS2 .... **29** F1
Jacob's Wells Rd *CFTN/FAIL* BS8 ...... **27** E2
Jamaica St *CBRISNE* BS2 .... **21** D3
James Cl *MANG/FISH* BS16 .... **80** B3 🖫
James Rd *MANG/FISH* BS16.............. **80** B4
James St *CBRISNE* BS2 .... **14** C4
EVILLE/WHL BS5 .... **22** B4
Jane St *EVILLE/WHL* BS5 .... **23** F5
Jarvis St *EVILLE/WHL* BS5 .... **31** E2
Jasmine Gv *AVONM* BS11 .... **62** B1 🖫
Jasper St *BMSTR* BS3 .... **35** F4
Jean Rd *BRSG/KWL/STAPK* BS4......... **41** E5
Jefferies Hill Bottom
KGWD/HNM BS15 .... **91** C2
Jersey Av *BRSG/KWL/STAPK* BS4 ...... **90** A3
Jessop Under/pass *BMSTR* BS3.......... **34** B1
Jocelyn Rd *HORF/LLZ* BS7 .... **67** C4
Jockey La *EVILLE/WHL* BS5 .... **84** B4
John Carr's Ter *CFTN/FAIL* BS8 .... **27** E2
Johnson Dr *OLD/WMLY/WICK* BS30 ... **93** C2
Johnsons La *EVILLE/WHL* BS5............ **24** C3
Johnsons Rd *EVILLE/WHL* BS5 .... **24** C3
John St *CBRIS/FH* BS1 .... **29** D1 🖫
CBRISNE BS2 .... **14** C5
KGWD/HNM BS15 .... **85** D3
John Wesley Rd *EVILLE/WHL* BS5 ...... **91** C1
Jordan Wk *ALMDB* BS32 .... **45** C3
Jubilee Crs *MANG/FISH* BS16 .... **81** D1
Jubilee Pl *CBRIS/FH* BS1 .... **29** D4 🖫
Jubilee Rd *BRSG/KWL/STAPK* BS4 ...... **98** B2
CBRISNE BS2 .... **22** C1
EVILLE/WHL BS5 .... **84** A4
KGWD/HNM BS15 .... **80** B4
Jubilee St *CBRISNE* BS2 .... **30** B2
Julian Cl *HNLZ/SM/SNYPK/WT* BS9 ... **77** C4
Julian Rd *HNLZ/SM/SNYPK/WT* BS9... **77** D4
Julius Rd *HORF/LLZ* BS7 .... **12** C2
Junction Rd *BRSG/KWL/STAPK* BS4 ... **40** A2
Juniper Ct *EVILLE/WHL* BS5................ **16** A4
Juniper Wy *ALMDB* BS32 .... **46** A4
Jupiter Rd *BRSTK/PCHW* BS34 .... **42** A4
Justice Rd *MANG/FISH* BS16 .... **78** B4 🖫
Jutland Rd *AVONM* BS11 .... **59** C2

K

Kathdene Gdns *HORF/LLZ* BS7 .... **14** B2

Keble Av *BMSTRD/HC/WWD* BS13 .... **104** A2
Keinton Wk *HNBRY/STHM* BS10...... **64** B1
Kellaway Av *HORF/LLZ* BS7................... **5** E1
RDLND/MONT BS6................................. **4** B4
Kellaway Crs *HORF/LLZ* BS7 .... **5** D2
Kelston Gdns *HNBRY/STHM* BS10 .. **66** A3 🖫
Kelston Gv *KGWD/HNM* BS15 .... **92** B1
Kelston Rd *HNBRY/STHM* BS10 .... **65** D3
KEYN BS31 .... **112** A3
Kelston Wk *MANG/FISH* BS16 .... **79** D3
Kemble Cl *KGWD/HNM* BS15 .... **92** B1 🖫
Kemperleye Wy *ALMDB* BS32 .... **45** C4 🖫
Kencot Wk
BMSTRD/HC/WWD BS13............... **105** C4
Kendall Gdns *MANG/FISH* BS16 .... **80** A3
Kendall Rd *MANG/FISH* BS16 .... **80** A3
Kendal Rd *HORF/LLZ* BS7 .... **67** D4
Kendon Dr *HNBRY/STHM* BS10 .... **66** A4
Kendon Wy *HNBRY/STHM* BS10........ **66** A3
Kenilworth Cl *KEYN* BS31 .... **112** A3
Kenilworth Rd *RDLND/MONT* BS6 .... **20** A2
Kenmare Rd *BRSG/KWL/STAPK* BS4 .. **96** B2
Kenmore Crs *HORF/LLZ* BS7 .... **66** B2
Kenmore Dr *HORF/LLZ* BS7 .... **66** B2
Kenmore Gv *HORF/LLZ* BS7 .... **66** B2 🖫
Kennard Ri *KGWD/HNM* BS15 .... **85** D4
Kennard Rd *KGWD/HNM* BS15 .... **85** D3
Kennel Lodge Rd *BMSTR* BS3........... **89** D3
Kenneth Rd *BRSG/KWL/STAPK* BS4 ... **99** C1
Kennet Rd *KEYN* BS31 .... **113** C3
Kennington Av *HORF/LLZ* BS7 .... **13** F1
KGWD/HNM BS15 .... **86** A2 🖫
Kennion Rd *EVILLE/WHL* BS5 .... **84** B4 🖫
Kennmoor Cl
OLD/WMLY/WICK BS30 .... **93** D1
Kenn Rd *EVILLE/WHL* BS5 .... **84** B4
Kensal Av *BMSTR* BS3 .... **37** E4
Kensal Rd *BMSTR* BS3 .... **37** E4
Kensington Pk *EVILLE/WHL* BS5 .... **23** D2
Kensington Park Rd
BRSG/KWL/STAPK BS4 .... **40** A5
Kensington Pl *CFTN/FAIL* BS8............ **27** E1
Kensington Rd *EVILLE/WHL* BS5 ..... **84** B3 🖫
MANG/FISH BS16 .... **80** A3 🖫
RDLND/MONT BS6........................ **20** A1
Kent Cl *BRSTK/PCHW* BS34 .... **53** C3
Kenton Ms
HNLZ/SM/SNYPK/WT BS9................... **4** A3
Kent Rd *HORF/LLZ* BS7 .... **13** F2
Kents Gn *KGWD/HNM* BS15............... **86** B1
Kent St *BMSTR* BS3 .... **36** B3 🖫
Kerry Rd *BRSG/KWL/STAPK* BS4......... **96** B2
Kersteman Rd *RDLND/MONT* BS6 ... **12** C1 🖫
Kestrel Cl *BRSTK/PCHW* BS34 .... **42** B3
Keswick Wk *HNBRY/STHM* BS10 ..... **65** D1 🖫
Ketch Rd *BMSTR* BS3 .... **38** B4
Kewstoke Rd
HNLZ/SM/SNYPK/WT BS9................ **77** D3
Kew Wk *BRSG/KWL/STAPK* BS4 .... **98** B3
Keynsham By-pass *KEYN* BS31 .... **102** B4
Keynsham Rd
OLD/WMLY/WICK BS30 .... **103** C4
Keys Av *HORF/LLZ* BS7 .... **67** C4
Kilbirnie Rd *HGRV/WHIT* BS14 .... **107** D4
Kilburn St *EVILLE/WHL* BS5............. **23** F3 🖫
Kildare Rd *BRSG/KWL/STAPK* BS4 ..... **96** A2
Kilkenny St *CBRISNE* BS2................... **30** B2
Kilmersdon Rd
BMSTRD/HC/WWD BS13............... **105** C3
Kilminster Rd *AVONM* BS11 .... **60** A4 🖫
Kiln Cl *KGWD/HNM* BS15 .... **85** C2
Kilnhurst Cl *OLD/WMLY/WICK* BS30... **103** C1

Kilvert Cl *BRSG/KWL/STAPK* BS4...... **32** C5
Kimberley Av *MANG/FISH* BS16 .... **79** D2
Kimberley Cl *MANG/FISH* BS16 ...... **73** C4 🗓
Kimberley Crs *MANG/FISH* BS16...... **79** D2
Kimberley Rd *KGWD/HNM* BS15 .... **86** A2 🗓
  MANG/FISH BS16.............................. **79** D2
Kingfisher Cl *ALMDB* BS32 .... **45** D1 🗓
Kingfisher Dr *MANG/FISH* BS16 .... **9** F1
King George's Rd
  BMSTRD/HC/WWD BS13................ **104** A2
King John's Rd *KGWD/HNM* BS15 .... **85** C1
King Rd *BRSG/KWL/STAPK* BS4........ **98** A2
King Road Av *AVONM* BS11.............. **58** B1
Kings Av *KGWD/HNM* BS15 .... **91** C3
  RDLND/MONT BS6............................ **4** A5
Kingscote Pk *EVILLE/WHL* BS5 .... **91** C1
Kingscourt Cl *HGRV/WHIT* BS14...... **107** D2
Kingsdown Pde *RDLND/MONT* BS6.... **20** C4
King's Dr *HORF/LLZ* BS7.................... **4** B4
  KGWD/HNM BS15 .... **91** C3
Kingsfield La *KGWD/HNM* BS15 ...... **92** B2
  OLD/WMLY/WICK BS30 .... **92** B3
Kingshill Rd *BRSG/KWL/STAPK* BS4 .. **98** A2
Kingsholme Rd *KGWD/HNM* BS15 .... **86** A2
Kingsholm Rd *HNBRY/STHM* BS10.... **66** A3
Kingsland Cl *CBRISNE* BS2.............. **30** C2
Kingsland Rd *CBRISNE* BS2 .... **30** C2
Kingsland Road Br *CBRISNE* BS2 ...... **30** C2
Kingsleigh Ct *KGWD/HNM* BS15 ...... **87** C4 🗓
Kingsleigh Gdns
  KGWD/HNM BS15 .... **87** C4 🗓
Kingsley Rd *EVILLE/WHL* BS5 .... **24** B1
  RDLND/MONT BS6.......................... **13** D5
Kingsmead Rd *EVILLE/WHL* BS5........ **84** B2
Kingsmead Wk *EVILLE/WHL* BS5........ **84** B2
Kingsmill *HNLZ/SM/SNYPK/WT* BS9.... **77** C2
King's Parade Av *CFTN/FAIL* BS8 ...... **19** E1
King's Parade Ms *CFTN/FAIL* BS8 ...... **19** E1
Kings Park Av *CBRISNE* BS2 .... **32** A3
King Sq *CBRISNE* BS2 .... **21** D3 🗓
King Square Av *CBRISNE* BS2 .... **21** D3
King's Rd *BRSG/KWL/STAPK* BS4 ...... **40** A3
  CFTN/FAIL BS8 .... **26** C1 🗓
Kingston Cl *MANG/FISH* BS16 .... **73** D4 🗓
Kingston Dr *MANG/FISH* BS16 .... **73** D4
Kingston Rd *BMSTR* BS3 .... **36** A1
Kingstree St
  BRSG/KWL/STAPK BS4 .... **38** C2 🗓
King St *AVONM* BS11 .... **58** B2
  CBRIS/FH BS1 .... **28** C3
  EVILLE/WHL BS5 .... **24** A2
  KGWD/HNM BS15 .... **85** C3
Kingsway *BRSTK/PCHW* BS34........... **52** B1
  EVILLE/WHL BS5 .... **85** C4
Kingsway Av *KGWD/HNM* BS15 .... **85** C3
Kingsway Crs *KGWD/HNM* BS15 ...... **85** C3
Kingswear Rd *BMSTR* BS3 .... **96** B3
Kings Weston Av *AVONM* BS11 .... **60** A4
Kings Weston La *AVONM* BS11........... **61** C3
Kings Weston Rd *AVONM* BS11 ...... **63** C1 🗓
King William Av *CBRIS/FH* BS1 .... **29** D3 🗓
King William St *BMSTR* BS3 .... **35** F2
Kinsale Rd *HGRV/WHIT* BS14.......... **98** B4
Kinsale Wk *BRSG/KWL/STAPK* BS4 .. **96** B2 🗓
Kinvara Rd *BRSG/KWL/STAPK* BS4 .. **96** B3 🗓
Kipling Rd *HORF/LLZ* BS7 .... **68** A2
Kirkby Rd *AVONM* BS11 .... **61** D2
Kirtlington Rd *EVILLE/WHL* BS5 ...... **15** F2
Kite Hay Cl *MANG/FISH* BS16 .... **9** F4 🗓
Kites Cl *ALMDB* BS32 .... **44** B1 🗓
Knapps La *EVILLE/WHL* BS5 .... **17** F5
Knighton Rd *HNBRY/STHM* BS10...... **66** B2

Knightwood Rd *BRSTK/PCHW* BS34 .. **54** A2
Knole La *HNBRY/STHM* BS10 .... **48** B4
Knoll Hl *HNLZ/SM/SNYPK/WT* BS9 .... **77** C4
Knovill Cl *AVONM* BS11 .... **62** A2
Knowle Rd *BRSG/KWL/STAPK* BS4 .... **38** B3
Knowsley Rd *MANG/FISH* BS16 ...... **17** E2 🗓
Kyght Cl *KGWD/HNM* BS15 .... **87** D3
Kylross Av *HGRV/WHIT* BS14.......... **108** A3
Kynges Mill Cl *MANG/FISH* BS16...... **70** B4

L

The Labbott *KEYN* BS31...................... **112** B2
Laburnum Gv *MANG/FISH* BS16 .... **79** C3
Laburnum Rd *KGWD/HNM* BS15 .... **91** D2 🗓
Lacey Rd *HGRV/WHIT* BS14.............. **109** D1
Lacock Dr *OLD/WMLY/WICK* BS30 .... **93** C2
Ladd Cl *KGWD/HNM* BS15 .... **87** C4 🗓
Ladies Mile
  HNLZ/SM/SNYPK/WT BS9.............. **18** A2
Ladman Gv *HGRV/WHIT* BS14.......... **109** D1
Ladman Rd *HGRV/WHIT* BS14.......... **109** D2
Ladysmith Rd *RDLND/MONT* BS6 .... **11** E1 🗓
Lakemead Gv
  BMSTRD/HC/WWD BS13................ **104** A1
Lake Rd *HNBRY/STHM* BS10 .... **65** D4
Lakeside *MANG/FISH* BS16 .... **17** F3
Lake View Rd *EVILLE/WHL* BS5.......... **25** D3
Lakewood Crs *HNBRY/STHM* BS10 .... **65** C3
Lakewood Rd *HNBRY/STHM* BS10...... **65** C3
Lambert Cl *BRSG/KWL/STAPK* BS4 .... **106** A1
Lambley Rd *EVILLE/WHL* BS5 .... **25** F4
Lambourn Rd *KEYN* BS31 .... **113** D3
Lambrook Rd *MANG/FISH* BS16 .... **78** B3
Lamb St *CBRISNE* BS2 .... **22** B5
Lamord Ga *BRSTK/PCHW* BS34........ **53** D2
Lampeter Rd
  HNLZ/SM/SNYPK/WT BS9.............. **64** A4
Lampton Av
  BMSTRD/HC/WWD BS13................ **106** B4
Lampton Gv
  BMSTRD/HC/WWD BS13................ **106** B4
Lanaway Rd *MANG/FISH* BS16 .... **79** C1 🗓
Lancashire Rd *HORF/LLZ* BS7 .... **13** C2
Lancaster Cl *BRSTK/PCHW* BS34 .... **53** C3 🗓
Lancaster Rd *CBRISNE* BS2 .... **15** D5
Lancaster St *EVILLE/WHL* BS5.......... **32** B1
Landseer Av *HORF/LLZ* BS7.............. **68** A4
Lanercost Rd *HNBRY/STHM* BS10 .... **65** D1
Lanesborough Ri *HGRV/WHIT* BS14.... **99** C4
Langdale Rd *MANG/FISH* BS16 .... **78** A3 🗓
Langfield Cl *HNBRY/STHM* BS10 ...... **48** A4 🗓
Langford Rd
  BMSTRD/HC/WWD BS13................ **94** A3
Langford Wy *KGWD/HNM* BS15 .... **86** B4
Langham Rd *BRSG/KWL/STAPK* BS4 .. **39** F5
Langhill Av *BRSG/KWL/STAPK* BS4 .. **96** A4 🗓
Langton Court Rd
  BRSG/KWL/STAPK BS4 .... **33** D4
Langton Pk *BMSTR* BS3.................... **36** A2
Langton Rd *BRSG/KWL/STAPK* BS4 .. **33** D5
Langton Wy *BRSG/KWL/STAPK* BS4.... **33** F2
Lansdown Cl *KGWD/HNM* BS15 ...... **86** A1
Lansdown Rd *CFTN/FAIL* BS8 .... **18** C5
  EVILLE/WHL BS5 .... **23** D2
  KGWD/HNM BS15 .... **86** A1
  RDLND/MONT BS6.......................... **4** C3
Lansdown Ter *RDLND/MONT* BS6 ...... **4** C3
Lansdown Vw *KGWD/HNM* BS15 .... **86** B3

Laphams Ct
  OLD/WMLY/WICK BS30 .... **93** C3 ⑪
Lapwing Cl *ALMDB* BS32 .... **45** C1
Lapwing Gdns *MANG/FISH* BS16 .... **9** F2
  MANG/FISH BS16 .... **78** A1 ②
Larch Rd *KGWD/HNM* BS15 .... **80** B4
Larch Wy *BRSTK/PCHW* BS34 .... **42** B4
Lark's Fld *MANG/FISH* BS16 .... **9** D3
Larksleaze Rd
  OLD/WMLY/WICK BS30 .... **102** B1
Lasbury Gv
  BMSTRD/HC/WWD BS13 ...... **105** D2 ③
Latimer Cl *BRSG/KWL/STAPK* BS4...... **41** F2
Latton Rd *HORF/LLZ* BS7 .... **67** C3
Launceston Av *KGWD/HNM* BS15 .... **91** C2
Launceston St *KGWD/HNM* BS15 .. **85** C2 ④
The Laurels *HNBRY/STHM* BS10 ...... **48** B1
  MANG/FISH BS16 .... **81** D1
Laurel St *KGWD/HNM* BS15 .... **86** A3
Laurie Crs *HNLZ/SM/SNYPK/WT* BS9 ... **4** C1
Laurie Lee Ct
  OLD/WMLY/WICK BS30 .... **93** D2 ⑦
Lavender Wy *ALMDB* BS32 .... **46** A4
Lavers Cl *KGWD/HNM* BS15 .... **92** B1
Lavington Rd *EVILLE/WHL* BS5 .... **91** C1
Lawford Av *BRSTK/PCHW* BS34 .... **52** B1
Lawfords Ga *CBRISNE* BS2 .... **22** B5
Lawn Av *MANG/FISH* BS16 .... **79** C2
Lawn Rd *MANG/FISH* BS16 .... **79** C2
Lawnwood Rd *EVILLE/WHL* BS5 ..... **23** F3 ④
Lawrence Av *EVILLE/WHL* BS5 .... **23** F1
Lawrence Cl *KGWD/HNM* BS15 .... **87** D1
Lawrence Gv
  HNLZ/SM/SNYPK/WT BS9.............. **3** F3
Lawrence Hl *CBRISNE* BS2 .... **22** C5
  EVILLE/WHL BS5 .... **23** E5
Lawrence Weston Rd
  AVONM BS11 .... **62** B2 ③
Laxey Rd *HORF/LLZ* BS7 .... **67** C4
Lays Dr *KEYN* BS31 .... **111** D3
Leaholme Gdns *HGRV/WHIT* BS14 ... **107** D4
Leap V *MANG/FISH* BS16 .... **73** D3
Leap Valley Crs *MANG/FISH* BS16..... **73** C3
Leda Av *HGRV/WHIT* BS14 .... **97** D4
Ledbury Rd *MANG/FISH* BS16 .... **79** D3
Lee Cl *BRSTK/PCHW* BS34 .... **43** C3
Leeming Wy *AVONM* BS11 .... **59** D3
Lees Hl *KGWD/HNM* BS15 .... **86** B1
Leicester Sq *MANG/FISH* BS16 ... **80** A4 ⑧
Leicester St *BMSTR* BS3 .... **36** C2 ⑨
Leicester Wk *BRSG/KWL/STAPK* BS4.. **90** A2
Leigh Cl *CFTN/FAIL* BS8.................. **19** D3
Leigh St *BMSTR* BS3 .... **35** D1
Leighton Rd *BMSTR* BS3 .... **35** F1
  BRSG/KWL/STAPK BS4 .... **39** F5
Leinster Av *BRSG/KWL/STAPK* BS4.... **96** B3
Lemon La *CBRISNE* BS2 .... **21** F5
Lena Av *EVILLE/WHL* BS5 .... **24** A2
Lena St *EVILLE/WHL* BS5 .... **23** F2
Lenover Gdns
  BMSTRD/HC/WWD BS13 ...... **105** C3 ⑥
Leonard La *CBRIS/FH* BS1 .... **28** C1
Leonard Rd *EVILLE/WHL* BS5 .... **24** B5
Leonards Av *EVILLE/WHL* BS5.......... **24** B2
Leopold Rd *RDLND/MONT* BS6 .... **13** F4
Lewington Rd *MANG/FISH* BS16 ...... **79** D3
Lewins Md *CBRIS/FH* BS1 .... **21** D5
Lewin St *EVILLE/WHL* BS5 .... **24** C5
Lewis Rd *BMSTRD/HC/WWD* BS13 ... **94** B3
Lewis St *CBRISNE* BS2 .... **31** D4
Leyland Wk
  BMSTRD/HC/WWD BS13............... **104** A3

Leyton Vls *RDLND/MONT* BS6.......... **11** F5
Lichfield Rd *BRSG/KWL/STAPK* BS4.... **33** F3
Lilac Cl *HNBRY/STHM* BS10 .... **65** D2
Lillian St *EVILLE/WHL* BS5 .... **24** B4
Lilstock Av *HORF/LLZ* BS7 .... **14** B1
Lilton Wk
  BMSTRD/HC/WWD BS13 .... **94** B2 ①
Lilymead Av *BRSG/KWL/STAPK* BS4.... **38** B3
Lime Cl *HNBRY/STHM* BS10 .... **49** C4
Lime Kiln Cl *BRSTK/PCHW* BS34 .... **69** C1
Limerick Rd *RDLND/MONT* BS6 .... **12** B4
Lime Rd *BMSTR* BS3 .... **35** E2
  KGWD/HNM BS15 .... **90** B2
Lime Tree Gv *PTSHD/EG* BS20......... **74** A4
Lincoln Cl *KEYN* BS31 .... **111** D3
Lincoln St *EVILLE/WHL* BS5 .... **31** F1
Lincombe Av *MANG/FISH* BS16 .... **80** A1
Lincombe Rd *MANG/FISH* BS16 .... **79** D2
Linden Cl *FRCTL/WBN* BS36............. **56** B1
  KGWD/HNM BS15 .... **85** C1
Linden Dr *ALMDB* BS32 .... **45** C3
Linden Rd *RDLND/MONT* BS6 .... **11** F1
Lindrea St *BMSTR* BS3 .... **35** F3 ②
Lindsay Rd *HORF/LLZ* BS7 .... **7** D5
Lines Wy *HGRV/WHIT* BS14 .... **108** B4
Lingfield Pk *FRCTL/WBN* BS36 .... **73** C2
Link Rd *BRSTK/PCHW* BS34 .... **51** C4
Linnell Cl *HORF/LLZ* BS7 .... **7** E1
Linnet Cl *BRSTK/PCHW* BS34........... **42** B3
Lintern Crs *OLD/WMLY/WICK* BS30 .. **93** D1
Lintham Dr *KGWD/HNM* BS15.......... **93** C1
Lisburn Rd *BRSG/KWL/STAPK* BS4 .... **96** B2
Litfield Rd *CFTN/FAIL* BS8 .... **18** A4
Little Ann St *CBRISNE* BS2 .... **22** B5
Little Birch Cft *HGRV/WHIT* BS14 .... **107** D4
Little Bishop St *CBRISNE* BS2 .... **21** F3
Little Caroline Pl *CFTN/FAIL* BS8 ...... **26** B4
Little Dowles
  OLD/WMLY/WICK BS30 .... **93** D3 ⑤
Little George St *CBRISNE* BS2........... **22** B4
Little Hayes *MANG/FISH* BS16 ...... **79** C1 ②
Little Headley Cl
  BMSTRD/HC/WWD BS13............... **95** C4
Little King St *CBRIS/FH* BS1 .... **29** D3 ③
Little Md *AVONM* BS11 .... **62** A2
Little Meadow *ALMDB* BS32 .... **54** A1
Little Paradise *BMSTR* BS3 .... **36** C2
Little Parr Cl *MANG/FISH* BS16 .... **8** B3
Little Paul St *CBRISNE* BS2 .... **20** B3
Little Stoke La *BRSTK/PCHW* BS34..... **44** B4
Little Stoke Rd
  HNLZ/SM/SNYPK/WT BS9............ **77** D3
Littleton Rd *BMSTR* BS3 .... **37** D5
Littleton St *EVILLE/WHL* BS5 .... **24** A1
Littlewood Cl *HGRV/WHIT* BS14 ...... **108** A4
Lockemor Rd
  BMSTRD/HC/WWD BS13............. **107** C3
Lockingwell Rd *KEYN* BS31 .... **112** A2
Lockleaze Rd *HORF/LLZ* BS7 .... **6** C1
Lodge Cswy *MANG/FISH* BS16 .... **78** B4
Lodge Hl *KGWD/HNM* BS15............. **85** D1
Lodge Rd *KGWD/HNM* BS15............. **85** D1
Lodgeside Av *KGWD/HNM* BS15 .. **85** D2 ③
Lodgeside Gdns *KGWD/HNM* BS15 ... **85** D2
Lodge St *CBRIS/FH* BS1 .... **28** B1
Lodge Wk *MANG/FISH* BS16 .... **80** A1
Lodore Rd *MANG/FISH* BS16 ...... **78** A4 ④
Lodway Rd *BRSG/KWL/STAPK* BS4..... **40** A5
Logan Rd *HORF/LLZ* BS7 .... **12** C2
Logus Ct *OLD/WMLY/WICK* BS30 .. **93** C3 ⑫
Lombard St *BMSTR* BS3 .... **36** C2 ②
Lomond Rd *HORF/LLZ* BS7 .... **67** C2

London Rd *CBRISNE* BS2 .... 22 B2
London St *KGWD/HNM* BS15 .... 86 A3
Longacre Rd *HGRV/WHIT* BS14 ...... 107 D4
Long Acres Cl
    HNLZ/SM/SNYPK/WT BS9 .... 63 C4
Long Beach Rd
    OLD/WMLY/WICK BS30 .... 103 D1
Long Cl *ALMDB* BS32 .... 53 D1
    MANG/FISH BS16 .... 79 D1
Long Cross *AVONM* BS11 .... 60 B3
Longden Rd *MANG/FISH* BS16 .... 81 C1
Long Eaton Dr *HGRV/WHIT* BS14 ...... 98 A3
Longfield Rd *HORF/LLZ* BS7 .... 13 E2
Longford Av *HNBRY/STHM* BS10 ...... 66 A3
Long Handstones
    OLD/WMLY/WICK BS30 .... 93 D3
Longleat Cl *HNLZ/SM/SNYPK/WT* BS9.. 4 A3
Longmead Av *HORF/LLZ* BS7 .... 4 C3
Long Meadow *HORF/LLZ* BS7 .... 4 C3
Longmeadow Rd *KEYN* BS31 .... 111 D3
Longmoor Rd *BMSTR* BS3 .... 35 D5
Longney Pl *BRSTK/PCHW* BS34 .... 43 C2
Longreach Gv *HGRV/WHIT* BS14 .... 99 C4
Long Rd *MANG/FISH* BS16 .... 81 D2
Long Rw *CBRIS/FH* BS1 .... 29 E3 ▣
Longway Av *HGRV/WHIT* BS14 .... 107 C3
Longwood *BRSG/KWL/STAPK* BS4 .... 100 B1
Lorain Wk *HNBRY/STHM* BS10 .... 64 A1
Lorton Rd *HNBRY/STHM* BS10 .... 65 C1
Louisa St *CBRISNE* BS2 .... 30 B2
Louise Av *MANG/FISH* BS16 .... 81 D2 ▣
Lovell's Hl *KGWD/HNM* BS15 .... 91 C2 ▣
Loveringe Cl *HNBRY/STHM* BS10 .... 48 A3
Lowbourne *HGRV/WHIT* BS14 .... 107 C3
Lower Ashley Rd *CBRISNE* BS2......... 22 B1
    EVILLE/WHL BS5 .... 22 C1 ▣
Lower Castle St *CBRIS/FH* BS1 .... 21 F5
Lower Chapel Rd
    KGWD/HNM BS15 .... 91 D2 ▣
Lower Cheltenham Pl
    RDLND/MONT BS6.................... 22 A1
Lower Church La *CBRISNE* BS2 .... 28 B1
Lower Clifton Hl *CFTN/FAIL* BS8......... 27 E2
Lower Cock Rd *KGWD/HNM* BS15 .... 87 C4
Lower College St *CBRIS/FH* BS1 .... 28 A3 ▣
Lower Fallow Cl
    HGRV/WHIT BS14 .... 107 C4 ▣
Lower Gay St *CBRISNE* BS2 .... 21 D3 ▣
Lower Grove Rd *MANG/FISH* BS16.... 17 F1
Lower Guinea St *CBRIS/FH* BS1 .... 29 D5
Lower Hanham Rd
    KGWD/HNM BS15 .... 91 D2
Lower High St *AVONM* BS11 .... 60 A3
Lower House Crs
    BRSTK/PCHW BS34 .... 52 A3
Lower Knole La *HNBRY/STHM* BS10 .. 48 B4
Lower Lamb St *CBRIS/FH* BS1 .... 28 A3
Lower Maudlin St *CBRIS/FH* BS1 ... 21 D5 ▣
Lower Park Rw *CBRIS/FH* BS1 .... 28 C1 ▣
Lower Redland Rd
    RDLND/MONT BS6 .... 11 E5
Lower Sidney St *BMSTR* BS3 .... 35 D1
Lower Station Approach Rd
    CBRIS/FH BS1 .... 30 A4 ▣
Lower Station Rd *MANG/FISH* BS16 .. 78 A3
Lowlis Cl *HNBRY/STHM* BS10 .... 48 A4 ▣
Lowther Rd *HNBRY/STHM* BS10 ... 65 D1 ▣
Loxton Sq *HGRV/WHIT* BS14 .... 107 D1
Lucas Cl *BRSG/KWL/STAPK* BS4 ...... 91 F5
Luccombe Hl *RDLND/MONT* BS6 .... 11 F4
Luckington Rd *HORF/LLZ* BS7 .... 66 B3

Luckley Av
    BMSTRD/HC/WWD BS13 .... 105 D2 ▣
Luckwell Rd *BMSTR* BS3 .... 35 E4
Lucky La *BMSTR* BS3 .... 36 C1
Ludlow Cl *CBRISNE* BS2 .... 22 A2
    KEYN BS31 .... 112 A2
Ludlow Rd *HORF/LLZ* BS7 .... 67 D4
Ludwell Cl *FRCTL/WBN* BS36 .... 56 A2 ▣
Lullington Rd
    BRSG/KWL/STAPK BS4 .... 39 F5
Luisgate Rd
    BMSTRD/HC/WWD BS13 .... 94 B3
Lulworth Crs *MANG/FISH* BS16 .... 73 C3
Lulworth Rd *KEYN* BS31 .... 112 B3
Lurgan Wk *BRSG/KWL/STAPK* BS4 ... 96 A2
Lux Furlong
    HNLZ/SM/SNYPK/WT BS9........... 62 A4
Luxton St *EVILLE/WHL* BS5 .... 23 F3
Lyddington Rd *HORF/LLZ* BS7 .... 66 B2
Lydford Wk *BMSTR* BS3 .... 95 D1
Lydiard Cft *KGWD/HNM* BS15 .... 91 D3
Lydney Rd *HNBRY/STHM* BS10 .... 66 A3
    MANG/FISH BS16 .... 80 B3
Lydstep Ter *BMSTR* BS3 .... 36 A2
Lynch Ct *OLD/WMLY/WICK* BS30 .. 93 C3 ▣
Lyncombe Wk *MANG/FISH* BS16 .... 85 C1 ▣
Lyndale Av
    HNLZ/SM/SNYPK/WT BS9............ 76 B2
Lyndale Rd *EVILLE/WHL* BS5 .... 24 C4
Lynde Cl *BMSTRD/HC/WWD* BS13 ... 105 C3
Lyndhurst Rd
    HNLZ/SM/SNYPK/WT BS9............ 64 A4
    KEYN BS31 .... 113 C4
Lynmouth Rd *CBRISNE* BS2 .... 14 B4
Lynn Rd *MANG/FISH* BS16 .... 9 D3
Lynton Pl *EVILLE/WHL* BS5 .... 24 B4
Lynton Rd *BMSTR* BS3 .... 96 A2
Lynton Wy *MANG/FISH* BS16 .... 71 C2
Lyons Court Rd *HGRV/WHIT* BS14 .... 99 C4
Lyppiatt Rd *EVILLE/WHL* BS5 .... 24 C4
Lyppincourt Rd *HNBRY/STHM* BS10 .. 48 B4
Lysander Rd *BRSTK/PCHW* BS34 ...... 49 C1
    HNBRY/STHM BS10 .... 49 C1
Lysander Wk *BRSTK/PCHW* BS34 .... 53 D2 ▣
Lytchet Dr *MANG/FISH* BS16 .... 73 C3 ▣
Lytton Gv *HORF/LLZ* BS7 .... 67 D3
    KEYN BS31 .... 113 D2
Lyveden Gdns
    BMSTRD/HC/WWD BS13 .... 105 C2 ▣

M

Macauley Rd *HORF/LLZ* BS7 .... 67 D3
Macey's Rd
    BMSTRD/HC/WWD BS13 .... 106 A4 ▣
Machin Cl *HNBRY/STHM* BS10 .... 48 A4
Machin Gdns *HNBRY/STHM* BS10 .. 48 B4 ▣
Machin Rd *HNBRY/STHM* BS10.......... 48 A4
Mackie Av *BRSTK/PCHW* BS34 .... 68 A1
Mackie Gv *BRSTK/PCHW* BS34 .... 68 A1
Mackie Rd *BRSTK/PCHW* BS34 .... 68 A1
Macrae Ct *KGWD/HNM* BS15 .... 86 B3 ▣
Madeline Rd *MANG/FISH* BS16 ...... 84 A1 ▣
Maesbury *KGWD/HNM* BS15.............. 92 B1
Maesknoll Rd *BRSG/KWL/STAPK* BS4. 38 C4
Magdalene Pl *CBRISNE* BS2 .... 14 B5
Maggs Cl *HNBRY/STHM* BS10 .... 49 D4
Maggs La *EVILLE/WHL* BS5 .... 17 F4
    HGRV/WHIT BS14 .... 108 A3
Magpie Bottom La *EVILLE/WHL* BS5 .. 91 C1

Maidenhead Rd
BMSTRD/HC/WWD BS13.................. **106** A4
Maiden Wy *AVONM* BS11 .... **59** D4 🬉
Maidstone St *BMSTR* BS3 .... **38** A3
Maisemore Av *BRSTK/PCHW* BS34.... **44** A2
Malago Rd *BMSTR* BS3 .... **36** C3
Maldowers La *EVILLE/WHL* BS5 .... **84** B2
Mallard Cl *ALMDB* BS32 .... **45** C1
EVILLE/WHL BS5 .... **84** A2
The Mall *CFTN/FAIL* BS8 .... **26** B1
Malmains Dr *MANG/FISH* BS16 .... **71** C2
Malmesbury Cl
OLD/WMLY/WICK BS30 .... **93** C2 🬉
RDLND/MONT BS6.................. **12** B1
Malvern Ct *EVILLE/WHL* BS5 .... **84** A4
Malvern Rd *BRSG/KWL/STAPK* BS4 ... **40** C4
EVILLE/WHL BS5 .... **84** A4
Mancroft Av *AVONM* BS11 .... **61** C4
Mangotsfield Rd *MANG/FISH* BS16 .... **81** C3
Manilla Rd *CFTN/FAIL* BS8 .... **18** C5
Manor Court Dr *HORF/LLZ* BS7 .... **66** B4
Manor Farm Crs *ALMDB* BS32 .... **45** C2
Manor Gv *ALMDB* BS32 .... **44** A1 🬉
MANG/FISH BS16 .... **81** D3
Manor Pk *RDLND/MONT* BS6 .... **11** E3
Manor Pl *MANG/FISH* BS16 .... **71** D2
Manor Rd *BMSTRD/HC/WWD* BS13 .. **104** A1
HORF/LLZ BS7 .... **13** E1
KEYN BS31 .... **113** D4
MANG/FISH BS16 .... **78** A2
MANG/FISH BS16 .... **81** D3
Mansfield St *BMSTR* BS3 .... **95** C1
Manston Cl *HGRV/WHIT* BS14 .... **98** B4
Manworthy Rd
BRSG/KWL/STAPK BS4 .... **41** D4
Manx Rd *HORF/LLZ* BS7 .... **67** C4
Maple Av *MANG/FISH* BS16 .... **79** D4
Maple Cl *BRSTK/PCHW* BS34 .... **44** B4
HGRV/WHIT BS14 .... **109** C2
Mapleleaze *BRSG/KWL/STAPK* BS4 .... **41** D3
Maplemeade *RDLND/MONT* BS6 .... **12** B1
Maple Rd *BRSG/KWL/STAPK* BS4 .... **33** D4
HORF/LLZ BS7 .... **5** D4
Maplestone Rd *HGRV/WHIT* BS14 .... **107** D4
Maple Wk *KEYN* BS31.................. **112** A3
Marbeck Rd *HNBRY/STHM* BS10 .... **65** C2
Mardale Cl *HNBRY/STHM* BS10 .... **65** D1 🬉
Marden Rd *KEYN* BS31 .... **113** D3
Mardon Rd *BRSG/KWL/STAPK* BS4.... **32** C3
Mardyke Ferry Rd *CBRIS/FH* BS1....... **27** E4
Margate St *BMSTR* BS3 .... **37** F3
Marguerite Rd
BMSTRD/HC/WWD BS13.......... **94** A3
Marigold Wk *BMSTR* BS3 .... **35** D5
Marina Gdns *MANG/FISH* BS16 .... **17** F3
Mariners Dr
HNLZ/SM/SNYPK/WT BS9........ **77** C3
Mariners' Pth
HNLZ/SM/SNYPK/WT BS9........ **77** C3
Marion Rd *KGWD/HNM* BS15 .... **91** C4
Marion Wk *EVILLE/WHL* BS5 .... **84** B4
Marjoram Pl *ALMDB* BS32 .... **46** A4
Market Sq *MANG/FISH* BS16 .... **79** D4 🬉
Markham Cl *AVONM* BS11 .... **59** D3
Mark La *CBRIS/FH* BS1 .... **28** B2
Marksbury Rd *BMSTR* BS3 .... **95** D1
Marlborough Av *EVILLE/WHL* BS5 ..... **17** E3 🬉
Marlborough Dr *MANG/FISH* BS16..... **71** C2
Marlborough Hl *RDLND/MONT* BS6..... **20** C4
Marlborough Hill Pl *CBRISNE* BS2 .. **20** C4 🬉
Marlborough St *CBRIS/FH* BS1.......... **21** D4
CBRISNE BS2 .... **20** C5

EVILLE/WHL BS5 .... **17** E3
Marlepit Gv
BMSTRD/HC/WWD BS13 .... **104** A1 🬉
Marling Rd *EVILLE/WHL* BS5 .... **84** B4 🬉
Marlwood Dr *HNBRY/STHM* BS10 .... **48** B4
Marmaduke St *BMSTR* BS3 .... **38** A3
Marmion Crs *HNBRY/STHM* BS10...... **48** A4
Marne Cl *HGRV/WHIT* BS14 .... **109** C2
Marsham Wy
OLD/WMLY/WICK BS30 .... **92** B2
Marsh Cl *FRCTL/WBN* BS36 .... **56** B3
Marshfield Rd *MANG/FISH* BS16....... **79** C3
Marsh La *EVILLE/WHL* BS5 .... **32** A2
PTSHD/EG BS20.................. **58** A4
Marsh Rd *BMSTR* BS3.................. **34** B3
Marsh St *AVONM* BS11 .... **59** D3
CBRIS/FH BS1.................. **28** C2
Marston Rd *BRSG/KWL/STAPK* BS4 ... **39** E5
Martin Cl *BRSTK/PCHW* BS34 .... **42** B3
Martingale Rd
BRSG/KWL/STAPK BS4 .... **40** C1
Martins Cl *KGWD/HNM* BS15 .... **91** D2 🬉
Martin's Rd *KGWD/HNM* BS15 .... **91** D2
Martin St *BMSTR* BS3.................. **35** E3
Martlock Crs *BMSTR* BS3.................. **95** D2
Martock Rd *BMSTR* BS3.................. **95** D2
KEYN BS31.................. **113** D4
Marwood Rd
BRSG/KWL/STAPK BS4 .... **96** B3 🬉
Marybush La *CBRISNE* BS2 .... **29** F1 🬉
Marygold Leaze
OLD/WMLY/WICK BS30 .... **93** D3 🬉
Mary St *EVILLE/WHL* BS5 .... **24** C4
Mascot Rd *BMSTR* BS3.................. **37** D4
Masefield Wy *HORF/LLZ* BS7 .... **67** D4 🬉
Maskelyne Av *HNBRY/STHM* BS10..... **66** A4
Materman Rd *HGRV/WHIT* BS14........ **109** D2
Matford Cl *FRCTL/WBN* BS36 .... **56** B2
HNBRY/STHM BS10 .... **50** A3
Matthews Cl *HGRV/WHIT* BS14........ **110** A1
Matthew's Rd *EVILLE/WHL* BS5 ..... **24** A5 🬉
Maules La *MANG/FISH* BS16 .... **70** A1
Maunsell Rd *AVONM* BS11 .... **62** A1
Maurice Rd *RDLND/MONT* BS6.......... **13** F4
Mautravers Cl *ALMDB* BS32 .... **45** C4
Maxse Rd *BRSG/KWL/STAPK* BS4 ... **39** E4
Maybec Gdns *EVILLE/WHL* BS5 .... **90** B1 🬉
Maybourne
BRSG/KWL/STAPK BS4 .... **100** B1 🬉
Maycliffe Pk *RDLND/MONT* BS6........ **14** B5
Mayfield Av *MANG/FISH* BS16 .... **84** B1
Mayfield Pk *MANG/FISH* BS16 .... **84** B1
Mayfield Pk North *MANG/FISH* BS16.. **84** B1
Mayfield Pk South
MANG/FISH BS16 .... **84** B1
Mayfields *KEYN* BS31.................. **112** B2
Maynard Cl *BMSTRD/HC/WWD* BS13 **105** D2
Maynard Rd *BMSTRD/HC/WWD* BS13 **105** D2
May St *KGWD/HNM* BS15.................. **85** D2
Maytree Av
BMSTRD/HC/WWD BS13.......... **95** C4
Maytree Cl *BMSTRD/HC/WWD* BS13 .. **95** C4
Mayville Av *BRSTK/PCHW* BS34 .... **51** D4
Maywood Crs *MANG/FISH* BS16........ **79** C3
Maywood Rd *MANG/FISH* BS16 .... **79** D3
Maze St *EVILLE/WHL* BS5.................. **31** F2
Mead Cl *AVONM* BS11 .... **74** B1 🬉
Meadow Cl *MANG/FISH* BS16 .... **73** C4
Meadowcroft *MANG/FISH* BS16 .... **73** D3 🬉
Meadow Gv *AVONM* BS11 .... **60** A4
Meadowside Dr *HGRV/WHIT* BS14..... **107** D4
The Meadows *KGWD/HNM* BS15 .... **92** A3

Meadow St *AVONM* BS11 .... 58 B2
   CBRISNE BS2 .... 21 F5 🔢
Meadowsweet Av
   BRSTK/PCHW BS34 .... 52 A4
Meadow V *EVILLE/WHL* BS5 .... 84 B2
Meadow Wy *ALMDB* BS32 .... 45 D4
Mead Ri *BMSTR* BS3 .... 38 A1
Mead Rd *BRSTK/PCHW* BS34 .... 54 A1
The Meads *MANG/FISH* BS16 .... 73 C4
Mead St *BMSTR* BS3 .... 38 A1
The Mead *BRSTK/PCHW* BS34 .... 52 A3
Meadway *HNLZ/SM/SNYPK/WT* BS9 .. 76 B1
Meardon Rd *HGRV/WHIT* BS14 ..... 109 D1 🔢
Mede Cl *CBRIS/FH* BS1 .... 29 E5 🔢
Medical Av *CFTN/FAIL* BS8 .... 28 B1
Medway Cl *KEYN* BS31 .... 113 C4
Medway Dr *KEYN* BS31 .... 113 D4
Meere Bank *AVONM* BS11 .... 62 A2
Meg Thatchers Cl
   EVILLE/WHL BS5 .... 85 C4 🔢
Melbourne Rd *HORF/LLZ* BS7 .... 13 D1
Melbury Rd *BRSG/KWL/STAPK* BS4 .... 97 D1
Melita Rd *RDLND/MONT* BS6 .... 13 F3
Mellent Av
   BMSTRD/HC/WWD BS13 .... 105 D4
Melrose Av *CFTN/FAIL* BS8 .... 19 E3
Melrose Cl *CFTN/FAIL* BS8 .... 19 E3 🔢
Melton Crs *HORF/LLZ* BS7 .... 67 D4
Melville Rd *RDLND/MONT* BS6 .... 19 F1
Melville Ter *BMSTR* BS3 .... 36 B3
Melvin Sq *BRSG/KWL/STAPK* BS4 ...... 96 B2
Memorial Cl *KGWD/HNM* BS15 .... 91 C3
Memorial Rd *KGWD/HNM* BS15 .... 91 C2
Mendip Cl *KEYN* BS31 .... 112 A1
Mendip Crs *MANG/FISH* BS16 .... 73 D4
Mendip Rd *BMSTR* BS3 .... 36 C4
Mendip View Av *KGWD/HNM* BS16..... 78 B4
Merchants Rd *CBRIS/FH* BS1 .... 26 B4
   CFTN/FAIL BS8 .... 26 C1
Merchant St *CBRIS/FH* BS1 .... 21 E5
Mercia Dr *CBRISNE* BS2 .... 14 C4
Merfield Rd *BRSG/KWL/STAPK* BS4 .... 39 F5
Meridian Pl *CFTN/FAIL* BS8 .... 27 E1
Meridian Rd *RDLND/MONT* BS6 .... 20 B1
Meridian V *CFTN/FAIL* BS8 .... 27 E1
Meriet Av *BMSTRD/HC/WWD* BS13 .. 105 A3
Merioneth St *BMSTR* BS3 .... 38 A3
Meriton St *CBRISNE* BS2 .... 31 E5
Merlin Cl *HNLZ/SM/SNYPK/WT* BS9 .. 64 A3
Merlin Rd *BRSTK/PCHW* BS34 .... 49 D1
Merrimans Rd *AVONM* BS11 .... 60 A3
Merryweather Cl *ALMDB* BS32 .... 44 B3
Merrywood Rd *BMSTR* BS3 .... 36 A1
Merstham Rd *CBRISNE* BS2 .... 15 D5
Merton Rd *HORF/LLZ* BS7 .... 5 F4
Mervyn Rd *HORF/LLZ* BS7 .... 13 E1
Metford Gv *RDLND/MONT* BS6 .... 11 F2
Metford Pl *RDLND/MONT* BS6 .... 11 F2
Metford Rd *RDLND/MONT* BS6........... 11 F2
Middle Av *CBRIS/FH* BS1 .... 28 C3 🔢
Middle Rd *KGWD/HNM* BS15............. 80 B4
Middleton Rd *AVONM* BS11 .... 61 C3
Midland Rd *CBRISNE* BS2................... 30 B1
   MANG/FISH BS16 .... 80 A3
Midland St *CBRISNE* BS2 .... 30 B2
Midland Ter *MANG/FISH* BS16 .... 78 A4 🔢
Mildred St *EVILLE/WHL* BS5 .... 32 A1
Miles Ct *OLD/WMLY/WICK* BS30 .... 93 C3 🔢
Miles Rd *CFTN/FAIL* BS8 .... 18 C2
Milford St *BMSTR* BS3 .... 36 A2
Millard Cl *HNBRY/STHM* BS10 .... 65 D1 🔢
Mill Av *CBRIS/FH* BS1 .... 29 D3

Millbank Cl *BRSG/KWL/STAPK* BS4 .... 41 E3
Millbrook Av
   BRSG/KWL/STAPK BS4 .... 90 A4 🔢
Milliman Cl
   BMSTRD/HC/WWD BS13............ 105 D2
Mill La *BMSTR* BS3 .... 36 C2
Millpond St *EVILLE/WHL* BS5........... 22 C1
Mill Rd *FRCTL/WBN* BS36 .... 56 A3
Millward Gv *MANG/FISH* BS16 .... 79 D3
Milner Gn *OLD/WMLY/WICK* BS30..... 93 D2
Milner Rd *HORF/LLZ* BS7 .... 6 A4
Milsom St *EVILLE/WHL* BS5 .... 22 C4
Milton Pk *EVILLE/WHL* BS5 .... 24 B5
Milton Rd *HORF/LLZ* BS7 .... 5 E1
Miltons Cl *BMSTRD/HC/WWD* BS13 .. 106 A3
Milverton Gdns
   RDLND/MONT BS6 .... 14 B5 🔢
Milward Rd *KEYN* BS31 .... 112 B1
Mina Rd *CBRISNE* BS2 .... 14 B3
Minehead Rd
   BRSG/KWL/STAPK BS4 .... 97 C2
Minsmere Rd *KEYN* BS31................... 113 C4
Minton Cl *HGRV/WHIT* BS14 .... 108 A2
Minto Rd *CBRISNE* BS2 .... 14 C5
Mitchell La *CBRIS/FH* BS1 .... 29 E3
Mivart St *EVILLE/WHL* BS5................. 15 F5
Modecombe Gv
   HNBRY/STHM BS10 .... 48 A4 🔢
Mogg St *CBRISNE* BS2 .... 14 C5
Molesworth Cl
   BMSTRD/HC/WWD BS13............ 104 B3
Molesworth Dr
   BMSTRD/HC/WWD BS13............ 104 B3
Monarch's Wy *EVILLE/WHL* BS5 .... 32 C2
   OLD/WMLY/WICK BS30 .... 102 B2
Monk Rd *HORF/LLZ* BS7 .... 13 D1
Monks Av *KGWD/HNM* BS15 .... 85 C3 🔢
Monk's Park Av *HORF/LLZ* BS7 .... 66 B2
Monks Park Wy *HNBRY/STHM* BS10 .. 66 B3
Monkton Rd *KGWD/HNM* BS15 .... 91 C3
Monmouth Rd *HORF/LLZ* BS7............ 13 D1
   KEYN BS31 .... 112 A2
Monmouth St *BMSTR* BS3 .... 38 A3
Monsdale Cl *HNBRY/STHM* BS10 ...... 64 B1
Monsdale Dr *HNBRY/STHM* BS10....... 48 B4
Montague Cl *BRSTK/PCHW* BS34 ..... 53 D2 🔢
Montague Hl *RDLND/MONT* BS6 .... 20 C3
Montague Hl South *CBRISNE* BS2 .. 21 D4 🔢
Montgomery St *BMSTR* BS3 .... 38 A2
Montreal Av *HORF/LLZ* BS7............... 67 C3
Montrose Av *RDLND/MONT* BS6 .... 20 A1
Montrose Pk *BRSG/KWL/STAPK* BS4 .. 40 C5
Montroy Cl *HNLZ/SM/SNYPK/WT* BS9 .. 4 B1
Moon St *CBRISNE* BS2 .... 21 E4
Moor Croft Dr
   OLD/WMLY/WICK BS30 .... 93 C3
Moorend Gdns *AVONM* BS11 .... 61 C4
Moorend Rd *MANG/FISH* BS16 .... 56 A4
Moor Gv *AVONM* BS11 .... 61 C3
Moorhill St *EVILLE/WHL* BS5 .... 23 E2 🔢
Moorlands Rd *MANG/FISH* BS16........ 84 B1
Moravian Rd *KGWD/HNM* BS15 .... 86 A3
Morden Wk *HGRV/WHIT* BS14 .... 99 C4 🔢
Moreton Cl *HGRV/WHIT* BS14 .... 107 D3
Morgan St *CBRISNE* BS2 .... 22 B2
Morley Av *MANG/FISH* BS16 .... 81 D3
Morley Cl *BRSTK/PCHW* BS34 .... 44 A4
   MANG/FISH BS16 .... 80 A4
Morley Rd *BMSTR* BS3 .... 38 A4
   MANG/FISH BS16 .... 80 A4
Morley Sq *HORF/LLZ* BS7.................. 13 E1
Morley St *CBRISNE* BS2 .... 22 B1

EVILLE/WHL BS5 .... **31** F1
Morley Ter *KGWD/HNM* BS15 .... **86** A2 🔟
Mornington Rd *CFTN/FAIL* BS8.......... **11** D5
Morpeth Rd *BRSG/KWL/STAPK* BS4 ... **96** A3
Morris Rd *HORF/LLZ* BS7 .... **6** C4
Morse Rd *EVILLE/WHL* BS5 .... **24** B5
Mortimer Rd *BRSTK/PCHW* BS34 ...... **68** A2
CFTN/FAIL BS8 .... **26** C1
Morton St *EVILLE/WHL* BS5............... **23** F5
Mount Crs *FRCTL/WBN* BS36............. **56** B2
Mount Gdns *KGWD/HNM* BS15........... **92** A1
Mount Hill Rd *KGWD/HNM* BS15 .... **91** D1
Mount Pleasant *PTSHD/EG* BS20 ...... **74** A3
Mount Pleasant Ter *BMSTR* BS3 .... **35** F2
Mowbray Rd *HGRV/WHIT* BS14 .... **98** B4
Mowcroft Rd
BMSTRD/HC/WWD BS13................ **105** D3
Moxham Dr
BMSTRD/HC/WWD BS13................ **105** D3
Muirfield *OLD/WMLY/WICK* BS30 ...... **93** D1
Mulberry Cl *KGWD/HNM* BS15 .... **86** B3
Mulberry Dr *KGWD/HNM* BS15 .... **87** C2
Mulberry Wk
HNLZ/SM/SNYPK/WT BS9 .... **62** B3 🔟
Muller Av *HORF/LLZ* BS7 .... **6** A5
Muller Rd *EVILLE/WHL* BS5 .... **16** B3
HORF/LLZ BS7 .... **6** A2
Mulready Cl *HORF/LLZ* BS7 .... **8** A2
Murford Av
BMSTRD/HC/WWD BS13................ **105** C3
Murford Wk
BMSTRD/HC/WWD BS13................ **105** C3
Murray St *BMSTR* BS3 .... **36** B2
Musgrove Cl *AVONM* BS11 .... **62** B1
Myrtle Dr *AVONM* BS11 .... **74** B2
Myrtle Hl *PTSHD/EG* BS20 .... **74** A2 🔟
Myrtle Rd *CBRISNE* BS2 .... **20** B4
Myrtle St *BMSTR* BS3 .... **35** F2

N

Nags Head Hl *EVILLE/WHL* BS5........... **90** B1
Nailsea Cl *BMSTRD/HC/WWD* BS13 ... **94** B4
Napier Miles Rd *AVONM* BS11............. **61** D3
Napier Rd *AVONM* BS11 .... **59** C2
EVILLE/WHL BS5 .... **15** F4
RDLND/MONT BS6............................ **11** F4
Napier Sq *AVONM* BS11 .... **58** B2
Napier St *EVILLE/WHL* BS5 .... **31** F3
Narroways Rd *CBRISNE* BS2 .... **15** D3
Narrow La *MANG/FISH* BS16............... **80** B3
Narrow Pln *CBRISNE* BS2 .... **29** F2
Narrow Quay *CBRIS/FH* BS1 .... **28** C3
Naseby Wk *EVILLE/WHL* BS5............... **84** A2
Nash Cl *KEYN* BS31 .... **113** D2 🔟
Nash Dr *HORF/LLZ* BS7 .... **68** B4
Neale Wy *AVONM* BS11 .... **59** D2 🔟
Neath Rd *EVILLE/WHL* BS5 .... **24** C3
Nelson Rd *MANG/FISH* BS16 .... **80** A2 🔟
MANG/FISH BS16 .... **80** A3 🔟
Nelson St *BMSTR* BS3 .... **94** B1 🔟
CBRIS/FH BS1 .... **29** D1
Neston Wk *BRSG/KWL/STAPK* BS4 ... **97** C3 🔟
Netham Rd *EVILLE/WHL* BS5............... **32** C2
Nevalan Dr *EVILLE/WHL* BS5............... **90** B1
Neville Rd *KGWD/HNM* BS15............... **86** B1
Nevil Rd *HORF/LLZ* BS7 .... **5** F5
Newbrick Rd *BRSTK/PCHW* BS34....... **54** B2
Newbridge Cl
BRSG/KWL/STAPK BS4 .... **32** C4

Newbridge Rd
BRSG/KWL/STAPK BS4 .... **33** E3
New Brunswick Av *EVILLE/WHL* BS5... **85** C4
New Buildings *MANG/FISH* BS16 .... **78** A3
Newbury Rd *HORF/LLZ* BS7 .... **67** D4
New Charlotte St *BMSTR* BS3 .... **37** D1
New Cheltenham Rd
KGWD/HNM BS15 .... **86** B2
Newcombe Dr
HNLZ/SM/SNYPK/WT BS9 .... **76** B3 🔟
Newcombe Rd
HNLZ/SM/SNYPK/WT BS9................ **64** A4
Newent Av *KGWD/HNM* BS15 .... **85** C4
New Fosseway Rd
HGRV/WHIT BS14............................ **108** A1
Newfoundland Rd *CBRISNE* BS2 .... **22** A4
Newfoundland St *CBRISNE* BS2 .... **21** F4
Newfoundland Wy *CBRISNE* BS2 .... **22** B4
Newgate *CBRIS/FH* BS1 .... **29** E1
New John St *BMSTR* BS3 .... **36** B3 🔟
New Kingsley Rd *CBRISNE* BS2 .... **30** A2 🔟
Newland Dr
BMSTRD/HC/WWD BS13................ **104** B3 🔟
Newland Rd
BMSTRD/HC/WWD BS13................ **104** B3
Newlands Rd *KEYN* BS31 .... **112** A3
The Newlands *MANG/FISH* BS16 .... **71** C4
Newland Wk
BMSTRD/HC/WWD BS13................ **104** B4
Newlyn Av
HNLZ/SM/SNYPK/WT BS9 .... **77** C2
Newlyn Wk
BRSG/KWL/STAPK BS4 .... **98** A2 🔟
Newnham Cl *HGRV/WHIT* BS14 .... **99** D3
Newnham Pl *BRSTK/PCHW* BS34 ..... **43** C2 🔟
Newport St *BMSTR* BS3 .... **37** F4
Newquay Rd *BRSG/KWL/STAPK* BS4 ... **97** C2
New Queen St *BMSTR* BS3 .... **37** C2
KGWD/HNM BS15 .... **85** C2
New Rd *BRSTK/PCHW* BS34 .... **51** C4
BRSTK/PCHW BS34.......................... **53** C4
Newry Rd *BRSG/KWL/STAPK* BS4 .... **96** B2
New Stadium Rd *EVILLE/WHL* BS5....... **15** E4
New Station Rd *MANG/FISH* BS16 .... **78** B3
New St *CBRISNE* BS2 .... **22** A5
New Thomas St *CBRISNE* BS2............. **30** A1
Newton Cl *KGWD/HNM* BS15 .... **87** C2
Newton Rd *OLD/WMLY/WICK* BS30 ... **93** D2
Newton St *EVILLE/WHL* BS5 .... **22** C4
New Wk *KGWD/HNM* BS15 .... **91** C2
New Walls *BRSG/KWL/STAPK* BS4 .... **38** C1
Niblett Cl *KGWD/HNM* BS15 .... **93** C1 🔟
Niblett's Hl *EVILLE/WHL* BS5 .... **90** B1
Nibley Rd *AVONM* BS11 .... **74** B2
Nicholas La *EVILLE/WHL* BS5............... **90** B1
Nicholas Rd *EVILLE/WHL* BS5 .... **23** E2
Nicholas St *BMSTR* BS3 .... **37** F1 🔟
Nigel Pk *AVONM* BS11 .... **60** B4
Nightingale Cl *FRCTL/WBN* BS36 .... **57** D1
Nine Tree Hl *CBRIS/FH* BS1 .... **21** D2
Ninth Av *HORF/LLZ* BS7 .... **68** A2
Norfolk Av *CBRISNE* BS2 .... **21** F4
RDLND/MONT BS6............................ **13** F4
Norfolk Gv *KEYN* BS31 .... **111** D3
Norfolk Pl *BMSTR* BS3 .... **36** B3 🔟
Norland Rd *CFTN/FAIL* BS8 .... **18** A4
Norley Rd *HORF/LLZ* BS7 .... **67** C4
Normanby Rd *EVILLE/WHL* BS5 .... **23** E2
Norman Gv *KGWD/HNM* BS15 .... **86** A1 🔟
Norman Rd *CBRISNE* BS2 .... **15** D5
Normanton Rd *CFTN/FAIL* BS8........... **10** C5
Norrisville Rd *RDLND/MONT* BS6 ..... **21** F2 🔟

Northcote Rd *CFTN/FAIL* BS8 .... 18 B2
   EVILLE/WHL BS5 .... 25 E4
   MANG/FISH BS16 .... 81 C1
Northcote St *EVILLE/WHL* BS5 .... 23 E2 **2**
North Devon Rd *MANG/FISH* BS16 ...... 78 B2
Northend Av *KGWD/HNM* BS15 .... 86 A1
Northend Rd *KGWD/HNM* BS15 .... 86 B1
Northfield Av *KGWD/HNM* BS15 .... 92 A2
Northfield Rd *EVILLE/WHL* BS5 .... 85 C4
North Green St *CFTN/FAIL* BS8 .... 26 B3
Northleach Wk *AVONM* BS11 .... 75 C2 **1**
Northover Rd
   HNLZ/SM/SNYPK/WT BS9 .... 64 A2
North Pk *KGWD/HNM* BS15 .... 86 B2
North Pk *BMSTR* BS3 .... 34 C2 **1**
   BRSTK/PCHW BS34 .... 53 D3
   CFTN/FAIL BS8 .... 89 C1
   RDLND/MONT BS6 .... 13 D5
North St *BMSTR* BS3 .... 35 E2
   CBRIS/FH BS1 .... 21 E4
   MANG/FISH BS16 .... 80 A2
Northumberland Rd
   RDLND/MONT BS6 .... 12 B4
Northumbria Dr
   HNLZ/SM/SNYPK/WT BS9 .... 3 E1
   RDLND/MONT BS6 .... 3 D5
North Vw *MANG/FISH* BS16 .... 80 A3 **1**
   RDLND/MONT BS6 .... 3 D5
Northville Rd *HORF/LLZ* BS7 .... 67 D2
Northway *BRSTK/PCHW* BS34 .... 52 A3
Northwick Rd *HORF/LLZ* BS7 .... 67 C3
Northwoods Wk
   HNBRY/STHM BS10 .... 50 A4 **1**
Norton Cl *KGWD/HNM* BS15 .... 87 C4 **1**
Norton Rd *BRSG/KWL/STAPK* BS4 ...... 73 H1
Norwich Dr *BRSG/KWL/STAPK* BS4 ...... 33 F3
Nottingham Rd *HORF/LLZ* BS7 .... 13 F2
Nottingham St *BMSTR* BS3 .... 37 F4
Nova Scotia Pl *CBRIS/FH* BS1 .... 26 C5
Novers Crs *BRSG/KWL/STAPK* BS4 ...... 95 D3
Novers Hl *BRSG/KWL/STAPK* BS4 ...... 95 D3
Novers La *BRSG/KWL/STAPK* BS4 ...... 95 D4
Novers Park Rd
   BRSG/KWL/STAPK BS4 .... 95 D3
Novers Park Rd
   BRSG/KWL/STAPK BS4 .... 96 A3
Novers Rd *BRSG/KWL/STAPK* BS4 ...... 95 D3
Nugent Hl *RDLND/MONT* BS6 .... 21 D2
Nursery Gdns *HNBRY/STHM* BS10 ...... 48 B4
The Nursery *BMSTR* BS3 .... 35 E3
Nutfield Gv *BRSTK/PCHW* BS34 .... 68 B1
Nutgrove Av *BMSTR* BS3 .... 37 E3
Nuthatch Dr *MANG/FISH* BS16 .... 78 B1
Nuthatch Gdns *MANG/FISH* BS16 ...... 78 B1
Nympsfield *KGWD/HNM* BS15 .... 86 B1

O

Oak Cl *BRSTK/PCHW* BS34 .... 45 C4
Oakdale Av *MANG/FISH* BS16 .... 72 A3
Oakdale Cl *MANG/FISH* BS16 .... 72 B4 **1**
Oakdale Ct *MANG/FISH* BS16 .... 72 B4 **1**
Oakdale Rd *HGRV/WHIT* BS14 .... 97 D3
   MANG/FISH BS16 .... 72 B3
Oakdene Av *EVILLE/WHL* BS5 .... 17 D2
Oakenhill Rd *BRSG/KWL/STAPK* BS4 ...... 99 D1
Oakenhill Wk *BRSG/KWL/STAPK* BS4... 99 D1
Oakfield Gv *CFTN/FAIL* BS8 .... 19 E4
Oakfield Pl *CFTN/FAIL* BS8... .... 19 E4
Oakfield Rd *CFTN/FAIL* BS8 .... 19 E3

   KEYN BS31 .... 113 C4
   KGWD/HNM BS15 .... 86 A4
Oakhanger Dr *AVONM* BS11 .... 62 A2
Oakhurst Rd
   HNLZ/SM/SNYPK/WT BS9 .... 2 A3
Oakland Rd *CFTN/FAIL* BS8 .... 19 E1
   EVILLE/WHL BS5 .... 25 F3
Oaklands Dr *MANG/FISH* BS16 .... 70 B3
Oaklands Rd *MANG/FISH* BS16 .... 81 D2 **2**
Oak La *EVILLE/WHL* BS5 .... 84 A1
Oakleigh Av *EVILLE/WHL* BS5 .... 24 C3
Oakley Rd *HORF/LLZ* BS7 .... 67 C4
Oakmeade Pk
   BRSG/KWL/STAPK BS4 .... 39 E5 **1**
Oakridge Cl *KGWD/HNM* BS15 .... 87 D4
Oak Rd *HORF/LLZ* BS7 .... 5 F4
Oak Tree Cl *KGWD/HNM* BS15 .... 91 D3
Oaktree Ct *AVONM* BS11 .... 60 B4
Oaktree Crs *ALMDB* BS32 .... 44 A1
Oak Tree Wk *KEYN* BS31 .... 112 A4
Oakwood Av
   HNLZ/SM/SNYPK/WT BS9 .... 3 F1
Oakwood Rd
   HNLZ/SM/SNYPK/WT BS9 .... 3 F1
Oatlands Av *HGRV/WHIT* BS14 .... 107 D3
Oberon Av *EVILLE/WHL* BS5 .... 17 E5
Okebourne Cl *HNBRY/STHM* BS10 ...... 49 D3
Okebourne Rd *HNBRY/STHM* BS10 ...... 49 D3
Old Ashley Hl *RDLND/MONT* BS6 ...... 14 A5
Old Barrow Hl *AVONM* BS11 .... 60 A4
Old Bread St *CBRISNE* BS2 .... 30 A2
Oldbridge Rd *HGRV/WHIT* BS14 .... 108 B3
Oldbury Cha
   OLD/WMLY/WICK BS30 .... 103 D1
Oldbury Court Dr
   MANG/FISH BS16 .... 79 C1 **3**
Oldbury Court Rd *MANG/FISH* BS16 .. 78 D2
Old Farm La *EVILLE/WHL* BS5 .... 91 C1 **3**
Oldfield Pl *CFTN/FAIL* BS8 .... 26 B4
Oldfield Rd *CFTN/FAIL* BS8 .... 26 C3
Old Gloucester Rd *FRCTL/WBN* BS36.. 47 C4
   MANG/FISH BS16 .... 55 D3
Old King Street Ct *CBRIS/FH* BS1 ...... 21 E5 **1**
Old Market St *CBRISNE* BS2 .... 30 A1
Old Pk *CBRISNE* BS2 .... 20 B5 **1**
Old Park Hl *CBRISNE* BS2 .... 28 B1
Old Park Rd *AVONM* BS11 .... 60 A4
Old Quarry Ri *AVONM* BS11 .... 60 B4
Old Quarry Rd *AVONM* BS11 .... 60 A4
Old Sneed Av
   HNLZ/SM/SNYPK/WT BS9 .... 77 C3
Old Sneed Pk
   HNLZ/SM/SNYPK/WT BS9 .... 77 C3
Old Sneed Rd
   HNLZ/SM/SNYPK/WT BS9 .... 77 C3
Olveston Rd *HORF/LLZ* BS7 .... 57 C3
Olympus Cl *BRSTK/PCHW* BS34 ...... 53 C3 **2**
Olympus Rd *BRSTK/PCHW* BS34 ...... 42 A4
Oram Ct *OLD/WMLY/WICK* BS30 ...... 93 C3
Orange St *CBRISNE* BS2 .... 22 A4
Orchard Av *CBRIS/FH* BS1 .... 28 B2 **1**
Orchard Cl *FRCTL/WBN* BS36 .... 56 B1
   HNLZ/SM/SNYPK/WT BS9 .... 2 B4
   KEYN BS31 .... 112 A1 **1**
   KGWD/HNM BS15 .... 86 B3
Orchard Crs *AVONM* BS11 .... 60 A4 **2**
Orchard Gdns *KGWD/HNM* BS15 ...... 87 C3
Orchard La *CBRIS/FH* BS1 .... 28 B2
Orchard Lea *PTSHD/EG* BS20 .... 74 A3
Orchard Rd *EVILLE/WHL* BS5 .... 88 A3 **3**
   HORF/LLZ BS7 .... 5 F5
   KGWD/HNM BS15 .... 86 B3

Orchard Sq *EVILLE/WHL* BS5................ 32 C1
The Orchards *KGWD/HNM* BS15......... 87 C3
Orchard St *CBRIS/FH* BS1 .... 28 B2
The Orchard *BRSTK/PCHW* BS34 .... 54 A2
Orchard V *KGWD/HNM* BS15............... 87 C4
Orion Dr *BRSTK/PCHW* BS34 .... 53 C1
Orland Wy *OLD/WMLY/WICK* BS30... 93 D4
Orlebar Gdns *AVONM* BS11 .... 62 A1
Ormerod Rd
    HNLZ/SM/SNYPK/WT BS9........... 77 D3
Ormonds Cl *ALMDB* BS32 .... 45 D1
Ormsley Cl *BRSTK/PCHW* BS34 .... 44 B3
Orpen Gdns *HORF/LLZ* BS7 .... 7 E3
Orpheus Av *BRSTK/PCHW* BS34 .... 53 C1
Orwell Dr *KEYN* BS31 .... 113 C3
Orwell St *BMSTR* BS3 .... 37 D3
Osborne Av *HORF/LLZ* BS7 .... 14 A2
Osborne Cl *BRSTK/PCHW* BS34 .... 53 C3
Osborne Rd *BMSTR* BS3 .... 36 A1
    CFTN/FAIL BS8 .... 19 D2
Osborne Ter *BMSTR* BS3 .... 35 F5
Osborne Vls *CBRISNE* BS2 .... 20 B4
Osprey Rd *EVILLE/WHL* BS5 .... 32 A1
Otterford Cl *HGRV/WHIT* BS14 .... 108 A2
Ottery Cl *AVONM* BS11 .... 61 D2
Overndale Rd *MANG/FISH* BS16 .... 79 D2
Overnhill Ct *MANG/FISH* BS16 .... 79 D2
Overnhill Rd *MANG/FISH* BS16 .... 79 D2
Overton Rd *RDLND/MONT* BS6........... 13 E4
Owen Gv *HNLZ/SM/SNYPK/WT* BS9... 3 F4
Owen St *EVILLE/WHL* BS5 .... 23 F3
Owls Head Rd *KGWD/HNM* BS15 .... 92 B1
Oxbarton *BRSTK/PCHW* BS34............. 54 A4
Oxen Leaze *ALMDB* BS32 .... 45 D1
Oxford Pl *CFTN/FAIL* BS8 .... 26 A2
    EVILLE/WHL BS5 .... 23 D1
Oxford St *BMSTR* BS3 .... 38 B2
    CBRISNE BS2 .... 30 C3
    EVILLE/WHL BS5 .... 32 B1
    RDLND/MONT BS6........................... 20 B3
Oxleaze *BMSTRD/HC/WWD* BS13...... 106 A3
Ozleworth *KGWD/HNM* BS15 .... 87 D3

P

Paddock Cl *ALMDB* BS32 .... 45 D1
Paddock Gdns *HGRV/WHIT* BS14 ..... 107 D3
Padstow Rd *BRSG/KWL/STAPK* BS4.... 96 B3
Page Rd *MANG/FISH* BS16 .... 80 A3
Pages Md *AVONM* BS11 .... 59 D3
Painswick Av *BRSTK/PCHW* BS34 .... 44 A3
Palmdale Cl
    OLD/WMLY/WICK BS30 .... 103 D1
Palmers Cl *OLD/WMLY/WICK* BS30.... 93 D1
Palmers Leaze *ALMDB* BS32 .... 46 B3
Palmerston Rd *RDLND/MONT* BS6 ...... 11 F1
Palmerston St *BMSTR* BS3 .... 35 F3
Palmyra Rd *BMSTR* BS3........................ 35 E5
The Parade *AVONM* BS11 .... 74 B1
The Paragon *CFTN/FAIL* BS8 .... 26 A2
Park Av *ALMDB* BS32 .... 43 D1
    BMSTR BS3 .... 37 F4
    EVILLE/WHL BS5 .... 17 D3
    EVILLE/WHL BS5 .... 25 F3
    FRCTL/WBN BS36 .... 56 B1
Park Cl *KEYN* BS31 .... 112 A2
    KGWD/HNM BS15 .... 86 B4
Park Crs *EVILLE/WHL* BS5 .... 25 D3
    MANG/FISH BS16 .... 71 D2
Parkers Barton *EVILLE/WHL* BS5 .... 31 F3

Parkers Cl *HNBRY/STHM* BS10 .... 50 B3
Parker St *BMSTR* BS3........................... 35 F3
Park Farm Ct
    OLD/WMLY/WICK BS30 .... 93 C3
Parkfield Av *EVILLE/WHL* BS5............. 25 D5
Park Gv *RDLND/MONT* BS6 .... 4 A4
Park Hl *AVONM* BS11 .... 74 B1
Parkhurst Av *MANG/FISH* BS16 .... 79 C3
Parklands *KGWD/HNM* BS15 .... 86 A3
Parklands Rd *BMSTR* BS3 .... 89 D3
Park La *FRCTL/WBN* BS36 .... 57 D2
Park Pl *CBRISNE* BS2 .... 20 B5
    CFTN/FAIL BS8 .... 19 F5
    EVILLE/WHL BS5 .... 17 C3
Park Rd *AVONM* BS11 .... 74 B1
    BMSTR BS3 .... 27 F5
    HORF/LLZ BS7 .... 67 C2
    KEYN BS31 .... 112 B2
    KGWD/HNM BS15 .... 86 A2
    MANG/FISH BS16 .... 8 C4
    MANG/FISH BS16 .... 80 B2
Park Rw *CBRIS/FH* BS1 .... 28 A1
Parkside Av *FRCTL/WBN* BS36 .... 56 B1
Parkside Gdns *EVILLE/WHL* BS5 .... 15 F1
Parkstone Av *HORF/LLZ* BS7 .... 6 A1
Park St *BRSG/KWL/STAPK* BS4 .... 39 D2
    CBRIS/FH BS1 .... 28 A1
    EVILLE/WHL BS5 .... 84 A3
Park Street Av *CBRIS/FH* BS1 .... 28 A1
The Park *KEYN* BS31 .... 112 B1
    KGWD/HNM BS15 .... 86 B3
    MANG/FISH BS16 .... 71 C2
Park Vw *KGWD/HNM* BS15 .... 86 B4
Park View Ter *EVILLE/WHL* BS5 .... 25 F4
Parkwall Crs *OLD/WMLY/WICK* BS30 . 93 C3
Parkwall Rd *OLD/WMLY/WICK* BS30 ... 93 C3
Parkway *BRSTK/PCHW* BS34 .... 54 B3
Park Wood Cl *HGRV/WHIT* BS14 .... 107 C3
Parliament St
    BRSG/KWL/STAPK BS4 .... 38 C2
Parnall Rd *MANG/FISH* BS16 .... 78 B4
Parry's Cl *HNLZ/SM/SNYPK/WT* BS9 .. 77 D2
Parrys Gv *HNLZ/SM/SNYPK/WT* BS9 .. 77 D2
Parry's La *HNLZ/SM/SNYPK/WT* BS9 ... 2 A4
Parslow Barton *EVILLE/WHL* BS5 .. 84 A4
Parsons Av *BRSTK/PCHW* BS34 .... 54 A2
Parsons Paddock
    HGRV/WHIT BS14 .... 97 D4
Parson St *BMSTR* BS3 .... 95 D2
Partition St *CBRIS/FH* BS1 .... 28 A3
Passage Leaze *AVONM* BS11 .... 74 A1
Passage Rd *HNBRY/STHM* BS10 .... 48 B4
    HNLZ/SM/SNYPK/WT BS9.............. 64 B3
Passage Road Brentry Hl
    HNBRY/STHM BS10 .... 48 B4
Passage St *CBRIS/FH* BS1 .... 29 F2
Paul St *CBRISNE* BS2 .... 20 B4
Paulton Dr *HORF/LLZ* BS7 .... 12 B1
Paultow Av *BMSTR* BS3 .... 37 E4
Paultow Rd *BMSTR* BS3 .... 37 E4
Pavey Cl *BMSTRD/HC/WWD* BS13 ..... 105 D3
Pavey Rd *BMSTRD/HC/WWD* BS13 ... 105 D3
Pawlett Rd
    BMSTRD/HC/WWD BS13.................. 105 D4
Pawlett Wk
    BMSTRD/HC/WWD BS13 .... 105 D4
Paybridge Rd
    BMSTRD/HC/WWD BS13.................. 104 A3
Payne Dr *EVILLE/WHL* BS5 .... 23 E5
Peache Rd *MANG/FISH* BS16 .... 80 B1
Peacocks La *KGWD/HNM* BS15 .... 85 D3
Pearces Hl *MANG/FISH* BS16.............. 71 C4

Pearl St *BMSTR* BS3 .... **35** E4
Pearsall Rd *OLD/WMLY/WICK* BS30 .. **102** B1
Peartree La *EVILLE/WHL* BS5 .... **91** C1
  KGWD/HNM BS15 .... **87** C1 ⬛
Pear Tree Rd *ALMDB* BS32 .... **44** B1
Pegasus Rd *BRSTK/PCHW* BS34 .... **42** A4
Pemberton Ct *MANG/FISH* BS16 ...... **79** D2 ⬛
Pembery Rd *BMSTR* BS3 .... **35** F4 ⬛
Pembroke Av *AVONM* BS11 .... **74** B1 ⬛
Pembroke Gv *CFTN/FAIL* BS8 .... **19** D5
Pembroke Pl *CFTN/FAIL* BS8 .... **27** C4 ⬛
Pembroke Rd *AVONM* BS11 .... **74** B1 ⬛
  BMSTR BS3 .... **36** A1
  CFTN/FAIL BS8 .... **18** C3
  KGWD/HNM BS15 .... **86** B1 ⬛
Pembroke St *CBRISE* BS2 .... **21** F4
Pembroke V *CFTN/FAIL* BS8 .... **18** C4
Penard Rd *KGWD/HNM* BS15 .... **87** C4 ⬛
Pendennis Av *MANG/FISH* BS16 ...... **80** A3 ⬛
Pendennis Pk
  BRSG/KWL/STAPK BS4 .... **41** D5
Pendennis Rd *MANG/FISH* BS16 .... **80** A1
Pendock Rd *FRCTL/WBN* BS36 .... **56** B2
  MANG/FISH BS16 .... **79** C1
Penfield Rd *CBRISNE* BS2 .... **14** C4
Penlea Ct *AVONM* BS11 .... **60** A4
Pennard Ct *HGRV/WHIT* BS14 .... **108** A2
Penn Dr *MANG/FISH* BS16 .... **71** D2
Penngrove
  OLD/WMLY/WICK BS30 .... **93** D4 ⬛
Pennlea *BMSTRD/HC/WWD* BS13 .... **95** C4
Penn St *CBRIS/FH* BS1 .... **21** F5
Pennyroyal Gv *MANG/FISH* BS16 .... **9** F4
Pennywell Rd *EVILLE/WHL* BS5 .... **22** C2
Pen Park Rd *HNBRY/STHM* BS10 .... **49** D4
Penpole Av *AVONM* BS11 .... **74** B1
Penpole Cl *AVONM* BS11 .... **60** A4 ⬛
Penpole La *AVONM* BS11 .... **60** B4
Penpole Pk *AVONM* BS11 .... **60** B4 ⬛
Penpole Pl *AVONM* BS11 .... **74** B1
Penrose *HGRV/WHIT* BS14 .... **107** C1
Penrose Dr *BRSTK/PCHW* BS34 ..... **45** C4 ⬛
Pensfield Pk *HNBRY/STHM* BS10 .... **50** A3
Pensford Ct *HGRV/WHIT* BS14 ...... **109** C2 ⬛
Pentire Av *BMSTRD/HC/WWD* BS13 .. **94** B4
Percival Rd *CFTN/FAIL* BS8 .... **18** A4
Perrott Rd *KGWD/HNM* BS15 .... **87** D2 ⬛
Perry Cl *FRCTL/WBN* BS36 .... **56** A3
Perrycroft Av
  BMSTRD/HC/WWD BS13 .... **104** B1
Perrycroft Rd
  BMSTRD/HC/WWD BS13 .... **104** B1
Perrymans Cl *MANG/FISH* BS16 .... **78** B1
Perry Rd *CBRIS/FH* BS1 .... **28** D1
Perrys Lea *ALMDB* BS32 .... **45** C1 ⬛
Perry St *EVILLE/WHL* BS5 .... **22** C3
Pesley Cl *BMSTRD/HC/WWD* BS13 ... **104** A3
Petercole Dr
  BMSTRD/HC/WWD BS13 .... **104** B1
Peterson Sq
  BMSTRD/HC/WWD BS13 .... **105** D4 ⬛
Peter's Ter *EVILLE/WHL* BS5 .... **31** E1
Petersway Gdns *EVILLE/WHL* BS5 .. **90** B1 ⬛
Petherton Cl *KGWD/HNM* BS15 .... **86** B4
Petherton Gdns *HGRV/WHIT* BS14 .... **98** A3 ⬛
Petherton Rd *HGRV/WHIT* BS14 .... **98** A3
Pettigrove Gdns *KGWD/HNM* BS15 ... **86** B3
Pettigrove Rd *KGWD/HNM* BS15 .... **92** B1
Pevensey Wk
  BRSG/KWL/STAPK BS4 .... **96** A4 ⬛
Peverell Cl *HNBRY/STHM* BS10 .... **48** A4

Peverell Dr *HNBRY/STHM* BS10 .... **48** A4
Philadelphia Ct *CBRIS/FH* BS1 .... **21** F5 ⬛
Philippa Cl *HGRV/WHIT* BS14 .... **97** D4
Philip St *BMSTR* BS3 .... **37** D2
  CBRISNE BS2 .... **31** E4
Phippen St *CBRIS/FH* BS1 .... **29** E4 ⬛
Phipps St *BMSTR* BS3 .... **35** E1
Phoenix Gv *RDLND/MONT* BS6 .... **4** B3
Picton La *RDLND/MONT* BS6 .... **21** E2
Picton St *RDLND/MONT* BS6 .... **21** E2
Pigeon House Dr
  BMSTRD/HC/WWD BS13 .... **106** A3 ⬛
Pigott Av *BMSTRD/HC/WWD* BS13 .. **104** B3 ⬛
Pile Marsh *EVILLE/WHL* BS5 .... **24** C5
Pilgrims Wy *AVONM* BS11 .... **59** D4 ⬛
  MANG/FISH BS16 .... **72** A3 ⬛
Pilkington Cl *BRSTK/PCHW* BS34 .... **68** B1
Pillingers Rd *KGWD/HNM* BS15 .... **85** D4
Pill Rd *PTSHD/EG* BS20 .... **74** A4
Pimpernel Md *ALMDB* BS32 .... **45** D4 ⬛
Pinecroft *HGRV/WHIT* BS14 .... **97** C4 ⬛
Pine Gv *HORF/LLZ* BS7 .... **67** C2
Pine Grove Pl *HORF/LLZ* BS7 .... **13** D4
Pine Ridge Cl
  HNLZ/SM/SNYPK/WT BS9 .... **76** B3 ⬛
Pine Rd *HNBRY/STHM* BS10 .... **49** C4
Pinewood *KGWD/HNM* BS15 .... **87** C2 ⬛
Pinewood Cl
  HNLZ/SM/SNYPK/WT BS9 .... **65** C4
Pinhay Rd
  BMSTRD/HC/WWD BS13 .... **105** C1 ⬛
Pioneer Pk *BRSG/KWL/STAPK* BS4 ..... **32** B5
Pipe La *CBRIS/FH* BS1 .... **28** B2
  CBRIS/FH BS1 .... **29** F4
Pippin Ct *OLD/WMLY/WICK* BS30 .. **93** C3 ⬛⬛
Pitch & Pay La
  HNLZ/SM/SNYPK/WT BS9 .... **77** D4
Pitchcombe Gdns
  HNLZ/SM/SNYPK/WT BS9 .... **63** C4
Pitch La *RDLND/MONT* BS6 .... **20** C2
Pithay Ct *CBRIS/FH* BS1 .... **29** D2 ⬛
Pitt Rd *HORF/LLZ* BS7 .... **5** F3
Players Cl *MANG/FISH* BS16 .... **55** C3
Playford Gdns *AVONM* BS11 .... **60** B3
Pleasant Rd *MANG/FISH* BS16 .... **80** A2
Plummer's Hl *EVILLE/WHL* BS5 .... **25** F3
Plumpton Ct *MANG/FISH* BS16 .... **73** C2 ⬛
Poets' Cl *EVILLE/WHL* BS5 .... **24** C3
Polly Barnes Cl *KGWD/HNM* BS15 .... **91** C1 ⬛
Polly Barnes Hl *KGWD/HNM* BS15 .... **91** C2
Polygon Rd *CFTN/FAIL* BS8 .... **26** B3 ⬛
Pomfrett Gdns
  HGRV/WHIT BS14 .... **109** D2 ⬛
Ponsford Rd *BRSG/KWL/STAPK* BS4 ... **98** A2
Ponting Ct *EVILLE/WHL* BS5 .... **84** B2 ⬛
Poole St *AVONM* BS11 .... **59** C3
Pooles Whf *CFTN/FAIL* BS8 .... **27** D4
Pooles Wharf Ct *CFTN/FAIL* BS8 .... **27** D4
Pool Rd *KGWD/HNM* BS15 .... **80** B4
Poplar Av
  HNLZ/SM/SNYPK/WT BS9 .... **77** C1 ⬛
Poplar Pl *MANG/FISH* BS16 .... **78** B4 ⬛
Poplar Rd *BMSTRD/HC/WWD* BS13 ... **94** A4
  EVILLE/WHL BS5 .... **84** A2
  KGWD/HNM BS15 .... **90** B2
Poplar Ter *KGWD/HNM* BS15 .... **87** C3 ⬛
Poppy Md *ALMDB* BS32 .... **45** D4
Porlock Rd *BMSTR* BS3 .... **36** C4
Portbury Gv *AVONM* BS11 .... **74** A1
Portbury Wk *AVONM* BS11 .... **74** A1 ⬛
Portland Pl *MANG/FISH* BS16 .... **80** A4 ⬛
Portland Sq *CBRISNE* BS2 .... **21** F4

Portland St *CBRISNE* BS2 .... 20 B3
  CFTN/FAIL BS8 .... 26 B1
  MANG/FISH BS16 .... 80 A4
Portmeirion Cl *HGRV/WHIT* BS14 .. 107 D2 🔟
Portview Rd *AVONM* BS11 .... 59 C3
Portwall La *CBRIS/FH* BS1 .... 29 E4
Portwall La East *CBRIS/FH* BS1 ...... 29 F4 🔟
Portway *AVONM* BS11 .... 59 D3
  HNLZ/SM/SNYPK/WT BS9 .... 76 B4
Pound Dr *MANG/FISH* BS16 .... 78 A2
Pound La *MANG/FISH* BS16 .... 78 A3
Pound Rd *KGWD/HNM* BS15 .... 87 C1
Pountney Dr *EVILLE/WHL* BS5 .... 23 E4 🔟
Pow's Rd *KGWD/HNM* BS15 .... 86 A4
Poyntz Ct *OLD/WMLY/WICK* BS30 .. 93 C4 🖪
Poyntz Rd *BRSG/KWL/STAPK* BS4 ..... 97 C3
Preddy's La *EVILLE/WHL* BS5 .... 90 B1
Press Moor Dr
  OLD/WMLY/WICK BS30 .... 93 C3 🔟🔼
Preston Wk
  BRSG/KWL/STAPK BS4 .... 97 D2 🔟
Prestwick Cl
  BRSG/KWL/STAPK BS4 .... 99 C2 🔟
Pretoria Rd *BRSTK/PCHW* BS34 .... 43 C3
Prewett St *CBRIS/FH* BS1 .... 29 E5
Priddy Ct *HGRV/WHIT* BS14 .... 108 A2
Priddy Dr *HGRV/WHIT* BS14 .... 108 A2
Priestwood Cl
  HNBRY/STHM BS10 .... 48 B4 🔟
Primrose Cl *ALMDB* BS32 .... 45 C1 🔟
  KGWD/HNM BS15 .... 85 C2
Primrose La *KGWD/HNM* BS15 .... 85 D3
Princes Ct *OLD/WMLY/WICK* BS30 ... 93 C3
Princes' La *CFTN/FAIL* BS8 .... 26 A2
Princes' Pl *HORF/LLZ* BS7 .... 13 E2
Princess Cl *KEYN* BS31 .... 112 C1
Princess Gdns *MANG/FISH* BS16 .... 9 D2 🔟
Princess Rw *CBRISNE* BS2 .... 21 D4
Princess St *BMSTR* BS3 .... 37 E1
  CBRISNE BS2 .... 30 C2
Prince's St *CBRISNE* BS2 .... 21 F3
Princess Victoria St *CFTN/FAIL* BS8 .. 26 A2
Prince St *CBRIS/FH* BS1 .... 28 C4
Priory Av *HNLZ/SM/SNYPK/WT* BS9 .. 64 B4
Priory Court Rd
  HNLZ/SM/SNYPK/WT BS9 .... 64 B4
Priory Dene
  HNLZ/SM/SNYPK/WT BS9 .... 64 B4 🔟
Priory Gdns *AVONM* BS11 .... 74 A1 🔟
  HORF/LLZ BS7 .... 67 C3
Priory Rd *AVONM* BS11 .... 74 A1
  CFTN/FAIL BS8 .... 19 F4
  KEYN BS31 .... 102 A3
Pritchard St *CBRISNE* BS2 .... 21 F4
Probyn Cl *MANG/FISH* BS16 .... 70 B4 🔟
Prospect Av *KGWD/HNM* BS15 ..... 85 C2 🔟
Prospect Cl *FRCTL/WBN* BS36 ..... 56 B3 🔟
Prospect Crs *KGWD/HNM* BS15 .... 87 C1
Prospect Pl *EVILLE/WHL* BS5 .... 24 B3
Providence Pl *CBRISNE* BS2 .... 30 A2 🔟
Prudham St *EVILLE/WHL* BS5 .... 24 A1 🔟
Pump La *CBRIS/FH* BS1 .... 29 E5
Pump Sq *PTSHD/EG* BS20 .... 74 A2 🔟
Purcell Wk
  BRSG/KWL/STAPK BS4 .... 96 A4 🔟🔟
Purdown Rd *HORF/LLZ* BS7 .... 6 A4
Pursey Dr *ALMDB* BS32 .... 53 D1
Purton Cl *KGWD/HNM* BS15 .... 92 B1
Purton Rd *HORF/LLZ* BS7 .... 13 D4
Puxley Cl *HGRV/WHIT* BS14 .... 109 D1 🔟
Pyecroft Av
  HNLZ/SM/SNYPK/WT BS9 .... 65 C4

Pylle Hill Crs *BMSTR* BS3 .... 38 A2
Pynne Cl *HGRV/WHIT* BS14 .... 109 D1
Pynne Rd *HGRV/WHIT* BS14 .... 110 A2

Q

Quadrant East *MANG/FISH* BS16 .... 79 D4 🔽
The Quadrant *RDLND/MONT* BS6 ...... 11 E2
Quadrant West *MANG/FISH* BS16 ..... 79 D4
Quaker's Cl *MANG/FISH* BS16 .... 72 A3 🔟
Quakers' Friars *CBRIS/FH* BS1 ..... 21 E5 🔟
Quaker's Rd *MANG/FISH* BS16 .... 72 A3
Quantock Rd *BMSTR* BS3 .... 36 C4
Quarrington Rd *HORF/LLZ* BS7 .... 5 F3
Quarry Barton *MANG/FISH* BS16 ..... 55 D3
Quarry La *AVONM* BS11 .... 62 B2
  FRCTL/WBN BS36 .... 56 B3
Quarry Rd *KGWD/HNM* BS15 .... 92 A1 🔟
  MANG/FISH BS16 .... 71 D4 🔟
Quarry Steps *CFTN/FAIL* BS8 .... 10 C5
Quarry Wy *MANG/FISH* BS16 .... 9 E4
  MANG/FISH BS16 .... 73 D2
Quayside La *EVILLE/WHL* BS5 .... 90 A1 🔟
Quay St *CBRIS/FH* BS1 .... 29 D1 🔟
Queen Ann Rd *CBRISNE* BS2 .... 31 E3
  EVILLE/WHL BS5 .... 31 F1
Queen Charlotte St
  CBRIS/FH BS1 .... 29 D2 🔟
Queen Charlton La
  HGRV/WHIT BS14 .... 109 C4
Queen's Av *CFTN/FAIL* BS8 .... 19 F5
Queensdale Crs
  BRSG/KWL/STAPK BS4 .... 97 D2
Queensdown Gdns
  BRSG/KWL/STAPK BS4 .... 40 A5
Queens Down Gdns
  BRSG/KWL/STAPK BS4 .... 40 A4
Queen's Dr *HORF/LLZ* BS7 .... 4 B5
  KGWD/HNM BS15 .... 91 C3
Queens Ga
  HNLZ/SM/SNYPK/WT BS9 .... 77 C2
Queenshill Rd
  BRSG/KWL/STAPK BS4 .... 97 D2
Queensholm Av *MANG/FISH* BS16 .. 72 B2 🔟
Queensholm Cl *MANG/FISH* BS16 .... 72 B2
Queensholm Crs *MANG/FISH* BS16 .. 72 A2
Queensholm Dr *MANG/FISH* BS16 .... 72 B3
Queens Pde *CBRIS/FH* BS1 .... 27 F3
Queen Sq *CBRIS/FH* BS1 .... 28 C3
Queen Square Av *CBRIS/FH* BS1 ... 29 D3 🔟
Queen's Rd
  BMSTRD/HC/WWD BS13 .... 104 A3
  BRSG/KWL/STAPK BS4 .... 98 B2
  CFTN/FAIL BS8 .... 19 D5
  EVILLE/WHL BS5 .... 84 A4
  HORF/LLZ BS7 .... 6 A5
  KEYN BS31 .... 112 A3
  LGASH BS41 .... 104 A4
  OLD/WMLY/WICK BS30 .... 93 C3
Queen St *AVONM* BS11 .... 58 B2
  CBRISNE BS2 .... 29 F1
  EVILLE/WHL BS5 .... 16 C4
  KGWD/HNM BS15 .... 85 C4
Queensway *BRSTK/PCHW* BS34 .... 52 B1
Queen Victoria Rd
  RDLND/MONT BS6 .... 11 D1
Queen Victoria St *CBRISNE* BS2 ..... 31 D2
Quickthorn Cl *HGRV/WHIT* BS14 .... 107 D1

R

Rackham Cl *HORF/LLZ* BS7 .... 7 F2
Rackhay *CBRIS/FH* BS1 .... 29 D2 ⊠
Radley Rd *MANG/FISH* BS16 .... 9 F3
Radnor Rd *HNLZ/SM/SNYPK/WT* BS9 .... 3 E3
HORF/LLZ BS7 .... 5 D4
Raeburn Rd *EVILLE/WHL* BS5 .... 85 C4
Raglan Pl *HORF/LLZ* BS7 .... 13 D4
Raglan Rd *HORF/LLZ* BS7 .... 13 D3
Railton Jones Cl *BRSTK/PCHW* BS34 .... 53 D4
Railway Ter *MANG/FISH* BS16 .... 79 D3
Raleigh Rd *BMSTR* BS3 .... 35 E2
Ralph Rd *HORF/LLZ* BS7 .... 6 A5
Ramsey Rd *HORF/LLZ* BS7 .... 67 C4
Randall Cl *KGWD/HNM* BS15 .... 87 C1
Randall Rd *CFTN/FAIL* BS8 .... 27 D3
Randolph Av
BMSTRD/HC/WWD BS13 .... 105 C2
Randolph Cl
BMSTRD/HC/WWD BS13 .... 105 C2
Rangers Wk *KGWD/HNM* BS15 .... 91 D3
Rannoch Rd *BRSTK/PCHW* BS34 .. 67 C1
Ratcliffe Dr *BRSTK/PCHW* BS34 .... 53 C2
Ravenglass Crs *HNBRY/STHM* BS10.... 65 D1
Ravenhead Dr *HGRV/WHIT* BS14 .... 98 A3
Ravenhill Av *BMSTR* BS3 .... 38 B5
Ravenhill Rd *BMSTR* BS3 .... 38 A3
Ravenswood Rd *RDLND/MONT* BS6 .. 20 A2
Rayleigh Rd
HNLZ/SM/SNYPK/WT BS9 .... 63 C4
Raymend Rd *BMSTR* BS3 .... 37 E4
Raymend Wk *BMSTR* BS3 .... 37 F5
Raymill *BRSG/KWL/STAPK* BS4 .. 100 B1 ⊠
Raynes Rd *BMSTR* BS3 .... 34 C3
Rectory La *BRSTK/PCHW* BS34 .... 51 D4
Redcar Cl *FRCTL/WBN* BS36 .... 73 C2 ⊠
Redcliff Backs *CBRIS/FH* BS1 .... 29 E3
Redcliffe Pde East *CBRIS/FH* BS1 .. 29 D4
Redcliffe Pde West *CBRIS/FH* BS1.. 29 D4
Redcliffe Wy *CBRIS/FH* BS1 .... 29 E4
Redcliff Hl *CBRIS/FH* BS1 .... 29 E5
Redcliff Mead La *CBRIS/FH* BS1 .. 29 F4
Redcliff St *CBRIS/FH* BS1 .... 29 E2
Redcross St *CBRISNE* BS2 .... 30 A1
The Reddings *KGWD/HNM* BS15 .... 87 C1
Redfield Rd *BRSTK/PCHW* BS34 .... 44 A4
Redford Wk
BMSTRD/HC/WWD BS13 .... 104 A4 ⊠
Redhill Cl *MANG/FISH* BS16 .... 17 E2
Redhill Dr *MANG/FISH* BS16 .... 17 E2
Red House La
HNLZ/SM/SNYPK/WT BS9 .... 77 D1
Redland Court Rd
RDLND/MONT BS6 .... 12 A3
Redland Green Rd
RDLND/MONT BS6 .... 12 A3
Redland Gv *RDLND/MONT* BS6 .... 12 B5
Redland Hl *RDLND/MONT* BS6 .... 11 F4
Redland Pk *RDLND/MONT* BS6 .... 11 E5
Redland Rd *RDLND/MONT* BS6 .... 11 F4
Redland Ter *RDLND/MONT* BS6 ..... 11 D5 ⊠
Redshelf Wk *HNBRY/STHM* BS10...... 49 D4
Redwick Cl *AVONM* BS11 .... 62 D1
Redwing Gdns *MANG/FISH* BS16 .... 9 F2
Redwood Cl
OLD/WMLY/WICK BS30 .... 93 D4 ⊠
Reed Cl *HNBRY/STHM* BS10 .... 5 D1
HNBRY/STHM BS10 .... 66 A4 ⊠
Reed Ct *OLD/WMLY/WICK* BS30 ...... 93 C4 ⊠

Reedley Rd *HNLZ/SM/SNYPK/WT* BS9.. 2 A3
Reedling Cl *MANG/FISH* BS16 .... 9 F2
Regency Dr
BRSG/KWL/STAPK BS4 .... 100 B1 ⊠
Regent Rd *BMSTR* BS3 .... 37 D1 ⊠
Regent St *CFTN/FAIL* BS8 .... 26 C1 ⊠
KGWD/HNM BS15 .... 85 D3
Remenham Dr
HNLZ/SM/SNYPK/WT BS9 .... 3 E4
Remenham Pk
HNLZ/SM/SNYPK/WT BS9 .... 3 F4
Rene Rd *EVILLE/WHL* BS5 .... 23 E2
Repton Rd *BRSG/KWL/STAPK* BS4 .. 40 B3
Reynolds Cl *KEYN* BS31 .... 113 D2
Reynold's Wk *HORF/LLZ* BS7 .... 67 D4
Richeson Cl *HNBRY/STHM* BS10...... 64 A1
Richeson Wk *HNBRY/STHM* BS10 ...... 64 A1
Richmond Av *BRSTK/PCHW* BS34 ...... 53 B2
RDLND/MONT BS6 .... 14 A5
Richmond Cl *KEYN* BS31 .... 112 A3
Richmond Dl *CFTN/FAIL* BS8 .... 10 C5
Richmond Hl *CFTN/FAIL* BS8 .... 19 E5
Richmond Hill Av *CFTN/FAIL* BS8 ...... 27 D1
Richmond La *CFTN/FAIL* BS8 .... 27 D1
Richmond Park Rd *CFTN/FAIL* BS8 .. 27 D1
Richmond Rd *EVILLE/WHL* BS5 .... 25 E4
MANG/FISH BS16 .... 81 D2
RDLND/MONT BS6 .... 13 F5
Richmond St *BMSTR* BS3 .... 38 B2
Richmond Ter *AVONM* BS11 .... 58 B2
CFTN/FAIL BS8 .... 27 D1
The Ride *KGWD/HNM* BS15 .... 87 D1
Ridgehill *HNLZ/SM/SNYPK/WT* BS9 .... 4 B2
The Ridge *AVONM* BS11 .... 60 B4
Ridgeway Ct *HNBRY/STHM* BS10...... 64 A2
Ridgeway Gdns *HGRV/WHIT* BS14.. 108 B2
Ridgeway La *HGRV/WHIT* BS14 ...... 108 A3
Ridgeway Pde *EVILLE/WHL* BS5...... 17 E3
Ridgeway Rd *MANG/FISH* BS16 ...... 17 F3
The Ridgeway *HNBRY/STHM* BS10 .. 64 B2
Ridingleaze *AVONM* BS11 .... 61 D2
Ringwood Crs *HNBRY/STHM* BS10 .. 66 A2
Ripley Rd *EVILLE/WHL* BS5 .... 84 B2
Ripon Ct *MANG/FISH* BS16 .... 73 C2
Ripon Rd *BRSG/KWL/STAPK* BS4 ...... 33 F3
Riverland Dr
BMSTRD/HC/WWD BS13 .... 104 A2
Riverleaze
HNLZ/SM/SNYPK/WT BS9 .... 76 A2
Riverside Cl *AVONM* BS11 .... 75 C2
Riverside Ct *BRSG/KWL/STAPK* BS4 .... 90 A1
Riverside Wk *EVILLE/WHL* BS5 ...... 90 A1 ⊠
Riverside Wy *KGWD/HNM* BS15 ...... 91 D4 ⊠
River St *CBRISNE* BS2 .... 22 A5
River Vw *MANG/FISH* BS16 .... 9 E5
Riverwood Rd *MANG/FISH* BS16 ...... 71 D2
Riviera Crs *MANG/FISH* BS16 .... 80 B3
Robbins Cl *ALMDB* BS32 .... 54 A1
Robertson Dr
BRSG/KWL/STAPK BS4 .... 90 A5
Robertson Rd *EVILLE/WHL* BS5 ...... 16 A5
Robert St *EVILLE/WHL* BS5 .... 15 E5
Robin Cl *HNBRY/STHM* BS10 .... 65 C1
Robinson Dr *EVILLE/WHL* BS5....... 22 C3
Rochester Rd
BRSG/KWL/STAPK BS4 .... 33 F4
Rock Cl *BRSG/KWL/STAPK* BS4 ...... 41 E5
Rockingham Gdns *AVONM* BS11 .. 61 D3 ⊠
Rockland Gv *MANG/FISH* BS16 .... 9 D2
Rockland Rd *MANG/FISH* BS16 ...... 71 D4
Rock La *BRSTK/PCHW* BS34 .... 54 A2
Rockleaze *HNLZ/SM/SNYPK/WT* BS9.. 83 D1

Rockleaze Av
  HNLZ/SM/SNYPK/WT BS9................. **77** D4
Rockleaze Rd
  HNLZ/SM/SNYPK/WT BS9................. **83** D1
Rock Rd *KEYN* BS31 .... **112** B2
Rockside Av *MANG/FISH* BS16 .... **73** C3
Rockside Dr
  HNLZ/SM/SNYPK/WT BS9................. **3** F1
Rockside Gdns *MANG/FISH* BS16 ..... **73** C3 🔢
Rockstowes Wy *HNBRY/STHM* BS10.. **50** A4
The Rock *BRSG/KWL/STAPK* BS4 .... **41** E4
Rockwell Av *AVONM* BS11 .... **62** A2
Rodbourne Rd *HNBRY/STHM* BS10 ..... **5** E1
Rodfords Md *HGRV/WHIT* BS14 .... **97** D4
Rodmead Wk
  BMSTRD/HC/WWD BS13 .... **104** B3 🔢
Rodney Av *KGWD/HNM* BS15 .... **84** B3
Rodney Crs *BRSTK/PCHW* BS34 .... **51** D3
Rodney Rd *KGWD/HNM* BS15 .... **84** B2
Rodney Wk *KGWD/HNM* BS15 .... **84** B2
Rodway HI *MANG/FISH* BS16 .... **81** D3
Rodway Rd *BRSTK/PCHW* BS34 .... **43** D3
  MANG/FISH BS16 .... **81** D2
Rodway Vw *KGWD/HNM* BS15 .... **81** C4
Roegate Dr *RDLND/MONT* BS6 .... **20** A1
Rokeby Av *RDLND/MONT* BS6 .... **20** A1
Roman Farm Ct *AVONM* BS11 .... **62** B1 🔢
Roman Rd *EVILLE/WHL* BS5 .... **23** F1
Roman Wk *BRSG/KWL/STAPK* BS4 ...... **40** B3
  BRSTK/PCHW BS34 .... **53** D2 🔢
Roman Wy
  HNLZ/SM/SNYPK/WT BS9................ **76** B3
Romney Av *HORF/LLZ* BS7 .... **7** D4
  HORF/LLZ BS7 .... **7** F2
Ronald Rd *MANG/FISH* BS16 .... **78** A1 🔢
Ronayne Wk *MANG/FISH* BS16............ **79** D1
Rookery Rd *BRSG/KWL/STAPK* BS4 ..... **38** C4
Rookery Wy *HGRV/WHIT* BS14 .... **107** C3
Rose Acre *HNBRY/STHM* BS10 .... **48** B4
Rosebay Md *MANG/FISH* BS16 .... **9** E4 🔢
Roseberry Pk *EVILLE/WHL* BS5............ **24** C4
Roseberry Rd *EVILLE/WHL* BS5 .... **32** B1
Rosebery Av *CBRISNE* BS2 .... **22** C1
Rosedale Rd *FRCTL/WBN* BS36 .... **56** B3
Rosedale Rd *MANG/FISH* BS16 .... **79** C4
Rose Green Cl *EVILLE/WHL* BS5 .... **17** E5
Rose Green Rd *EVILLE/WHL* BS5 .... **17** E5
Roselarge Gdns
  HNBRY/STHM BS10 .... **64** B1 🔢
Rosemary Cl *ALMDB* BS32 .... **46** A4
Rosemary La *EVILLE/WHL* BS5 .... **16** A5
Rose Md *HORF/LLZ* BS7 .... **67** D4 🔢
Rosemont Ter *CFTN/FAIL* BS8 .... **27** D3
Rose Rd *EVILLE/WHL* BS5 .... **25** F5
Rosery Cl *HNLZ/SM/SNYPK/WT* BS9 .... **64** B3
The Rosery *MANG/FISH* BS16 .... **79** D4 🔢
Rose St *CBRIS/FH* BS1 .... **29** F4
Roseville Av
  OLD/WMLY/WICK BS30 .... **103** D1
Rose Wk *MANG/FISH* BS16 .... **79** D4
Rosling Rd *HORF/LLZ* BS7 .... **5** F2
Roslyn Rd *RDLND/MONT* BS6 .... **12** A5
Rossall Av *BRSTK/PCHW* BS34 .... **52** B1
Rossall Rd *BRSG/KWL/STAPK* BS4 ...... **40** C4
Rossiter's La *EVILLE/WHL* BS5 .... **90** B1
Roundmoor Gdns
  HGRV/WHIT BS14 .... **99** C4 🔢
Rousham Rd *EVILLE/WHL* BS5 .... **15** D3
Rowacres *HGRV/WHIT* BS14 .... **107** C1
Rowan Cl *MANG/FISH* BS16................ **84** B1
Rowan Wy *KGWD/HNM* BS15 .... **91** C4 🔢
Rowberrow *HGRV/WHIT* BS14 .... **97** C4

Rowland Av *MANG/FISH* BS16 .... **16** C1
Rowlandson Gdns *HORF/LLZ* BS7 .... **7** E1 🔢
Rowley St *BMSTR* BS3 .... **36** A4 🔢
Rownham Cl *BMSTR* BS3 .... **89** D1 🔢
Rownham HI *CFTN/FAIL* BS8 .... **89** D1 🔢
Rownham Md *CFTN/FAIL* BS8 .... **26** C4 🔢
Royal Albert Rd *RDLND/MONT* BS6.... **11** D1
Royal Fort Rd *CFTN/FAIL* BS8 .... **20** B5
Royal Pk *CFTN/FAIL* BS8 .... **18** C5
Royal Rd *MANG/FISH* BS16 .... **81** D1
Royal York Crs *CFTN/FAIL* BS8 .... **26** B2
Royal York VIs *CFTN/FAIL* BS8 .... **26** C2
Royate HI *EVILLE/WHL* BS5 .... **17** D4
Roycroft Rd *BRSTK/PCHW* BS34 .... **68** A1
Royston Wk *HNBRY/STHM* BS10 .... **66** A1
Rozel Rd *HORF/LLZ* BS7 .... **5** E2
Rubens Cl *KEYN* BS31 .... **113** D2 🔢
Ruby St *BMSTR* BS3 .... **35** E4
Rudford Cl *BRSTK/PCHW* BS34 .... **44** A3
Rudge Cl *KGWD/HNM* BS15................ **87** C1
Rudgewood Cl
  BMSTRD/HC/WWD BS13 .... **106** A3 🔢
Rudhall Gv *HNBRY/STHM* BS10 .... **66** B4
Rudthorpe Rd *HORF/LLZ* BS7 .... **5** F3
Rugby Rd *BRSG/KWL/STAPK* BS4 .... **40** C3
Runnymead Av
  BRSG/KWL/STAPK BS4 .... **99** C2
Runnymede *KGWD/HNM* BS15 .... **86** B2 🔢
Runswick Rd *BRSG/KWL/STAPK* BS4 ... **40** A4
Rupert St *CBRIS/FH* BS1 .... **29** D1
  EVILLE/WHL BS5 .... **32** A1
Rush Cl *ALMDB* BS32 .... **45** C1
Rushy *OLD/WMLY/WICK* BS30............ **93** D3
Rushy Wy *MANG/FISH* BS16 .... **73** D2
Ruskin Gv *HORF/LLZ* BS7 .... **67** D3
Russell Av *KGWD/HNM* BS15.............. **86** A4
Russell Gv *RDLND/MONT* BS6 .... **4** A4
Russell Rd *MANG/FISH* BS16 .... **85** C1
  RDLND/MONT BS6 .... **3** F5
Russell Town Av *EVILLE/WHL* BS5 ...... **23** F4
Russ St *CBRISNE* BS2 .... **30** A2
Rutherford Cl
  OLD/WMLY/WICK BS30 .... **93** D4 🔢
Ruthven Rd *BRSG/KWL/STAPK* BS4 .... **96** B3
Rutland Av *OLD/WMLY/WICK* BS30 .... **103** D1
Rutland Rd *HORF/LLZ* BS7 .... **13** F2 🔢
Ryde Rd *BRSG/KWL/STAPK* BS4 .... **39** E5 🔢
Ryland Pl *CBRISNE* BS2 .... **14** C4 🔢
Rylestone Gv
  HNLZ/SM/SNYPK/WT BS9................. **2** A4
Rysdale Rd *HNLZ/SM/SNYPK/WT* BS9 .. **2** A1

S

Sabrina Wy
  HNLZ/SM/SNYPK/WT BS9................ **76** B3
  PTSHD/EG BS20 .... **74** A3 🔢
Sadlier Cl *AVONM* BS11 .... **61** C3
Sages Md *ALMDB* BS32 .... **45** D3 🔢
St Agnes Av *BRSG/KWL/STAPK* BS4 .... **38** B5
St Agnes Cl *BRSG/KWL/STAPK* BS4 .. **38** B5
St Agnes Wk *BRSG/KWL/STAPK* BS4 ... **38** B5
St Aidan's Cl *EVILLE/WHL* BS5 .... **91** C1 🔢
St Aidan's Rd *EVILLE/WHL* BS5 .... **90** B1
St Alban's Rd *RDLND/MONT* BS6 .... **11** E1
St Aldwyn's Cl *HORF/LLZ* BS7 .... **67** C3 🔢
St Andrew's Rd *AVONM* BS11 .... **59** C2
  RDLND/MONT BS6 .... **13** F5 🔢
St Anne's Av *KEYN* BS31 .... **112** A1

St Anne's Park Rd
    BRSG/KWL/STAPK BS4 .... 33 E5
St Anne's Rd BRSG/KWL/STAPK BS4 .. 33 D2
    EVILLE/WHL BS5 .... 91 C1
St Anne's Ter BRSG/KWL/STAPK BS4 ... 91 C1
St Aubin's Av BRSG/KWL/STAPK BS4 .. 90 A4
St Augustine's Pde CBRIS/FH BS1 ...... 28 C2
St Augustine's Pl CBRIS/FH BS1 .... 28 C2 🔢
St Bartholomew's Rd
    HORF/LLZ BS7 .... 14 A3 🔢
St Bede's Rd KGWD/HNM BS15 .... 85 D1
St Bernard's Rd AVONM BS11............ 74 B1
St Brelades Gv BRSG/KWL/STAPK BS4 33 F5
St Brendan's Wy AVONM BS11 .... 59 C2
St Catherine's Md
    PTSHD/EG BS20 .... 74 A4 🔢
St Clements Ct KEYN BS31 .... 112 B3
St Clements Rd KEYN BS31 .... 112 B2
St David's Crs
    BRSG/KWL/STAPK BS4 .... 33 F4
St Dunstan's Rd BMSTR BS3................ 36 B5
St Edward's Rd CFTN/FAIL BS8 .... 27 E3 🔢
St Edyth's Rd
    HNLZ/SM/SNYPK/WT BS9.................. 44 A1
St Francis Dr FRCTL/WBN BS36 .... 57 C1
St Francis Rd BMSTR BS3 .... 35 D2 🔢
    KEYN BS31 .... 111 D1
St Gabriel's Rd EVILLE/WHL BS5......... 23 E3
St Georges Av EVILLE/WHL BS5 .... 90 A1 🔢
St Georges Rd CBRIS/FH BS1 .... 28 A3
    KEYN BS31 .... 112 A2
St Gregory's Rd HORF/LLZ BS7............ 67 C3
St Gregory's Wk HORF/LLZ BS7 ...... 67 D3 🔢
St Helena Rd RDLND/MONT BS6 .... 11 E1
St Helen's Wk EVILLE/WHL BS5 .... 84 B2
St Helier Av
    BRSG/KWL/STAPK BS4 .... 90 A4 🔢
St Hilary Cl
    HNLZ/SM/SNYPK/WT BS9.................. 77 C2
St James's St MANG/FISH BS16 .... 81 D2
St John's Br CBRIS/FH BS1 .... 20 C5 🔢
St Johns Ct KEYN BS31 .... 112 B1
St John's Crs BMSTR BS3.................... 37 E5
St John's La BMSTR BS3 .... 36 B4
    BRSG/KWL/STAPK BS4 .... 38 B3
St John's Rd BMSTR BS3 .... 36 C1
    CFTN/FAIL BS8 .... 19 D1
St John's St BMSTR BS3..................... 36 B3
St Joseph's Rd HNBRY/STHM BS10 .... 49 C4
St Keyna Rd KEYN BS31..................... 112 B2
St Ladoc Rd KEYN BS31 .... 112 A1
St Laud Cl HNLZ/SM/SNYPK/WT BS9 .. 76 B2
St Leonard's Rd EVILLE/WHL BS5 .... 16 B5
    HORF/LLZ BS7 .... 5 E2
St Lucia Cl HORF/LLZ BS7 .... 66 B3
St Lucia Crs HORF/LLZ BS7 .... 66 B4
St Luke's Crs BMSTR BS3.................... 38 C1
St Luke's Gdns
    BRSG/KWL/STAPK BS4 .... 41 E5
St Luke's Rd BMSTR BS3 .... 37 F1
St Margaret's Cl KEYN BS31 .... 112 A1 🔢
St Margaret's Dr
    HNLZ/SM/SNYPK/WT BS9 .... 4 A3 🔢
St Marks Cl KEYN BS31 .... 112 B1 🔢
St Mark's Gv EVILLE/WHL BS5............ 23 E1
St Mark's Rd EVILLE/WHL BS5 .... 23 E1
St Mark's Ter EVILLE/WHL BS5 .... 23 E1
St Martin's Gdns
    BRSG/KWL/STAPK BS4 .... 98 A2 🔢
St Martin's Rd
    BRSG/KWL/STAPK BS4 .... 98 A1

St Martin's Wk
    BRSG/KWL/STAPK BS4 .... 98 A2 🔢
St Mary's Rd AVONM BS11 .... 60 A4
    CFTN/FAIL BS8 .... 89 C1 🔢
St Mary's Wk AVONM BS11 .... 74 A1
St Matthew's Av RDLND/MONT BS6 .. 21 C3
St Matthew's Rd RDLND/MONT BS6 .. 20 C3
St Matthias Pk CBRISNE BS2.............. 22 A5
St Michaels Ct KGWD/HNM BS15 ..... 85 C3 🔢
St Michael's Hl RDLND/MONT BS6 ..... 20 A3
St Michael's Pk CFTN/FAIL BS8 .... 20 A4
St Nicholas Pk EVILLE/WHL BS5 .... 23 E1
St Nicholas' Rd CBRISNE BS2 .... 22 A2
    HGRV/WHIT BS14 .... 108 B3
St Nicholas St CBRIS/FH BS1 .... 29 D2 🔢
St Oswald's Rd RDLND/MONT BS6.... 11 E3
St Paul's Rd BMSTR BS3 .... 36 C1
    CFTN/FAIL BS8 .... 19 E5
St Paul St CBRISNE BS2 .... 21 F4
St Peter's Ri
    BMSTRD/HC/WWD BS13.................. 94 B4
St Peter's Wk
    HNLZ/SM/SNYPK/WT BS9.................. 3 F2
St Philips Cswy
    BRSG/KWL/STAPK BS4 .... 40 A1
    CBRISNE BS2 .... 31 E3
St Philips Rd CBRISNE BS2 .... 30 B1
St Phillips Rd CBRISNE BS2 .... 30 C1
St Ronan's Av RDLND/MONT BS6 ...... 20 A1
St Silas St CBRISNE BS2 .... 31 D4
St Stephen's Av CBRIS/FH BS1 ...... 28 C2 🔢
St Stephens Cl KGWD/HNM BS15 ..... 80 B4 🔢
St Stephen's Rd MANG/FISH BS16 ..... 80 A4
St Stephen's St CBRIS/FH BS1 .... 28 C1
St Thomas St CBRIS/FH BS1 .... 29 E3
St Vincent's Hl CFTN/FAIL BS8 .... 11 D4
St Vincent's Rd CFTN/FAIL BS8.......... 26 C3
St Werburgh's Pk CBRISNE BS2 .... 14 C4
St Werburgh's Rd CBRISNE BS2 .... 14 B4
St Whytes Rd BRSG/KWL/STAPK BS4.. 96 A3
Salcombe Rd BRSG/KWL/STAPK BS4 .. 97 D3
Salisbury Av KGWD/HNM BS15.......... 85 C3
Salisbury Gdns MANG/FISH BS16 ...... 80 B2
Salisbury Rd BRSG/KWL/STAPK BS4 .. 33 D5
    MANG/FISH BS16 .... 80 B1
    RDLND/MONT BS6............................ 12 C4
Salisbury St EVILLE/WHL BS5............. 25 E4
    EVILLE/WHL BS5 .... 31 F3
Sallybarn Cl OLD/WMLY/WICK BS30.. 102 B1
Sallysmead Cl
    BMSTRD/HC/WWD BS13.................. 105 C3 🔢
Salmons Wy MANG/FISH BS16 .... 73 D3
Salthrop Rd HORF/LLZ BS7 .... 13 E2
Saltmarsh Dr AVONM BS11 .... 61 D2
Saltwell Av HGRV/WHIT BS14 .... 108 B3
Samian Wy BRSTK/PCHW BS34 .... 53 D2
Sampsons Rd
    BMSTRD/HC/WWD BS13.................. 105 D3
Samuel St EVILLE/WHL BS5................. 24 A4
Samuel White Rd KGWD/HNM BS15 .. 91 D4
Sandbach Rd BRSG/KWL/STAPK BS4 .. 40 C2
Sandbed Rd CBRISNE BS2 .... 14 C5
Sandburrows Wk
    BMSTRD/HC/WWD BS13.................. 104 A1 🔢
Sandcroft HGRV/WHIT BS14 .... 107 C1
Sandford Rd CFTN/FAIL BS8 .... 26 C4
Sandgate Rd BRSG/KWL/STAPK BS4 .. 40 C3
Sand Hl BRSG/KWL/STAPK BS4 .... 40 B2
Sandholme Cl MANG/FISH BS16 ..... 72 B3 🔢
Sandholme Rd
    BRSG/KWL/STAPK BS4 .... 40 C2
Sandhurst Cl BRSTK/PCHW BS34 .... 44 A2

Sandhurst Rd
  BRSG/KWL/STAPK BS4 .... **40** B3
Sandling Av *HORF/LLZ* BS7 .... **67** D4
Sandown Cl *MANG/FISH* BS16 ...... **73** C2
Sandown Rd *BRSG/KWL/STAPK* BS4 .. **40** C2
  BRSTK/PCHW BS34 .... **52** B4 🔟
Sandringham Av *MANG/FISH* BS16 .. **72** B3
Sandringham Pk
  MANG/FISH BS16 .... **72** B3 🔟
Sandringham Rd
  BRSG/KWL/STAPK BS4 .... **40** C3
  BRSTK/PCHW BS34 .... **53** C3
Sandstone Ri *FRCTL/WBN* BS36 ..... **56** A3
Sandwich Rd *BRSG/KWL/STAPK* BS4 .. **40** C2
Sandy Cl *ALMDB* BS32 .... **53** D1
Sandy La *EVILLE/WHL* BS5 .... **16** A3
Sandyleaze
  HNLZ/SM/SNYPK/WT BS9 .... **63** D4
Sandy Park Rd
  BRSG/KWL/STAPK BS4 .... **40** B2
Sarah St *EVILLE/WHL* BS5 .... **23** E5
Sargent St *BMSTR* BS3 .... **37** E1
Sarum Crs *HNBRY/STHM* BS10 .... **65** D2
Sassoon Ct
  OLD/WMLY/WICK BS30 .... **93** C2 🔟
Satchfield Cl *HNBRY/STHM* BS10 ... **64** A1
Satchfield Crs *HNBRY/STHM* BS10 .. **64** A1
Sates Wy *HNLZ/SM/SNYPK/WT* BS9 .. **4** B2
Saunders Rd *MANG/FISH* BS16 ...... **80** B3 🔟
Saunton Wk
  BRSG/KWL/STAPK BS4 .... **96** B3 🔟
Savages Wood Rd *ALMDB* BS32 ..... **45** C3
Saville Gate Cl
  HNLZ/SM/SNYPK/WT BS9 .... **10** B1
Saville Pl *CFTN/FAIL* BS8 .... **4** C4 🔟
Saville Rd *HNLZ/SM/SNYPK/WT* BS9 .. **10** C1
Savoy Rd *BRSG/KWL/STAPK* BS4 ...... **40** C1
Saxon Rd *CBRISNE* BS2 .... **15** D5
Saxon Wy *ALMDB* BS32 .... **44** B2
Scantleberry Cl *MANG/FISH* BS16 .. **72** A3 🔟
School Cl *BRSTK/PCHW* BS34 .... **44** B3
  EVILLE/WHL BS5 .... **17** D4
  HGRV/WHIT BS14 .... **107** C3
School Rd *BRSG/KWL/STAPK* BS4 .... **38** C3
  BRSG/KWL/STAPK BS4 .... **41** E5
  KGWD/HNM BS15 .... **85** D3
  OLD/WMLY/WICK BS30 .... **93** D3
School Wk *EVILLE/WHL* BS5 .... **25** D2
Scott Ct *OLD/WMLY/WICK* BS30 ..... **93** C2 🔟
Scott Lawrence Cl
  MANG/FISH BS16 .... **70** B4 🔟
Seagry Ct *HNBRY/STHM* BS10 .... **66** B2
Sea Mills La
  HNLZ/SM/SNYPK/WT BS9 .... **76** B3
Searle Court Av
  BRSG/KWL/STAPK BS4 .... **41** F1
Seaton Rd *EVILLE/WHL* BS5 .... **24** A2
Seawalls Rd
  HNLZ/SM/SNYPK/WT BS9 .... **83** C1
Seddon Rd *CBRISNE* BS2 .... **14** B4
Sedgefield Gdns
  MANG/FISH BS16 .... **73** C2 🔟
Sefton Park Rd *HORF/LLZ* BS7 ...... **13** F3
Selborne Rd *HORF/LLZ* BS7 .... **6** A4
Selbrooke Crs *MANG/FISH* BS16 ..... **79** D1
Selby Rd *EVILLE/WHL* BS5 .... **84** A2
Selden Rd *HGRV/WHIT* BS14 .... **109** D2
Selkirk Rd *KGWD/HNM* BS15.......... **85** D1
Selley Wk *BRSTRD/HC/WWD* BS13 .. **104** B2
Selworthy *KGWD/HNM* BS15 .... **86** B4
Selworthy Cl *KEYN* BS31 .... **112** A2

Selworthy Rd
  BRSG/KWL/STAPK BS4 .... **39** F5
Seneca Pl *EVILLE/WHL* BS5 .... **25** D5 🔟
Seneca St *EVILLE/WHL* BS5 .... **25** D5
Seventh Av *HORF/LLZ* BS7 .... **68** A2 🔟
Severn Rd *AVONM* BS11 .... **74** A1 🔟
Severn Wy *BRSTK/PCHW* BS34 ...... **43** C2
  KEYN BS31 .... **113** C2
Sevier St *CBRISNE* BS2 .... **14** B5
Seymour Av *HORF/LLZ* BS7 .... **5** F5
Seymour Rd *EVILLE/WHL* BS5 .... **23** D1
  HORF/LLZ BS7 .... **5** F5
  KGWD/HNM BS15 .... **85** D2 🔟
  MANG/FISH BS16 .... **80** A3
Seyton Wk *BRSTK/PCHW* BS34 ...... **53** D2
Shadwell Rd *HORF/LLZ* BS7 .... **13** D3
Shaftesbury Av *RDLND/MONT* BS6 ... **21** F1
Shaftesbury Ter *EVILLE/WHL* BS5 .... **24** C5
Shakespeare Av *HORF/LLZ* BS7 ...... **67** D3
Shaldon Rd *HORF/LLZ* BS7 .... **6** C5
Shamrock Rd *EVILLE/WHL* BS5 .... **17** D3
Shanklin Dr *BRSTK/PCHW* BS34 ..... **52** A4 🔟
Shapcott Cl
  BRSG/KWL/STAPK BS4 .... **98** A2 🔟
Shaplands *HNLZ/SM/SNYPK/WT* BS9 .. **2** A5
Shearmore Cl *HORF/LLZ* BS7 .... **67** D3 🔟
Sheene La *BMSTR* BS3 .... **36** B4
Sheeps Cft
  BMSTRD/HC/WWD BS13............ **104** B3
Sheepwood Cl *HNBRY/STHM* BS10 ... **64** B2
Sheepwood Rd *HNBRY/STHM* BS10 .. **64** B1
Sheldare Barton *EVILLE/WHL* BS5 .... **85** C4 🔟
Sheldrake Dr *MANG/FISH* BS16 ...... **9** F2
Shellard Rd *BRSTK/PCHW* BS34 ...... **51** D4
Shellards Rd *OLD/WMLY/WICK* BS30 .. **93** C4
Shelley Cl *EVILLE/WHL* BS5 .... **84** A1
Shelley Wy *HORF/LLZ* BS7 .... **67** D3
Shellmor Av *BRSTK/PCHW* BS34...... **44** A2
Shellmor Cl *ALMDB* BS32 .... **45** C2 🔟
  BRSTK/PCHW BS34 .... **44** B2
Shepherds Cl *MANG/FISH* BS16 ...... **80** B2
Sheppard Rd *MANG/FISH* BS16 ...... **79** D1
Shepton Wk *BMSTR* BS3 .... **36** A5
Sherbourne Av *ALMDB* BS32 .... **45** D4
Sherbourne Cl *KGWD/HNM* BS15 ..... **87** C1
Sherbourne St *EVILLE/WHL* BS5 ...... **25** E4
Sheridan Rd *HORF/LLZ* BS7 .... **67** D2
Sheridan Wy
  OLD/WMLY/WICK BS30 .... **103** D1
Sherston Cl *MANG/FISH* BS16 .... **79** C2
Sherston Rd *HORF/LLZ* BS7 .... **66** B3 🔟
Sherwell Rd *BRSG/KWL/STAPK* BS4 ... **41** E4
Sherwood Rd *KEYN* BS31 .... **112** B2
Sherwood Rd *KEYN* BS31 .... **112** B2
  KGWD/HNM BS15 .... **84** B2
Shetland Rd *HNBRY/STHM* BS10 ..... **66** A2
Shields Av *HORF/LLZ* BS7 .... **67** D1
Shiels Dr *ALMDB* BS32 .... **45** C4 🔟
Shilton Cl *KGWD/HNM* BS15 .... **87** C4 🔟
Shimsey Cl *MANG/FISH* BS16 .... **79** D1 🔟
Shipham Cl *HGRV/WHIT* BS14 .... **108** A2
Ship La *CBRIS/FH* BS1................. **29** E5
Shipley Rd
  HNLZ/SM/SNYPK/WT BS9 .... **64** B3
Shipnran Ct *MANG/FISH* BS16 .... **80** B3 🔟
Shire Gdns *AVONM* BS11 .... **60** A3
Shirehampton Rd *AVONM* BS11....... **61** C4 🔟
  HNLZ/SM/SNYPK/WT BS9 .... **76** B1 🔟
Shortlands Rd *AVONM* BS11 .... **61** D2 🔟
Short St *CBRISNE* BS2 .... **31** D4
Shortwood Rd
  BMSTRD/HC/WWD BS13............ **106** B4

Shortwood Vw *KGWD/HNM* BS15 .. **87** C3 🔟
Shortwood Wk
  BMSTRD/HC/WWD BS13 .... **106** B4 🔢
Showering Cl *HGRV/WHIT* BS14 ... **109** C2 🔢
Showering Rd *HGRV/WHIT* BS14 ..... **109** C2
Shrubbery Cottages
  RDLND/MONT BS6................. **11** E4
Shrubbery Rd *MANG/FISH* BS16.... **80** D2
Shuter Rd
  BMSTRD/HC/WWD BS13 .... **104** A2 🔟
Sidcot *BRSG/KWL/STAPK* BS4 ...... **100** B1
Sideland Cl *HGRV/WHIT* BS14 ..... **109** D1
Sidelands Rd *MANG/FISH* BS16...... **79** D1
Sidmouth Gdns *BMSTR* BS3 .... **37** D5
Sidmouth Rd *BMSTR* BS3 .... **37** D5
Signal Rd *MANG/FISH* BS16........... **80** B3
Silcox Rd
  BMSTRD/HC/WWD BS13 .... **105** D3 🔢
Silklands Gv
  HNLZ/SM/SNYPK/WT BS9 ...... **76** B1 🔢
Silverbirch Cl *BRSTK/PCHW* BS34... **45** C4
Silver St *CBRIS/FH* BS1 .... **21** D5 🔢
Silverthorne La *CBRISNE* BS2 .... **31** E3 🔢
Silverton Ct
  BRSG/KWL/STAPK BS4 .... **97** C2 🔢
Simmonds Vw *BRSTK/PCHW* BS34 .... **54** A3
Sion Hl *CFTN/FAIL* BS8 .... **26** A2
Sion La *CFTN/FAIL* BS8 .... **26** A1
Sion Pl *CFTN/FAIL* BS8 .... **26** B1
Sion Rd *BMSTR* BS3 .... **36** A3
Sir John's La *EVILLE/WHL* BS5....... **15** F1
  HORF/LLZ BS7 .... **7** E5
Siston Cl *KGWD/HNM* BS15 .... **87** D1
Siston Pk *KGWD/HNM* BS15 .... **87** D1
Sixth Av *HORF/LLZ* BS7 .... **67** D2
Skippon Ct *KGWD/HNM* BS15 .... **92** B2 🔢
Sleep La *HGRV/WHIT* BS14........... **109** C4
Sloan St *EVILLE/WHL* BS5 .... **25** D4
Slymbridge Av *HNBRY/STHM* BS10 ... **48** B3
Small La *MANG/FISH* BS16............... **9** E4
Small St *CBRIS/FH* BS1 .... **29** D1 🔢
  CBRISNE BS2 .... **31** D4
Smeaton Rd *CBRIS/FH* BS1 .... **26** B5
Smithmead
  BMSTRD/HC/WWD BS13............ **105** C2
Smythe Cft *HGRV/WHIT* BS14....... **107** D4
Smyth Rd *BMSTR* BS3 .... **34** C4
Smyths Cl *AVONM* BS11 .... **59** C2 🔢
Snowberry Wk *EVILLE/WHL* BS5 .... **25** F3
Snowdon Cl *MANG/FISH* BS16 .... **78** A3
Snowdon Rd *MANG/FISH* BS16....... **78** A3
Somerby Cl *ALMDB* BS32 .... **45** C4 🔢
Somerdale Av
  BRSG/KWL/STAPK BS4 .... **97** C2
Somerdale Rd *KEYN* BS31 .... **103** D4
Somerdale Rd North *KEYN* BS31 ..... **103** C4
Somermead *BMSTR* BS3 .... **95** D2
Somerset Crs *BRSTK/PCHW* BS34 .. **54** A2 🔢
Somerset Rd *BRSG/KWL/STAPK* BS4 .. **39** E4
Somerset Sq *CBRIS/FH* BS1 .... **29** E5
Somerset St *CBRIS/FH* BS1 .... **29** F5
  CBRISNE BS2 .... **21** D3
Somerset Ter *BMSTR* BS3 .... **37** D4
Somerton Cl *KGWD/HNM* BS15 ..... **86** B4
Somerton Rd *HORF/LLZ* BS7 .... **57** D1
Sommerville Rd *RDLND/MONT* BS6... **13** E2
Sommerville Rd South
  RDLND/MONT BS6................. **14** A4
Soundwell Rd *KGWD/HNM* BS15 .... **85** D2 🔢
South Cft *HNLZ/SM/SNYPK/WT* BS9 .. **65** D4
South Dene
  HNLZ/SM/SNYPK/WT BS9........ **77** D1

Southdown Rd
  HNLZ/SM/SNYPK/WT BS9................. **64** A3
Southernhay *CFTN/FAIL* BS8 .... **27** E3 🔢
  MANG/FISH BS16...................... **79** D3
Southernhay Av *CFTN/FAIL* BS8....... **27** E3
Southey Av *KGWD/HNM* BS15 .... **86** A2
Southey St *CBRISNE* BS2 .... **14** B5
Southfield Av *KGWD/HNM* BS15 ..... **86** D2
Southfield Ct
  HNLZ/SM/SNYPK/WT BS9 .... **64** B4 🔢
Southfield Rd
  HNLZ/SM/SNYPK/WT BS9.......... **64** B4
  RDLND/MONT BS6................... **20** C1
South Green St *CFTN/FAIL* BS8 ...... **26** B3 🔢
South Gv *RDLND/MONT* BS6 .... **4** B4
South Hayes *EVILLE/WHL* BS5 .... **15** F1
Southleigh Rd *CFTN/FAIL* BS8........ **19** E1
South Liberty La
  BMSTRD/HC/WWD BS13 .... **95** C1 🔟
Southmead Rd *BRSTK/PCHW* BS34 .... **66** B2
  HNBRY/STHM BS10................. **65** D3
  HNLZ/SM/SNYPK/WT BS9 .... **65** C4
Southmead Wy *HNBRY/STHM* BS10 .. **66** A3
Southover Cl
  HNLZ/SM/SNYPK/WT BS9.......... **64** B3
South Rd *BMSTR* BS3 .... **36** A4
  KGWD/HNM BS15 .... **86** A3
  RDLND/MONT BS6 .... **12** B5
Southsea Rd *BRSTK/PCHW* BS34 ..... **43** D4
Southside Cl *AVONM* BS11 .... **62** A4
South St *BMSTR* BS3 .... **35** F3
South Vw *MANG/FISH* BS16........... **80** B2
Southville Pl *BMSTR* BS3.............. **36** C1
Southville Rd *BMSTR* BS3 .... **36** B1
Southwell St *CBRISNE* BS2 .... **20** B4
Southwood Av
  HNLZ/SM/SNYPK/WT BS9.......... **62** B3
Southwood Dr
  HNLZ/SM/SNYPK/WT BS9 .... **62** A3
Southwood Dr East
  HNLZ/SM/SNYPK/WT BS9.......... **62** B3
Spalding Cl *HORF/LLZ* BS7 .... **14** C3
Spartley Dr
  BMSTRD/HC/WWD BS13.......... **104** A1
Spartley Wk
  BMSTRD/HC/WWD BS13 .... **104** A1 🔟
Speedwell Av *EVILLE/WHL* BS5 ...... **25** D5
Speedwell Rd *EVILLE/WHL* BS5 ...... **25** F2
  KGWD/HNM BS15 .... **85** C2
The Spinney *ALMDB* BS32 .... **45** D4
Spires Vw *MANG/FISH* BS16........... **9** E4
Springfield Av *AVONM* BS11 .... **74** A1 🔢
  HORF/LLZ BS7 .... **6** A4
  MANG/FISH BS16.................... **81** D1
Springfield Cl *MANG/FISH* BS16 ..... **73** D4 🔢
Springfield Gv *RDLND/MONT* BS6 ..... **3** F3
Springfield Rd *MANG/FISH* BS16 ..... **81** D1 🔢
  RDLND/MONT BS6.................. **21** D2
Springfields *BRSTK/PCHW* BS34..... **67** D1
Spring Gdns *BRSG/KWL/STAPK* BS4 .. **97** D2
Spring Hl *KGWD/HNM* BS15 .... **86** B1
  RDLND/MONT BS6.................. **21** D3
Springleaze *BRSG/KWL/STAPK* BS4 ... **97** D2
  MANG/FISH BS16.................... **73** D4
Spring St *BMSTR* BS3 .... **37** F1
Spring Street Pl *BMSTR* BS3........... **37** F1
Springville Cl
  OLD/WMLY/WICK BS30 .... **93** D4 🔢
Spruce Wy *BRSTK/PCHW* BS34 .... **42** B1 🔢
The Square
  BRSG/KWL/STAPK BS4 .... **97** D2 🔢
Squires Ct *OLD/WMLY/WICK* BS30 .. **93** C4 🔢

Stackpool Rd *BMSTR* BS3 .... 36 A1
Stadium Rd *RDLND/MONT* BS6 .... 4 B4
Stafford Rd *CBRISNE* BS2 .... 14 C5
Staffords Ct
   OLD/WMLY/WICK BS30 .... 93 D1 🔟
Stafford St *BMSTR* BS3 .... 36 A4
Stainer Cl *BRSG/KWL/STAPK* BS4 .. 106 A1 🔟
Stanbridge Cl *MANG/FISH* BS16 ...... 81 C1 🔟
Stanbridge Rd *MANG/FISH* BS16 ...... 81 C1
Stanbury Av *MANG/FISH* BS16 .... 79 C2
Stanbury Rd *BMSTR* BS3 .... 37 E4
Standfast Rd *HNBRY/STHM* BS10 ... 48 A4
Standish Av *BRSTK/PCHW* BS34 ...... 44 A2
Standish Cl *HNBRY/STHM* BS10 ...... 64 A2 🔟
Standon Wy *HNBRY/STHM* BS10 ...... 65 D1 🔟
Stane Wy *AVONM* BS11 .... 59 D4 🔟
Stanfield Cl *HORF/LLZ* BS7 .... 7 F1
Stanhope Rd
   OLD/WMLY/WICK BS30 .... 103 C1
Stanhope St *CBRISNE* BS2 .... 30 C5
Stanley Av *BRSTK/PCHW* BS34 .... 68 A1
   HORF/LLZ BS7 .... 13 F2
Stanley Cha *EVILLE/WHL* BS5 .... 17 D5
Stanley Crs *BRSTK/PCHW* BS34 ...... 68 A1
Stanley Hl *BRSG/KWL/STAPK* BS4.... 38 C5
Stanley Md *ALMDB* BS32 .... 45 D1 🔟
Stanley Pk *EVILLE/WHL* BS5 .... 23 F1
Stanley Park Rd *MANG/FISH* BS16..... 80 B4
Stanley Rd *RDLND/MONT* BS6 .... 12 A5
Stanley St *BMSTR* BS3 .... 36 A3 🔟
Stanley St North *BMSTR* BS3 .... 36 A4 🔟
Stanley St South *BMSTR* BS3 .... 36 A4
Stanley Ter *BMSTR* BS3 .... 36 A5
Stanshaw Rd *MANG/FISH* BS16 .... 70 B4
Stanshaws Cl *BRSTK/PCHW* BS34 .... 44 A1
Stanton Cl *KGWD/HNM* BS15 .... 87 C2
Stanton Rd *HNBRY/STHM* BS10 ...... 66 B2
Staple Gv *KEYN* BS31 .... 112 A2
Staple Grove Crs *EVILLE/WHL* BS5 .. 84 B4 🔟
Staplehill Rd *MANG/FISH* BS16 .... 79 C3
Stapleton Cl *MANG/FISH* BS16 .... 8 A1
Stapleton Rd *EVILLE/WHL* BS5 .... 16 A4
Star La *MANG/FISH* BS16 .... 78 A4
   PTSHD/EG BS20 .... 74 A3 🔟
Station Av *MANG/FISH* BS16 .... 78 B3
Station La *HORF/LLZ* BS7 .... 14 C1
Station Rd *AVONM* BS11 .... 74 A2
   BRSG/KWL/STAPK BS4 .... 99 C1
   BRSTK/PCHW BS34 .... 51 D4
   BRSTK/PCHW BS34 .... 52 B1
   BRSTK/PCHW BS34 .... 68 B1
   FRCTL/WBN BS36 .... 56 B3
   HNBRY/STHM BS10 .... 48 A4
   HORF/LLZ BS7 .... 14 B1
   KEYN BS31 .... 112 B1
   KGWD/HNM BS15 .... 81 C4
   MANG/FISH BS16 .... 78 B3
   RDLND/MONT BS6 .... 13 D5
Station Wy *MANG/FISH* BS16 .... 78 B3
Staunton Flds *HGRV/WHIT* BS14 ..... 108 B4
Staunton La *HGRV/WHIT* BS14 .... 108 B3
Staunton Wy *HGRV/WHIT* BS14 ..... 109 C3 🔟
Staveley Crs *HNBRY/STHM* BS10 ..... 65 D1
Stavordale Gv *HGRV/WHIT* BS14 .... 108 A1
Staynes Crs *KGWD/HNM* BS15 .... 86 B3 🔟
Stean Bridge La *ALMDB* BS32 .... 53 C1
Steel Cl *OLD/WMLY/WICK* BS30 ...... 93 C2
Steel Mills *KEYN* BS31 .... 113 C3
Stella Gv *BMSTR* BS3 .... 34 C5
Stephens Dr *OLD/WMLY/WICK* BS30 .. 93 C2
Stephen St *EVILLE/WHL* BS5 .... 24 B3
Stepney Rd *EVILLE/WHL* BS5 .... 24 B2

Stepney Wk *EVILLE/WHL* BS5 .... 24 B2
The Stepping Stones
   BRSG/KWL/STAPK BS4 .... 33 F2
Sterncourt Rd *MANG/FISH* BS16 ..... 70 B4
Stevens Crs *BMSTR* BS3 .... 38 A2
Stevens Wk *ALMDB* BS32 .... 45 C3
Stibbs Ct *OLD/WMLY/WICK* BS30 ... 93 C3 🔟🔟
Stibbs Hl *EVILLE/WHL* BS5 .... 84 B4
Stile Acres *AVONM* BS11 .... 61 D2
Stillhouse La *BMSTR* BS3 .... 37 D1
Stillingfleet Rd
   BMSTRD/HC/WWD BS13 .... 105 D2
Stirling Rd *BRSG/KWL/STAPK* BS4 ... 40 B2
Stirling Wy *KEYN* BS31 .... 112 B3 🔟
Stockton Cl *HGRV/WHIT* BS14 .... 107 C3 🔟
Stockwell Av *MANG/FISH* BS16 .... 81 C1
Stockwell Cl *MANG/FISH* BS16 .... 73 C4
Stockwell Dr *MANG/FISH* BS16....... 81 C1
Stockwood Crs
   BRSG/KWL/STAPK BS4 .... 97 C1
Stockwood Hl *KEYN* BS31 .... 101 D4
Stockwood La *HGRV/WHIT* BS14 .... 109 D2
Stockwood Ms
   BRSG/KWL/STAPK BS4 .... 90 A2 🔟
Stockwood Rd
   BRSG/KWL/STAPK BS4 .... 100 A2
   HGRV/WHIT BS14.................. 109 D2
Stoke Bridge Av *BRSTK/PCHW* BS34.. 53 C1
Stoke Gv *HNLZ/SM/SNYPK/WT* BS9 .... 77 D1
Stoke Hamlet
   HNLZ/SM/SNYPK/WT BS9........ 2 B1
Stoke Hl *HNLZ/SM/SNYPK/WT* BS9 .... 77 D3
Stoke La *BRSTK/PCHW* BS34 .... 44 B3
   HNLZ/SM/SNYPK/WT BS9 .... 2 A1 🔟
   MANG/FISH BS16 .... 69 D4
Stokeleigh Wk
   HNLZ/SM/SNYPK/WT BS9 ...... 76 B2 🔟
Stokemead *BRSTK/PCHW* BS34 ...... 44 B3 🔟
Stoke Mdw *ALMDB* BS32 .... 45 C2
Stoke Paddock Rd
   HNLZ/SM/SNYPK/WT BS9 ...... 77 C1
Stoke Park Rd
   HNLZ/SM/SNYPK/WT BS9 ...... 77 D3
Stoke Park Rd South
   HNLZ/SM/SNYPK/WT BS9 ...... 77 D4
Stoke Rd *CFTN/FAIL* BS8 .... 11 D4
   HNLZ/SM/SNYPK/WT BS9........ 10 B3
Stokes Ct *OLD/WMLY/WICK* BS30 ... 93 D3 🔟
Stokes Cft *CBRIS/FH* BS1 .... 21 E3
Stoke View Rd *MANG/FISH* BS16 ..... 78 A4 🔟
Stoneberry Rd *HGRV/WHIT* BS14 .... 107 C4
Stonebridge Pk *EVILLE/WHL* BS5...... 17 C4
Stonechat Gdns *MANG/FISH* BS16 .... 9 F2 🔟
Stonehill *OLD/WMLY/WICK* BS30 ..... 92 B3
Stone La *FRCTL/WBN* BS36 .... 56 B3
Stoneleigh Crs
   BRSG/KWL/STAPK BS4 .... 38 C5
Stoneleigh Dr
   OLD/WMLY/WICK BS30 .... 93 C2
Stoneleigh Rd
   BRSG/KWL/STAPK BS4 .... 38 C5
Stoneleigh Wk
   BRSG/KWL/STAPK BS4 .... 97 D1 🔟
Stothard Rd *HORF/LLZ* BS7............... 68 A4
Stottbury Rd *HORF/LLZ* BS7 .... 15 D2
Stoulton Gv *HNBRY/STHM* BS10 ..... 48 B4 🔟
Stourden Cl *MANG/FISH* BS16 .... 70 B4 🔟
Stourton Dr *OLD/WMLY/WICK* BS30 .. 93 C3
Stowick Crs *AVONM* BS11 .... 62 B2
Stradbrook Av *EVILLE/WHL* BS5........ 85 C4
Stradling Rd *AVONM* BS11 .... 62 B1
Straight St *CBRISNE* BS2 .... 30 A2

Stratford Cl *HGRV/WHIT* BS14 ...... 107 C4 ⑥
Strathmore Rd *HORF/LLZ* BS7 .... 5 F2
Stratton St *CBRISNE* BS2..................... 21 F4
Strawbridge Rd *EVILLE/WHL* BS5 ...... 31 F1
Stream Cl *HNBRY/STHM* BS10 .... 50 A4
Stream Side *MANG/FISH* BS16 .... 81 C1
The Stream *MANG/FISH* BS16 .... 71 C1
Stretford Av *EVILLE/WHL* BS5 ...... 25 D3 ⑥
Stretford Rd *EVILLE/WHL* BS5 .... 25 D3
Stroud Rd *AVONM* BS11........................ 74 B2
    BRSTK/PCHW BS34 .... 42 B3
Stuart St *EVILLE/WHL* BS5 .... 32 A1
Sturden La *MANG/FISH* BS16 .... 55 D4
Sturdon Rd *BMSTR* BS3....................... 35 D4
Sturminster Cl *HGRV/WHIT* BS14 ... 109 C1
Sturminster Rd *HGRV/WHIT* BS14 .... 99 C4
Summer HI *BRSG/KWL/STAPK* BS4... 38 C2
Summerhill Rd *EVILLE/WHL* BS5 .... 84 A3
Summerhill Ter *EVILLE/WHL* BS5 ... 84 A4 ⑥
Summerleaze *KEYN* BS31 .... 102 B4 ⑨
    MANG/FISH BS16.......................... 79 D4
Summers Rd *CBRISNE* BS2 .... 22 C1 ⑥
Summer St *BMSTR* BS3 .... 36 A2
Sunderland Pl *CFTN/FAIL* BS8 .... 19 E4
Sunny Bank *KGWD/HNM* BS15.......... 85 C2
Sunnydene *BRSG/KWL/STAPK* BS4... 40 C2
Sunny HI *HNLZ/SM/SNYPK/WT* BS9 .. 62 B4
Sunnyhill Dr *AVONM* BS11................. 74 B1 ⑥
Sunnymead *KEYN* BS31 .... 113 C4
Sunnyside
    HNLZ/SM/SNYPK/WT BS9 .... 77 D2 ⑥
Sunnyside La *MANG/FISH* BS16 .... 71 C1
Sunny Wk *KGWD/HNM* BS15............. 85 C2
Sunridge *MANG/FISH* BS16 .... 80 A1
Sunrise Gv *BRSG/KWL/STAPK* BS4 ... 40 C1
Surrey Rd *HORF/LLZ* BS7 .... 13 F2
Surrey St *CBRISNE* BS2 .... 21 F4
Suspension Br *CFTN/FAIL* BS8 .... 83 D4
Sussex Pl *CBRISNE* BS2 .... 22 B1
Sussex St *CBRISNE* BS2 .... 30 C2
Sutherland Av *MANG/FISH* BS16 ...... 72 B4
Sutherland Pl *CFTN/FAIL* BS8 .... 10 C5
Sutton Av *BRSG/KWL/STAPK* BS4...... 41 D2
Swainswick *HGRV/WHIT* BS14 .... 107 C4
Swaish Dr *OLD/WMLY/WICK* BS30 ... 93 C3
Swallow Dr *BRSTK/PCHW* BS34 .... 42 B3
Swallows Ct *BRSTK/PCHW* BS34 ...... 53 D3
Swane Rd *HGRV/WHIT* BS14 ...... 110 A1 ⑥
Swan La *FRCTL/WBN* BS36 .... 47 D3
Swanmoor Crs *HNBRY/STHM* BS10.... 48 B3
Sweets Cl *KGWD/HNM* BS15 .... 86 B1
Sweets Rd *KGWD/HNM* BS15 .... 86 A1
Swiss Rd *BMSTR* BS3 .... 94 A1
Sycamore Cl *EVILLE/WHL* BS5........... 25 F2
    KGWD/HNM BS15 .... 91 C4 ⑥
Sycamore Dr *BRSTK/PCHW* BS34...... 42 B4
Sydenham HI *RDLND/MONT* BS6....... 21 D1
Sydenham La *RDLND/MONT* BS6....... 21 D1
Sydenham Rd
    BRSG/KWL/STAPK BS4 .... 39 D3
    RDLND/MONT BS6........................ 21 D2
Sydenham Wy *KGWD/HNM* BS15...... 91 D4
Sydney Rw *CBRIS/FH* BS1 .... 27 E5
Sylvan Wy
    HNLZ/SM/SNYPK/WT BS9............ 76 A1
Sylvia Av *BMSTR* BS3 .... 38 A4
Symes Av *HGRV/WHIT* BS13 .... 105 D4
Symington Rd *MANG/FISH* BS16 ...... 79 C2
Syston Wy *KGWD/HNM* BS15 .... 86 A2

T

Tabernacle Rd *KGWD/HNM* BS15....... 91 D1
Tackley Rd *EVILLE/WHL* BS5 .... 15 E2 ⑥
Talbot Av *KGWD/HNM* BS15............... 85 C2
Talbot Rd *BRSG/KWL/STAPK* BS4 ..... 39 E5
Talgarth Rd *HORF/LLZ* BS7 .... 6 A5
Tallis Gv *BRSG/KWL/STAPK* BS4...... 106 A1
Tamar Dr *KEYN* BS31 .... 113 D3
Tamar Rd *CBRISNE* BS2 .... 32 A3
Tamworth Rd *KEYN* BS31 .... 112 B3 ⑥
Tankard's Cl *CFTN/FAIL* BS8 .... 20 B5
Tanner Cl *OLD/WMLY/WICK* BS30...... 93 C2
Tanorth Cl *HGRV/WHIT* BS14............ 107 D4
Tanorth Rd *HGRV/WHIT* BS14 ... 107 D4 ⑥
Tapsters *OLD/WMLY/WICK* BS30 .... 93 D3 ⑥
Tarnock Av *HGRV/WHIT* BS14 .... 97 D4
Tarragon Pl *ALMDB* BS32 .... 46 A4
Taunton Wk *HORF/LLZ* BS7 .... 67 D4 ⑥
Taverner Cl
    BRSG/KWL/STAPK BS4 .... 96 A4 ⑯
Tavistock Rd *BRSG/KWL/STAPK* BS4 .. 97 C2
Tavistock Wk
    BRSG/KWL/STAPK BS4 .... 97 C2
Taylor Cl *KGWD/HNM* BS15 .... 87 C3 ⑥
Taylor Gdns
    BMSTRD/HC/WWD BS13 .... 104 A3 ⑥
Tayman Cl *HNBRY/STHM* BS10 .... 5 E1
Teal Cl *ALMDB* BS32 .... 45 C1 ⑥
Teasel Md *ALMDB* BS32 .... 45 D4 ⑥
Teewell Av *MANG/FISH* BS16............. 80 B3
Teewell Cl *MANG/FISH* BS16 .... 80 B3 ⑥
Teewell HI *MANG/FISH* BS16 .... 80 B3
Teignmouth Rd
    BRSG/KWL/STAPK BS4 .... 97 D2 ⑨
Telephone Av *CBRIS/FH* BS1 .... 28 C2
Telford Wy *EVILLE/WHL* BS5 .... 84 B2
Temple Back *CBRIS/FH* BS1 .... 29 F2
Temple Ga *CBRIS/FH* BS1.................. 29 F4
Templeland Rd
    BMSTRD/HC/WWD BS13 .... 104 A2 ⑥
Temple Rose St *CBRIS/FH* BS1 .... 29 F3
Temple St *BMSTR* BS3 .... 95 C1 ⑯
    CBRIS/FH BS1................................ 29 F3
    KEYN BS31 .... 112 B2
Temple Wy *CBRIS/FH* BS1 .... 29 F3
Temple Way U/P *CBRISNE* BS2 ...... 30 A1 ⑨
Tenby Rd *KEYN* BS31 .... 112 A3
Tenby St *EVILLE/WHL* BS5 .... 23 E5
Tennessee Gv *RDLND/MONT* BS6........ 4 A4
Tenniscourt Rd *KGWD/HNM* BS15 .... 87 D2
Tennis Rd *BRSG/KWL/STAPK* BS4 ..... 38 C5
Tennyson Cl *KEYN* BS31 .... 113 C1
Tennyson Rd *HORF/LLZ* BS7 .... 5 F3
Tenth Av *HORF/LLZ* BS7 .... 68 A2
Tereslake Gn *HNBRY/STHM* BS10 ..... 50 A3
Terrell Gdns *EVILLE/WHL* BS5 .... 24 C5
Terrell St *CBRISNE* BS2 .... 20 C5
Tetbury Cl *BRSTK/PCHW* BS34 .... 44 B3
Tetbury Rd *KGWD/HNM* BS15............ 85 C3
Teviot Rd *KEYN* BS31 .... 113 D3
Tewkesbury Rd *CBRISNE* BS2 .... 15 D5
Tewther Rd
    BMSTRD/HC/WWD BS13 .... 105 D4
Teyfant Rd
    BMSTRD/HC/WWD BS13 .... 106 B4
Teyfant Wk
    BMSTRD/HC/WWD BS13 ..... 106 B3 ⑥
Thackeray Wk *HORF/LLZ* BS7 .... 67 D3 ⑥
Thanet Rd *BMSTR* BS3....................... 95 C1

Thatchers Cl *EVILLE/WHL* BS5 .... 85 C4 🔟

There-and-back-again La
  CFTN/FAIL BS8 .... 28 A1 🛛

Theresa Av *HORF/LLZ* BS7 .... 13 F1

Thicket Av *MANG/FISH* BS16 .... 79 D4

Thicket Rd *MANG/FISH* BS16 .... 79 D3

Thiery Rd *BRSG/KWL/STAPK* BS4 ..... 40 B5

Thingwall Pk *MANG/FISH* BS16 .... 17 E2

Third Av *HORF/LLZ* BS7 .... 67 D2

Third Wy *AVONM* BS11 .... 59 D1

Thirlmere Rd *BRSTK/PCHW* BS34 .... 43 E5 🛛

Thistle St *BMSTR* BS3 .... 35 E3 🛽

Thomas Pring Wk
  EVILLE/WHL BS5 .... 84 B2 🛛

Thomas St *CBRIS/FH* BS1 .... 21 E3
  CBRISNE BS2 .... 22 B2
  EVILLE/WHL BS5 .... 23 F5 🛛

Thomas St North *CBRISNE* BS2 ...... 21 D2 🛛

Thompson Rd *HGRV/WHIT* BS14 .... 109 D1 🛛

Thomson Rd *EVILLE/WHL* BS5 .... 23 E3

Thorndale *CFTN/FAIL* BS8 .... 19 D3 🛛

The Thornhills *MANG/FISH* BS16 .... 79 C1

Thornleigh Rd *HORF/LLZ* BS7 .... 5 E4

Thornmead Gv
  HNBRY/STHM BS10 .... 64 B1 🛽

Thornycroft Cl *HORF/LLZ* BS7 .... 68 A4

Three Queens' La *CBRIS/FH* BS1 ..... 29 E3

Three Wells Rd
  BMSTRD/HC/WWD BS13 .... 104 A3

Thrissell St *EVILLE/WHL* BS5 .... 22 C4

Throgmorton Rd
  BRSG/KWL/STAPK BS4 .... 97 C4

Thurlestone Rd *HGRV/WHIT* BS14 . 107 C2

Thurlow Rd *EVILLE/WHL* BS5 .... 16 B5

Thurston's Barton
  EVILLE/WHL BS5 .... 25 D2 🛛

Tibberton Rd *MANG/FISH* BS15 ...... 87 D3

Tibbott Rd *HGRV/WHIT* BS14 .... 108 B3

Tibbott Wk *HGRV/WHIT* BS14 .... 108 B2

Tichborne Rd *EVILLE/WHL* BS5 .... 32 A1

Tide Gv *AVONM* BS11 .... 37 C4

Tidenham Wy *BRSTK/PCHW* BS34 ... 43 C2

Tilling Rd *HNBRY/STHM* BS10 .... 66 B4

Tilling Wk *HNBRY/STHM* BS10 .... 66 B4

Timber Dene *MANG/FISH* BS16 .... 9 D5

Timberscombe Wk
  HGRV/WHIT BS14 .... 108 B2 🛛

Tindell Ct *OLD/WMLY/WICK* BS30 .. 93 C3 🛛🛛

Tintern Av *EVILLE/WHL* BS5 .... 24 C4

Tintern Cl *OLD/WMLY/WICK* BS30 .. 93 C1 🛽

Tippetts Rd *KGWD/HNM* BS15 .... 92 A3

Tiverton Wk *MANG/FISH* BS16 .... 84 D1

Tormarton Crs *HNBRY/STHM* BS10 .. 48 A3

Toronto Rd *HORF/LLZ* BS7 .... 67 D3

Torpoint Rd *BMSTR* BS3 .... 96 A1

Torridge Rd *KEYN* BS31 .... 113 D3

Torrington Av
  BRSG/KWL/STAPK BS4 .... 97 C3

Tortworth Rd *HORF/LLZ* BS7 .... 5 F3

Totshill Dr *BMSTRD/HC/WWD* BS13 106 B3

Totshill Gv
  BMSTRD/HC/WWD BS13 .... 106 B3 🛛

Touchstone Av *BRSTK/PCHW* BS34 .. 53 D2

Tower Hl *CBRISNE* BS2 .... 29 F2

Tower La *CBRIS/FH* BS1 .... 29 D1
  OLD/WMLY/WICK BS30 .... 93 D1

Tower Rd *KGWD/HNM* BS15 .... 85 D2

Tower St *CBRIS/FH* BS1 .... 29 F3

Townsend Cl *HGRV/WHIT* BS14 .... 110 A2

Townsend Rd *HGRV/WHIT* BS14 ... 110 A2

Tozers Hl *BRSG/KWL/STAPK* BS4 .... 98 B1 🛛

Trafalgar Ter *BMSTR* BS3 .... 95 C1 🛛🛛

Tralee Wk *BRSG/KWL/STAPK* BS4 ...... 96 A2

Tramway Rd
  BRSG/KWL/STAPK BS4 .... 40 B4 🛛

Tranmere Av *HNBRY/STHM* BS10 ..... 48 B3

Tranmere Gv *HNBRY/STHM* BS10 .... 48 B4

Tratman Wk *HNBRY/STHM* BS10 .... 48 A4 🛛

Travers Cl *BRSG/KWL/STAPK* BS4 .. 106 A1 🛛

Travers Wk *BRSTK/PCHW* BS34 .... 53 D2

Tredegar Rd *MANG/FISH* BS16 .... 79 C4

Treefield Pl *CBRISNE* BS2 .... 15 D4 🛛

Tregarth Rd *BMSTR* BS3 .... 94 A2

Trelawney Av *EVILLE/WHL* BS5 .... 24 C2 🛛

Trelawney Pk
  BRSG/KWL/STAPK BS4 .... 41 D4

Trelawney Rd *RDLND/MONT* BS6 .... 20 A2

Trenchard St *CBRIS/FH* BS1 .... 28 B2

Trench La *FRCTL/WBN* BS36 .... 46 A1

Trendlewood Pk *MANG/FISH* BS16 ... 9 E5

Trent Gv *KEYN* BS31 .... 113 D3

Trentham Cl *CBRISNE* BS2 .... 14 C4 🛛

Tresham Cl *ALMDB* BS32 .... 45 C1

Trevanna Rd *BMSTR* BS3 .... 94 A2

Trevelyan Wk *HNBRY/STHM* BS10 .. 48 A4 🛛

Trevethin Cl *KGWD/HNM* BS15 .... 85 D4 🛛

Trevisa Gv *HNBRY/STHM* BS10 .... 49 D3

Triangle South *CFTN/FAIL* BS8 .... 27 F1

Triangle West *CFTN/FAIL* BS8 .... 27 F1

Trident Cl *MANG/FISH* BS16 .... 73 D2

Trinity Rd *CBRISNE* BS2 .... 22 C5

Trinity St *CBRISNE* BS2 .... 22 C5

Trinity Wk *CBRISNE* BS2 .... 22 B5

Troopers' Hill Rd *EVILLE/WHL* BS5 .. 90 A1

Trowbridge Rd *HNBRY/STHM* BS10 .. 65 D2

Trowbridge Wk
  HNBRY/STHM BS10 .... 65 D2 🛛

Truro Rd *BMSTR* BS3 .... 35 E3

Trym Cross Rd
  HNLZ/SM/SNYPK/WT BS9 .... 76 B2

Trymleaze
  HNLZ/SM/SNYPK/WT BS9 .... 76 B2 🛛

Trym Rd *HNLZ/SM/SNYPK/WT* BS9 .. 64 B4

Trym Side *HNLZ/SM/SNYPK/WT* BS9 76 B2

Trymwood Cl *HNBRY/STHM* BS10 ... 64 A1

Tucker St *CBRISNE* BS2 .... 22 A4

Tuckett La *MANG/FISH* BS16 .... 71 D4 🛛

Tudor Rd *CBRISNE* BS2 .... 22 B2
  EVILLE/WHL BS5 .... 24 A1
  KGWD/HNM BS15 .... 91 D2

Tuffley Rd *HNBRY/STHM* BS10 .... 65 D3

Tufton Av *AVONM* BS11 .... 61 D3

Tugela Rd *BMSTRD/HC/WWD* BS13 .. 94 A4

Tunstall Cl *HNLZ/SM/SNYPK/WT* BS9 .. 77 D3

Turley Rd *EVILLE/WHL* BS5 .... 24 C1

Turnbridge Rd *HNBRY/STHM* BS10 .. 49 D3

Turner Cl *KEYN* BS31 .... 113 D3

Turner Gdns *HORF/LLZ* BS7 .... 7 E1

Turners Ct
  OLD/WMLY/WICK BS30 .... 93 C3 🛛🛛

Turville Dr *HORF/LLZ* BS7 .... 6 C1

Twenty Acres Rd
  HNBRY/STHM BS10 .... 65 D1 🛛

Twickenham Rd
  RDLND/MONT BS6 .... 4 B3 🛛

Two Acres Rd *HGRV/WHIT* BS14 ..... 97 D4

Two Mile Ct *KGWD/HNM* BS15 ...... 85 C3 🛛

Twomile Hill Rd *KGWD/HNM* BS15 .. 85 C3

The Twynings *KGWD/HNM* BS15 ..... 86 B1

Tybalt Wy *BRSTK/PCHW* BS34 .... 53 D2

Tyler Cl *KGWD/HNM* BS15 .... 92 B1

Tyler's La *MANG/FISH* BS16 .... 80 A2 🛛

Tyler St *CBRISNE* BS2 .... 30 C3

Tyndale Av *MANG/FISH* BS16 .... 78 B3

Tyndale Rd *KGWD/HNM* BS15 .... 86 B1 🔟
Tyndall Av *CFTN/FAIL* BS8 .... 20 A5
Tyndall Rd *EVILLE/WHL* BS5 .... 23 F4
Tyndalls Park Ms *CFTN/FAIL* BS8 ..... 20 A4
Tyndall's Park Rd *CFTN/FAIL* BS8 ...... 19 F4
Tyndalls Wy *HNBRY/STHM* BS10 ...... 66 B3
Tyne Rd *HORF/LLZ* BS7 .... 13 D3
Tyne St *CBRISNE* BS2 .... 14 C5
Tyning Cl *HGRV/WHIT* BS14 .... 97 D4
Tyning Rd *BMSTR* BS3 .... 38 A4
Tynte Av *BMSTRD/HC/WWD* BS13 .. 106 A4
Tyntesfield Rd
  BMSTRD/HC/WWD BS13................ 94 B4
Tyrone Wk *BRSG/KWL/STAPK* BS4 .. 96 B3 🔟
Tyrrel Wy *BRSTK/PCHW* BS34 .... 53 D1

U

Ullswater Rd *HNBRY/STHM* BS10.... 65 C2
Underbanks *PTSHD/EG* BS20 .... 74 A3
Union Rd *CBRISNE* BS2 .... 30 C1
Union St *CBRIS/FH* BS1 .... 21 D5
Unity Rd *KEYN* BS31 .... 113 D2
Unity St *CBRIS/FH* BS1 .... 28 B2 🔟
  CBRISNE BS2 .... 30 A1
  KGWD/HNM BS15 .... 85 D3
University Rd *CFTN/FAIL* BS8 .... 27 F1
University Wk *CFTN/FAIL* BS8 .... 20 A5
Uphill Rd *HORF/LLZ* BS7 .... 6 A4
Upjohn Crs
  BMSTRD/HC/WWD BS13 .... 106 A4
Uplands Rd *MANG/FISH* BS16 .... 79 D4
Upper Belgrave Rd
  CFTN/FAIL BS8 .... 11 D4 🔟
Upper Belmont Rd
  RDLND/MONT BS6 .... 13 E2
Upper Byron Pl *CFTN/FAIL* BS8 ...... 27 F1
Upper Cheltenham Pl
  RDLND/MONT BS6 .... 21 F1
Upper Cranbrook Rd
  RDLND/MONT BS6..................... 3 F5
Upper Maudlin St *CBRISNE* BS2 .... 20 C5
Upper Perry Hl *BMSTR* BS3 .... 36 A1
Upper Sandhurst Rd
  BRSG/KWL/STAPK BS4 .... 40 C2
Upper Station Rd *MANG/FISH* BS16 .. 79 D3
Upper St *BRSG/KWL/STAPK* BS4 ...... 39 D2
Upper Sydney St *BMSTR* BS3 .... 35 E3
Upper Wells St *CBRIS/FH* BS1 ...... 28 B2 🔟
Upper York St *CBRISNE* BS2 .... 21 E3
Upton Rd *BMSTR* BS3 .... 35 E1
Urfords Dr *MANG/FISH* BS16 ...... 79 D1 🔟

V

Vale La *BMSTRD/HC/WWD* BS13 .... 95 D3
Valentine Cl *HGRV/WHIT* BS14 ...... 108 A3 🔟
Valerian Cl *AVONM* BS11 .... 75 C1
Vale St *BRSG/KWL/STAPK* BS4.......... 39 D3
Valley Gdns *MANG/FISH* BS16.......... 73 C3
Valley Rd *BMSTRD/HC/WWD* BS13 .... 94 B3
  CFTN/FAIL BS8 .... 82 B4
  MANG/FISH BS16 .... 81 D2
The Valls *ALMDB* BS32 .... 54 A1
Valma Rocks *EVILLE/WHL* BS5 .... 90 B1 🔟
Vandyck Av *KEYN* BS31 .... 113 E5
Vassall Ct *MANG/FISH* BS16.......... 79 C2
Vassall Rd *MANG/FISH* BS16 .... 79 C2

Vaughan Cl *HNBRY/STHM* BS10 ...... 48 A4
Ventnor Rd *BRSTK/PCHW* BS34 ...... 52 A4
  EVILLE/WHL BS5 .... 84 A2
Vera Rd *MANG/FISH* BS16 .... 84 A1
Vernon St *BRSG/KWL/STAPK* BS4 .... 38 B1 🔟
Verrier Rd *EVILLE/WHL* BS5.............. 24 B5
Vicarage Ct *KGWD/HNM* BS15 ...... 91 C2 🔟
Vicarage Rd *BMSTR* BS3 .... 35 F2
  BMSTRD/HC/WWD BS13............. 104 A1
  CFTN/FAIL BS8 .... 89 C1
  EVILLE/WHL BS5 .... 24 A3
  KGWD/HNM BS15 .... 91 C2
Vicars Cl *MANG/FISH* BS16 .... 79 C3 🔟
Victoria Av *EVILLE/WHL* BS5 .... 24 A5
Victoria Gdns *RDLND/MONT* BS6...... 20 C2
Victoria Gv *BMSTR* BS3 .... 37 E1
Victoria Pde *EVILLE/WHL* BS5.......... 24 B4
Victoria Pk *KGWD/HNM* BS15 ...... 86 A3
  MANG/FISH BS16 .... 78 B2
Victoria Pl *BMSTR* BS3 .... 36 A2
Victoria Rd *AVONM* BS11 .... 59 C3
  CBRISNE BS2 .... 30 C5
  KGWD/HNM BS15 .... 91 C2
Victoria Sq *CFTN/FAIL* BS8............ 26 C1
Victoria St *CBRIS/FH* BS1 .... 29 E2
  MANG/FISH BS16 .... 80 A3
Victoria Ter *CBRISNE* BS2 .... 31 D4
  CFTN/FAIL BS8 .... 26 B3
Victoria Wk *RDLND/MONT* BS6 ...... 21 C2
Victor Rd *BMSTR* BS3 .... 36 A4
Victor St *CBRISNE* BS2 .... 38 B1
  EVILLE/WHL BS5 .... 31 F2
Vigor Rd
  BMSTRD/HC/WWD BS13 .... 105 C2 🔟
Villiers Rd *EVILLE/WHL* BS5 .... 23 E2
Vimpany Cl *HNBRY/STHM* BS10 ...... 48 A4
Vincent Cl *AVONM* BS11 .... 62 B1
Vining Wk *EVILLE/WHL* BS5.............. 23 E5
Vinny Av *MANG/FISH* BS16 .... 73 D4
Vintery Leys
  HNLZ/SM/SNYPK/WT BS9.......... 65 C4
Vivian St *BMSTR* BS3 .... 37 D3
Vowell Cl *BMSTRD/HC/WWD* BS13.. 105 C3
Vyvyan Rd *CFTN/FAIL* BS8 .... 18 C5
Vyvyan Ter *CFTN/FAIL* BS8 .... 18 C5

W

Wades Rd *BRSTK/PCHW* BS34 ...... 52 A4
Wade St *CBRISNE* BS2 .... 22 A4
Wadham Dr *MANG/FISH* BS16 ...... 71 C2
Wainbrook Dr *EVILLE/WHL* BS5 ...... 17 D4
Wakeford Rd *MANG/FISH* BS16 ...... 73 D4 🔟
Walden Rd *KEYN* BS31 .... 113 D3
Walker Cl *EVILLE/WHL* BS5 .... 23 E5
  MANG/FISH BS16 .... 73 D4
Walker St *CBRISNE* BS2 .... 20 B4
Wallingford Rd
  BRSG/KWL/STAPK BS4 .... 96 A4
Walliscote Av
  HNLZ/SM/SNYPK/WT BS9.............. 4 A2
Walliscote Rd
  HNLZ/SM/SNYPK/WT BS9.............. 4 A2
Wallscourt Rd *BRSTK/PCHW* BS34 ...... 68 A1
Wallscourt Rd South
  BRSTK/PCHW BS34 .... 68 A2
Walnut Cl *KEYN* BS31 .... 111 D3
Walnut Crs *KGWD/HNM* BS15 ...... 87 C3
Walnut La *KGWD/HNM* BS15 .... 87 D3 🔟

Walnut Wk
  BMSTRD/HC/WWD BS13 .... **104** B1
Walsh Av *HGRV/WHIT* BS14 .... **97** D4
Walsingham Rd *RDLND/MONT* BS6 ..... **13** F4
Walter St *BMSTR* BS3 .... **35** D1
Walton Av *BRSG/KWL/STAPK* BS4 ...... **33** D5
Walton CI *KEYN* BS31 .... **112** A3
Walton Ri *HNLZ/SM/SNYPK/WT* BS9 .. **64** B3
Walton Rd *AVONM* BS11 .... **74** A1
Walton St *EVILLE/WHL* BS5 .... **23** E2
Wansbeck Rd *KEYN* BS31 .... **113** D3
Wanscow Wk
  HNLZ/SM/SNYPK/WT BS9................ **3** F2
Wapping Rd *CBRIS/FH* BS1 .... **28** C4
Warden Rd *BMSTR* BS3 .... **36** B2
Wardour Rd *BRSG/KWL/STAPK* BS4 .... **96** A3
Warman CI *HGRV/WHIT* BS14 .... **110** A1
Warman Rd *HGRV/WHIT* BS14 .... **110** A1
Warmington Rd *HGRV/WHIT* BS14 .... **98** B3
Warminster Rd *CBRISNE* BS2 .... **15** D5
Warner CI *KGWD/HNM* BS15 .... **93** C1
The Warns *OLD/WMLY/WICK* BS30 ... **93** D1
Warren Gdns *HGRV/WHIT* BS14 .... **110** A2
Warren Rd *BRSTK/PCHW* BS34 .... **52** A4
Warrington Rd
  BRSG/KWL/STAPK BS4 .... **99** C1
Warwick Av *EVILLE/WHL* BS5 .... **23** E1
Warwick Rd *EVILLE/WHL* BS5 .... **23** E1
  KEYN BS31 .... **112** A3
  RDLND/MONT BS6 .... **19** F2
Washing Pound La
  HGRV/WHIT BS14 .... **108** A3
Washington Av *EVILLE/WHL* BS5 .... **24** A1
Watch Elm CI *ALMDB* BS32 .... **53** D1
Watchhouse Rd *PTSHD/EG* BS20 .... **74** A3
Watchill Av
  BMSTRD/HC/WWD BS13.................. **104** A1
Watchill CI
  BMSTRD/HC/WWD BS13.................. **104** A1
Waterbridge Rd
  BMSTRD/HC/WWD BS13.................. **104** A2
Watercress Rd *CBRISNE* BS2 .... **14** B3
Waterdale CI *HNBRY/STHM* BS10........ **65** D4
Waterdale Gdns
  HNLZ/SM/SNYPK/WT BS9................ **65** D4
Waterford Rd
  HNLZ/SM/SNYPK/WT BS9................ **3** E2
Water La *BMSTR* BS3 .... **38** A3
  BRSG/KWL/STAPK BS4 .... **99** C2
  CBRIS/FH BS1 .... **29** F2
  KGWD/HNM BS15 .... **101** C1
Waterloo Pl *CBRISNE* BS2 .... **30** B1
Waterloo Rd *CBRISNE* BS2 .... **30** B1
Waterloo St *CBRISNE* BS2 .... **22** B5
  CFTN/FAIL BS8 .... **26** B1
Waterside Dr *ALMDB* BS32 .... **43** D2
Water's La
  HNLZ/SM/SNYPK/WT BS9................ **64** B4
Waters Rd *KGWD/HNM* BS15 .... **85** D3
Wathen Rd *RDLND/MONT* BS6 .... **14** B3
Watkins Yd
  HNLZ/SM/SNYPK/WT BS9................ **64** B3
Watling Wy *AVONM* BS11 .... **60** A4
Watson Av *BRSG/KWL/STAPK* BS4 ...... **41** D2
Watson's Rd *OLD/WMLY/WICK* BS30 ... **93** C4
Waveney Rd *KEYN* BS31 .... **113** D4
Waverley Rd *AVONM* BS11 .... **74** A1
  RDLND/MONT BS6............................ **20** A1
Waverley St *EVILLE/WHL* BS5 .... **23** D1
Wayford CI *KEYN* BS31 .... **113** D4
Webb St *EVILLE/WHL* BS5 .... **22** C3
Webbs Wood Rd *ALMDB* BS32 .... **46** A4

Wedgewood Rd *MANG/FISH* BS16...... **72** A2
Wedgwood CI *HGRV/WHIT* BS14 .... **108** A2
Wedmore CI *KGWD/HNM* BS15.......... **87** C4
Wedmore V *BMSTR* BS3 .... **37** E5
Weedon CI *CBRISNE* BS2 .... **14** C4
Weight Rd *EVILLE/WHL* BS5 .... **24** B5
Welland Rd *KEYN* BS31 .... **113** C3
Wellgarth Rd *BRSG/KWL/STAPK* BS4 .. **97** D1
Wellgarth Wk
  BRSG/KWL/STAPK BS4 .... **97** D2
Well House CI
  HNLZ/SM/SNYPK/WT BS9................ **83** D1
Wellington Av *RDLND/MONT* BS6 .... **21** F1
Wellington Crs *HORF/LLZ* BS7 .... **5** F2
Wellington Dr
  HNLZ/SM/SNYPK/WT BS9................ **4** C1
Wellington HI *HORF/LLZ* BS7 .... **5** E2
Wellington HI West
  HNLZ/SM/SNYPK/WT BS9................ **65** D4
Wellington La *RDLND/MONT* BS6 .... **21** E2
Wellington Ms *AVONM* BS11 .... **74** A3
Wellington Pk *CFTN/FAIL* BS8............ **19** E1
Wellington Rd *CBRISNE* BS2 .... **21** F5
  KGWD/HNM BS15 .... **86** A1
Wellington Wk *HNBRY/STHM* BS10..... **65** D4
Wells CI *HGRV/WHIT* BS14 .... **108** B1
Wells Rd *BRSG/KWL/STAPK* BS4 .... **38** B1
  HGRV/WHIT BS14............................ **98** A3
Wells St *BMSTR* BS3 .... **34** C2
Wellsway *KEYN* BS31 .... **113** C3
Welsford Av *MANG/FISH* BS16 .... **16** C1
Welsford Rd *MANG/FISH* BS16 .... **16** B1
Welsh Back *CBRIS/FH* BS1 .... **29** D4
Welton Wk *KGWD/HNM* BS15 .... **85** D1
Wenmore CI *MANG/FISH* BS16 .... **72** A2
Wentforth Dr *KGWD/HNM* BS15 .... **85** D1
Wentworth
  OLD/WMLY/WICK BS30 .... **93** D1
Wentworth Rd *HORF/LLZ* BS7 .... **13** D2
Wesley Av *KGWD/HNM* BS15 .... **92** A2
Wesley CI *MANG/FISH* BS16 .... **80** A4
Wesley HI *KGWD/HNM* BS15 .... **86** A2
Wesley Pl *CFTN/FAIL* BS8 .... **11** D4
Wesley Rd *HORF/LLZ* BS7 .... **13** E1
Wesley St *BMSTR* BS3 .... **36** B3
Wessex Av *HORF/LLZ* BS7 .... **67** C4
Westacre CI *HNBRY/STHM* BS10 .... **64** B1
Westbourne Av *KEYN* BS31 .... **112** B2
Westbourne CI *MANG/FISH* BS16 .... **73** C4
Westbourne Gv *BMSTR* BS3 .... **36** A3
Westbourne Pl *CFTN/FAIL* BS8 .... **19** E4
Westbourne Rd *EVILLE/WHL* BS5......... **23** F3
  MANG/FISH BS16 .... **73** C3
West Broadway
  HNLZ/SM/SNYPK/WT BS9................ **4** C1
Westbrook Rd
  BRSG/KWL/STAPK BS4 .... **99** C3
Westbury Court Rd
  HNLZ/SM/SNYPK/WT BS9................ **64** A4
Westbury HI
  HNLZ/SM/SNYPK/WT BS9................ **64** B4
Westbury La
  HNLZ/SM/SNYPK/WT BS9................ **62** A4
Westbury Pk *RDLND/MONT* BS6 .... **11** D1
Westbury Rd
  HNLZ/SM/SNYPK/WT BS9................ **3** D1
  HNLZ/SM/SNYPK/WT BS9................ **11** D2
West Coombe
  HNLZ/SM/SNYPK/WT BS9................ **77** C1
West Cft *HNLZ/SM/SNYPK/WT* BS9 ... **65** D4
West Dene
  HNLZ/SM/SNYPK/WT BS9................ **77** D1

West End *BMSTR* BS3 .... **36** B1
  CBRISNE BS2 .... **20** C4
Westering CI *MANG/FISH* BS16 ...... **81** D2 🔲
Westerleigh CI *MANG/FISH* BS16 ...... **73** C4 🔲
Westerleigh Rd *MANG/FISH* BS16 .... **80** B1 🔲
Western Dr *HGRV/WHIT* BS14.......... **96** B4
Western Rd *HORF/LLZ* BS7 .... **5** F1
Westfield CI *KEYN* BS31 .... **111** D2
  KGWD/HNM BS15 .... **92** A2
Westfield La *BRSTK/PCHW* BS34 ...... **53** D4
Westfield Pk *RDLND/MONT* BS6 ...... **11** E5
Westfield PI *CFTN/FAIL* BS8............. **26** A1
Westfield Rd
  HNLZ/SM/SNYPK/WT BS9............ **64** B3
Westfield Wy *ALMDB* BS32............... **45** C1
West Gv *RDLND/MONT* BS6............. **22** A1
West Leaze PI *ALMDB* BS32 .... **53** D1
Westleigh CI *HNBRY/STHM* BS10 .... **66** A2 🔲
Westleigh Pk *HGRV/WHIT* BS14........ **97** D3
Westleigh Rd *HNBRY/STHM* BS10 .... **65** D2
West MI *CFTN/FAIL* BS8 .... **26** B1
Westmead Rd *EVILLE/WHL* BS5 .... **85** C4
Westminster CI
  HNLZ/SM/SNYPK/WT BS9............ **64** B4 🔲
Westminster Rd *EVILLE/WHL* BS5 ...... **24** C3
Westmoreland Rd
  RDLND/MONT BS6 .... **11** D3
Weston Av *EVILLE/WHL* BS5 .... **25** D5
Weston CI *HNLZ/SM/SNYPK/WT* BS9.. **62** B4
Weston Crs *HORF/LLZ* BS7 .... **5** F1
Westons Brake *MANG/FISH* BS16 ...... **73** D2
Westons Hill Dr *MANG/FISH* BS16 .... **73** D3
Westons Wy *KGWD/HNM* BS15 .... **87** C4
Westover CI
  HNLZ/SM/SNYPK/WT BS9............ **64** A2
Westover Dr
  HNLZ/SM/SNYPK/WT BS9............ **64** B3
Westover Gdns
  HNLZ/SM/SNYPK/WT BS9............ **64** A3 🔳
Westover Ri
  HNLZ/SM/SNYPK/WT BS9............ **64** B2
Westover Rd
  HNLZ/SM/SNYPK/WT BS9............ **64** B3
West Pde *HNLZ/SM/SNYPK/WT* BS9 .. **62** B4
West Pk *CFTN/FAIL* BS8 .... **19** F3
West Park Rd *MANG/FISH* BS16 .... **80** D2
West Priory CI
  HNLZ/SM/SNYPK/WT BS9............ **64** B4 🔳
West Rocke Av
  HNLZ/SM/SNYPK/WT BS9............ **63** C4
West Shrubbery *RDLND/MONT* BS6 .. **11** E4
West St *BMSTR* BS3 .... **36** A4
  CBRISNE BS2 .... **30** B1
  KGWD/HNM BS15 .... **86** A3 🔳
West Town Dr
  BRSG/KWL/STAPK BS4 .... **99** C2 🔳
West Town Gv
  BRSG/KWL/STAPK BS4 .... **99** C3
West Town La
  BRSG/KWL/STAPK BS4 .... **99** C2
  HGRV/WHIT BS14.......................... **98** A3
West Town Pk
  BRSG/KWL/STAPK BS4 .... **99** C2
West Town Rd *AVONM* BS11 .... **59** D4 🔳
West View Rd *BMSTR* BS3................. **35** E4
  KEYN BS31 .... **112** B3
Westward Rd
  BMSTRD/HC/WWD BS13................ **94** A4
Westwood Crs
  BRSG/KWL/STAPK BS4 .... **33** D4
Westwood Rd
  BRSG/KWL/STAPK BS4 .... **99** C3

Wetherby Ct *FRCTL/WBN* BS36 .... **73** C2 🔳
Wetherell PI *CFTN/FAIL* BS8 .... **27** E1
Wexford Rd *BRSG/KWL/STAPK* BS4 .... **96** A3
Weymouth Rd *BMSTR* BS3 .... **37** D5
Wharf Rd *MANG/FISH* BS16 .... **78** A3 🔳
Wharnecliffe CI
  HGRV/WHIT BS14.......................... **108** A2 🔳
Wharnecliffe Gdns
  HGRV/WHIT BS14.......................... **108** A2
Whatley Rd *CFTN/FAIL* BS8 .... **19** E2
Wheatfield Dr *ALMDB* BS32 .... **45** C2
Wheathill CI *KEYN* BS31 .... **111** D2
Whinchat Gdns *MANG/FISH* BS16 .. **78** A1 🔳
Whippington Ct *CBRIS/FH* BS1 .... **21** E5 🔳
Whitby Rd *BRSG/KWL/STAPK* BS4 ...... **32** B5
Whitchurch La
  BMSTRD/HC/WWD BS13................ **104** B2
  HGRV/WHIT BS14.......................... **106** B2
Whitecross Av *HGRV/WHIT* BS14 .... **108** B1 🔳
Whitefield Av *EVILLE/WHL* BS5 .... **84** B2
  KGWD/HNM BS15 .... **92** A2 🔳
Whitefield Rd *EVILLE/WHL* BS5 .... **84** B1
Whitehall Av *EVILLE/WHL* BS5 .... **25** F2
Whitehall Gdns *EVILLE/WHL* BS5 .... **24** C3 🔳
Whitehall Rd *EVILLE/WHL* BS5 .... **23** F4
Whitehouse La *BMSTR* BS3............... **37** D2
Whitehouse PI *BMSTR* BS3 .... **37** E1
Whitehouse St *BMSTR* BS3 .... **37** E2
Whiteladies Rd *CFTN/FAIL* BS8 .... **11** D5
  CFTN/FAIL BS8 .... **19** F5
Whiteleaze *HNBRY/STHM* BS10 ...... **65** D4 🔳
White Lodge Rd *MANG/FISH* BS16.... **81** C3
Whites HI *EVILLE/WHL* BS5 .... **90** B1
Whiteshill *MANG/FISH* BS16 .... **56** A4
White St *EVILLE/WHL* BS5 .... **22** B4
White Tree Rd
  HNLZ/SM/SNYPK/WT BS9............ **3** E5
Whiteway CI
  BRSG/KWL/STAPK BS4 .... **33** F2 🔳
  EVILLE/WHL BS5 .... **84** B3
Whiteway Ms *EVILLE/WHL* BS5 .... **84** B3
Whiteway Rd *EVILLE/WHL* BS5.......... **84** B2
Whitewood Rd *EVILLE/WHL* BS5 ...... **84** B2
Whitfield CI *KGWD/HNM* BS15 .... **86** A1 🔳
Whiting Rd
  BMSTRD/HC/WWD BS13................ **104** B2
Whitland Av
  BMSTRD/HC/WWD BS13................ **105** C2 🔳
Whitland Rd
  BMSTRD/HC/WWD BS13................ **105** C2
Whitley Md *BRSTK/PCHW* BS34 .... **53** D4
Whitmead Gdns
  BMSTRD/HC/WWD BS13................ **105** D3 🔳
Whitmore Av *BRSG/KWL/STAPK* BS4 .. **90** B4
Whitson St *CBRIS/FH* BS1 .... **21** D4
Whittington Rd *MANG/FISH* BS16 .... **79** D1
Whittock Rd *HGRV/WHIT* BS14........ **109** C2
Whittock Sq *HGRV/WHIT* BS14 .... **99** C4
Whittucks Rd *KGWD/HNM* BS15 ...... **92** A2 🔳
Whitwell Rd *HGRV/WHIT* BS14 .... **98** A3
Whytes CI *HNLZ/SM/SNYPK/WT* BS9.. **64** B3
Wick Crs *BRSG/KWL/STAPK* BS4 ...... **41** D3
The Wickets *HORF/LLZ* BS7............. **67** C2
  KGWD/HNM BS15 .... **86** A1 🔳
Wickham Gln *MANG/FISH* BS16 ...... **8** C4
Wickham HI *MANG/FISH* BS16 .... **9** D4
Wickham Vw *MANG/FISH* BS16 .... **9** D5
Wicklow Rd *BRSG/KWL/STAPK* BS4 .... **96** B3
Wick Rd *BRSG/KWL/STAPK* BS4 ...... **40** C5
Widcombe *HGRV/WHIT* BS14 .... **107** D2
Widcombe CI *EVILLE/WHL* BS5 .... **84** B4 🔳
Wigton Crs *HNBRY/STHM* BS10 .... **65** D1

Wilbye Gv *BRSG/KWL/STAPK* BS4 .. **106** A1 ⬚

Wilcox Cl *KGWD/HNM* BS15 .... **85** D4

Wildcroft Rd
HNLZ/SM/SNYPK/WT BS9............. **3** E4

Wilder St *CBRISNE* BS2.................... **21** E3

Willada Cl *BMSTR* BS3 .... **95** C1

William Mason Cl
EVILLE/WHL BS5 .... **31** E1 ⬚

Williams Cl *OLD/WMLY/WICK* BS30 .. **103** C1

Williamson Rd *HORF/LLZ* BS7 .... **14** A3

William St *BMSTR* BS3 .... **37** E1
CBRISNE BS2 .... **22** A2
CBRISNE BS2 .... **30** C2
EVILLE/WHL BS5 .... **24** B4
MANG/FISH BS16 .... **79** C4 ⬚

Willinton Rd *BRSG/KWL/STAPK* BS4.... **97** C4

Willis Rd *KGWD/HNM* BS15 .... **87** C1

Willmott Cl *HGRV/WHIT* BS14 ...... **107** C4 ⬚

Willoughby Cl
BMSTRD/HC/WWD BS13............... **94** B4

Willoughby Rd *HORF/LLZ* BS7 .... **5** E4

Willow Bed Cl *MANG/FISH* BS16 ..... **79** C1

Willow Cl *BRSTK/PCHW* BS34 .... **42** B4

Willow Gv *MANG/FISH* BS16 .... **85** D1 ⬚

Willow Rd *KGWD/HNM* BS15 .... **91** D4 ⬚

The Willows *ALMDB* BS32 .... **45** C3

Willow Wk *HNBRY/STHM* BS10....... **49** C4
KEYN BS31 .... **112** A3

Willsbridge Hl
OLD/WMLY/WICK BS30 .... **103** D1

Wills Dr *EVILLE/WHL* BS5 .... **23** D3

Willway St *BMSTR* BS3.................... **37** E2
CBRISNE BS2 .... **30** B1

Wilmot Ct *OLD/WMLY/WICK* BS30 .. **93** D1 ⬚

Wilmots Wy *PTSHD/EG* BS20 .... **74** A3 ⬚

Wilshire Av *KGWD/HNM* BS15......... **92** A2

Wilson Pl *CBRISNE* BS2 .... **22** A3

Wilson St *CBRISNE* BS2 .... **21** F4

Wilton Cl *HNBRY/STHM* BS10 .... **65** D3

Wiltshire Pl *KGWD/HNM* BS15 ...... **80** B4 ⬚

Wimbledon Rd *RDLND/MONT* BS6..... **4** B3

Wimborne Rd *BMSTR* BS3 .... **95** D2 ⬚

Winash Cl *HGRV/WHIT* BS14 .... **99** C4

Wincanton Cl *FRCTL/WBN* BS36 ...... **73** C2 ⬚

Winchester Av
BRSG/KWL/STAPK BS4 .... **40** C4

Winchester Rd
BRSG/KWL/STAPK BS4 .... **40** C4

Windcliff Crs *AVONM* BS11 .... **60** B3

Windermere Rd *BRSTK/PCHW* BS34 .. **43** D3

Windmill Cl *BMSTR* BS3 .... **37** E2

Windmill Hl *BMSTR* BS3 .... **37** D3

Windrush Rd *KEYN* BS31 .... **113** D3

Windsor Av *EVILLE/WHL* BS5 .... **91** C1
KEYN BS31 .... **112** B3 ⬚

Windsor Cl *BRSTK/PCHW* BS34 .... **53** D3 ⬚

Windsor Ct *MANG/FISH* BS16 .... **72** B4

Windsor Gv *EVILLE/WHL* BS5 .... **23** F4 ⬚

Windsor Pl *MANG/FISH* BS16 .... **81** D2

Windsor Rd
OLD/WMLY/WICK BS30 .... **103** C1 ⬚
RDLND/MONT BS6........................ **13** E4

Windsor Ter *BMSTR* BS3 .... **38** A2
CFTN/FAIL BS8 .... **26** A3

Wineberry Cl *EVILLE/WHL* BS5 .... **25** D2

Wine St *CBRIS/FH* BS1 .... **29** C1

Winford Gv *BMSTRD/HC/WWD* BS13.. **94** B1

Wingfield Rd *BMSTR* BS3 .... **96** B1

Winkworth Pl *CBRISNE* BS2 .... **22** A2

Winsbury Wy *ALMDB* BS32 .... **44** B3

Winscombe Cl *KEYN* BS31 .... **112** A1

Winsford St *EVILLE/WHL* BS5 .... **22** C4 ⬚

Winsham Cl *HGRV/WHIT* BS14 ...... **108** A2 ⬚

Winsley Rd *RDLND/MONT* BS6 .... **21** D1

Winterbourne Hl *FRCTL/WBN* BS36.... **56** A2

Winterbourne Rd
BRSTK/PCHW BS34 .... **53** D1

Winterstoke Cl *BMSTR* BS3 .... **95** C1 ⬚⬚

Winterstoke Rd *BMSTR* BS3 .... **34** B4

Winterstoke U/P *BMSTR* BS3 .... **34** A3 ⬚

Winton St *BRSG/KWL/STAPK* BS4 .... **38** B2

Witchell Rd *EVILLE/WHL* BS5 .... **24** B5

Witch Hazel Rd
BMSTRD/HC/WWD BS13............... **106** B4

Witcombe Cl *KGWD/HNM* BS15 ...... **86** B2

Witham Rd *KEYN* BS31 .... **113** D4

Witherlies Rd *MANG/FISH* BS16 ..... **78** A1 ⬚

Withey Cl West
HNLZ/SM/SNYPK/WT BS9............. **77** D2

The Witheys *HGRV/WHIT* BS14 ...... **108** B3

Withleigh Rd *BRSG/KWL/STAPK* BS4 .. **39** F5

Withy Cl East
HNLZ/SM/SNYPK/WT BS9............. **2** A3

Withypool Gdns
HGRV/WHIT BS14 .... **108** A2 ⬚⬚

Withywood Rd
BMSTRD/HC/WWD BS13............... **104** A3

Woburn Cl *OLD/WMLY/WICK* BS30 .. **93** C2 ⬚

Woburn Rd *EVILLE/WHL* BS5 .... **15** F2

Wolferton Rd *RDLND/MONT* BS6...... **14** A4

Wolfridge Gdns *HNBRY/STHM* BS10 .. **48** B3

Wolseley Rd *HORF/LLZ* BS7 .... **13** D3

Woodbine Rd *EVILLE/WHL* BS5 .... **24** B3

Woodborough St *EVILLE/WHL* BS5 .. **23** E2

Woodbridge Rd
BRSG/KWL/STAPK BS4 .... **39** D5

Woodbury La *EVILLE/WHL* BS8 .... **11** D5 ⬚

Woodchester *KGWD/HNM* BS15 ...... **80** B4 ⬚

Woodchester Rd
HNBRY/STHM BS10 .... **65** D4 ⬚

Woodcote Rd *KGWD/HNM* BS15 ..... **92** A1 ⬚

Woodcote Rd *MANG/FISH* BS16 ..... **85** C1

Woodcote Wk *MANG/FISH* BS16 ..... **85** C1

Woodcroft Av *EVILLE/WHL* BS5 .... **24** C3

Woodcroft Cl *BRSG/KWL/STAPK* BS4.. **41** F1

Woodcroft Rd
BRSG/KWL/STAPK BS4 .... **41** F1

Woodend *KGWD/HNM* BS15 .... **92** A1 ⬚

Wood End Wk
HNLZ/SM/SNYPK/WT BS9............. **76** B1

Woodfield Rd *RDLND/MONT* BS6...... **19** F1

Woodgrove Rd *HNBRY/STHM* BS10 .. **63** C1

Woodhall Cl *MANG/FISH* BS16 .... **81** C1 ⬚

Woodhouse Gv *HORF/LLZ* BS7 .... **5** E2

Woodington Ct
OLD/WMLY/WICK BS30 .... **93** C3 ⬚⬚

Woodland Av *KGWD/HNM* BS15 ..... **86** A1 ⬚

Woodland Cl *MANG/FISH* BS16 ...... **85** D1 ⬚

Woodland Gv
HNLZ/SM/SNYPK/WT BS9............. **77** C1

Woodland Rd *CFTN/FAIL* BS8 .... **20** A5

Woodlands *MANG/FISH* BS16 .... **80** B1 ⬚

Woodlands La *ALMDB* BS32 .... **44** B1

Woodlands Ri *MANG/FISH* BS16...... **80** A1

Woodland Ter *KGWD/HNM* BS15 ..... **86** A4
RDLND/MONT BS6........................ **11** E5

Woodland Wy *KGWD/HNM* BS15 ..... **85** D1

Woodleaze
HNLZ/SM/SNYPK/WT BS9............. **76** A1

Woodleigh Gdns *HGRV/WHIT* BS14 .. **108** B1

Woodmancote Rd
RDLND/MONT BS6........................ **21** F1 ⬚

Woodmarsh Cl *HGRV/WHIT* BS14...... **107** D3

Woodmead Gdns
  BMSTRD/HC/WWD BS13............... **105** D3
Wood Rd *KGWD/HNM BS15* **86** A3
Woodside Rd *BRSG/KWL/STAPK BS4* .. **33** E3
  KGWD/HNM BS15 .... **85** D3
  MANG/FISH BS16 .... **71** D4
Woodstock Av *RDLND/MONT BS6* **20** A1
Woodstock Cl *KGWD/HNM BS15* ... **87** C3 🔢
Woodstock Rd *KGWD/HNM BS15* **87** C4 🔢
  RDLND/MONT BS6........................ **12** A4
Wood St *EVILLE/WHL BS5* **15** F5
Woodview Cl *AVONM BS11* **60** B3
Woodward Dr
  OLD/WMLY/WICK BS30 .... **93** C3
Woodwell Rd *AVONM BS11*............... **74** B1
Woodyleaze Dr *KGWD/HNM BS15* **91** D1
Woolcot St *RDLND/MONT BS6* **11** F4
Woolley Rd *HGRV/WHIT BS14* .... **109** D2 🔢
Wootton Crs *BRSG/KWL/STAPK BS4* .. **33** E2
Wootton Pk *HGRV/WHIT BS14* **98** A2
Wootton Rd *BRSG/KWL/STAPK BS4*.. **33** F2
Worcester Cl *MANG/FISH BS16*......... **49** C1
Worcester Crs *CFTN/FAIL BS8* .... **18** C4 🔢
Worcester Rd *CFTN/FAIL BS8* **18** C4
  KGWD/HNM BS15 .... **86** A2 🔢
Worcester Ter *CFTN/FAIL BS8*........... **18** C4
Wordsworth Rd *HORF/LLZ BS7* **7** D1
Worrall Rd *CFTN/FAIL BS8*................ **10** C5
Worrel's La *MANG/FISH BS16* **56** A4
Worsley St *EVILLE/WHL BS5* **24** C5
Worth Cl *KGWD/HNM BS15* .... **93** C1 🔢
Worthing Rd *BRSTK/PCHW BS34*....... **43** C3
The Worthys *ALMDB BS32* **54** B1
Wraxall Gv *BMSTRD/HC/WWD BS13* .. **94** A3
Wraxall Rd *KGWD/HNM BS15*........... **93** D1
  OLD/WMLY/WICK BS30 .... **93** D1
Wrenbert Rd *MANG/FISH BS16* **80** A2
Wren Dr *MANG/FISH BS16*................ **78** A1
Wrington Cl *BRSTK/PCHW BS34*......... **44** B4
Wrington Crs
  BMSTRD/HC/WWD BS13................. **94** B4
Wroughton Dr
  BMSTRD/HC/WWD BS13 .... **106** A3
Wroughton Gdns
  BMSTRD/HC/WWD BS13 .... **106** A3 🔢
Wroxham Dr *BRSTK/PCHW BS34* .... **44** B3 🔢
Wyatt Av *BMSTRD/HC/WWD BS13*.... **104** A2
Wyatt Cl *BMSTRD/HC/WWD BS13* **104** A2

Wychwood *KGWD/HNM BS15* **92** A1
Wyck Beck Rd *HNBRY/STHM BS10* **48** B3
Wycliffe Rd
  HNLZ/SM/SNYPK/WT BS9............. **65** C4
Wycombe Gv
  BRSG/KWL/STAPK BS4 .... **99** C1 🔢
Wye Croft Cl *HNBRY/STHM BS10* **50** A1
Wyedale Av
  HNLZ/SM/SNYPK/WT BS9............. **62** A4
Wykis Ct *KGWD/HNM BS15* .... **92** B2 🔢
Wymbush Crs
  BMSTRD/HC/WWD BS13............. **105** D2
Wymbush Gdns
  BMSTRD/HC/WWD BS13 .... **105** D2 🔢
Wyndham Crs
  BRSG/KWL/STAPK BS4 .... **90** A4
The Wynstones *KGWD/HNM BS15*... **85** D4
Yeomans Cl
  HNLZ/SM/SNYPK/WT BS9 .... **77** C2 🔢

Y

Yeomanside Cl *HGRV/WHIT BS14*...... **108** B2
Yewcroft Cl *HGRV/WHIT BS14* **107** D3
Yew Tree Dr *KGWD/HNM BS15*......... **81** C4
York Av *HORF/LLZ BS7* **14** B1
York Cl *BRSTK/PCHW BS34* **53** C3
  FRCTL/WBN BS36......................... **73** C2
York Gdns *CFTN/FAIL BS8* **26** B2
York Pl *CBRIS/FH BS1*..................... **28** A3
  CFTN/FAIL BS8 .... **27** E1
York Rd *BMSTR BS3* **37** E1
  EVILLE/WHL BS5 .... **24** A2
  MANG/FISH BS16 .... **80** B3
  RDLND/MONT BS6 .... **21** F1
York St *CBRISNE BS2* **14** B5
  CBRISNE BS2 .... **21** E4
  CFTN/FAIL BS8 .... **11** D4 🔢
  EVILLE/WHL BS5 .... **32** B1

Z

Zetland Rd *RDLND/MONT BS6* **12** C5

Index - featured places

3-D Gallery
  CBRISNE BS2 .... **20** C5
ABC Cinema
  CFTN/FAIL BS8............................ **19** E3
Air Balloon Hill Junior &
  Infant School
  EVILLE/WHL BS5 .... **84** B4
Allen School House
  OLD/WMLY/WICK BS30 .... **93** D2
All Saints Exhibition Centre
  CBRIS/FH BS1............................. **29** D1
Amberley House School
  CFTN/FAIL BS8............................ **19** D1
Amelia Nutt Clinic
  BMSTRD/HC/WWD BS13 .... **104** A3
Amphitheatre
  CBRIS/FH BS1 .... **28** B4

Anchor Business Centre
  CFTN/FAIL BS8............................ **19** E2
Aretians RFC Clubhouse
  BRSTK/PCHW BS34...................... **44** A4
Arnolfini Gallery
  CBRIS/FH BS1 .... **28** C4
Arts Centre Cinema
  CBRISNE BS2 .... **21** D3
Ashley Down Junior School
  HORF/LLZ BS7 .... **6** A4
Ashley Down OB Rugby Club
  HORF/LLZ BS7 .... **68** A3
Ashley Trading Estate
  CBRISNE BS2 .... **14** B5
Ashton Gate Primary School
  BMSTR BS3 .... **35** D2

Ashton Park School
  BMSTR BS3 .... **89** D4
Ashton Vale Primary School
  BMSTR BS3 .... **94** A1
Avonbank Industrial Centre
  AVONM BS11 .... **59** C4
Avonbridge Trading Estate
  AVONM BS11 .... **59** D3
Avon Business Park
  MANG/FISH BS16 .... **78** B4
Avondale Business Centre
  MANG/FISH BS16 .... **85** D1
Avon Gorge Industrial Estate
  AVONM BS11 .... **59** D4
Avonmouth C of E School
  AVONM BS11 .... **59** D3
Avonmouth Group Practice
  Health Centre Doctors Surgery
  AVONM BS11 .... **59** C3
Avonmouth Medical Centre
  AVONM BS11 .... **59** C3
Avon Primary School
  AVONM BS11 .... **60** A3
Avon Riverside Estate
  AVONM BS11 .... **59** C4
Avon & Somerset Constabulary
  CBRIS/FH BS1 .... **21** D5
Avon Trading Estate
  CBRISNE BS2 .... **30** C4
Azure Gallery
  HNLZ/SM/SNYPK/WT BS9 .... **64** A4
Badminton School
  HNLZ/SM/SNYPK/WT BS9 .... **2** C3
Badocks Wood Primary School
  HNBRY/STHM BS10 .... **65** D3
Baileys Court Primary School
  ALMDB BS32 .... **54** A1
Balaclava Industrial Estate
  MANG/FISH BS16 .... **78** A4
Bank Leaze Primary School
  AVONM BS11 .... **62** A1
Bannerman Road Primary School
  EVILLE/WHL BS5 .... **23** F2
Barley Close Primary School
  MANG/FISH BS16 .... **81** D1
Barnack Trading Centre
  BMSTR BS3 .... **95** D2
Barrs Court Primary School
  OLD/WMLY/WICK BS30 .... **93** C2
Barton Hill Primary School
  EVILLE/WHL BS5 .... **31** E2
Barton Hill Trading Estate
  EVILLE/WHL BS5 .... **31** F3
Beacon Rise Junior School
  KGWD/HNM BS15 .... **92** A1
Bedminster Down School
  BMSTRD/HC/WWD BS13 .... **94** A4
Beehive Trading Estate
  EVILLE/WHL BS5 .... **33** F1
Begbrook Primary School
  MANG/FISH BS16 .... **78** A1
Bishop Road Primary School
  HORF/LLZ BS7 .... **5** D5
Bishopston House Clinic
  HORF/LLZ BS7 .... **13** E1
Bishopsworth C of E School
  BMSTRD/HC/WWD BS13 ...... **104** A1
Bishopsworth Swimming Pool
  BMSTRD/HC/WWD BS13 ...... **104** B1
Blackberry Hill Hospital
  MANG/FISH BS16 .... **78** A2

Blackhorse CP School
  MANG/FISH BS16 .... **73** D3
Blaise Hamlet (NT)
  HNBRY/STHM BS10 .... **63** C1
Bonville Business Centre
  BRSG/KWL/STAPK BS4 .... **100** A1
Bradgate Surgery
  HNBRY/STHM BS10 .... **48** B4
Brentry Hospital
  HNBRY/STHM BS10 .... **65** C1
Brentry Primary School
  HNBRY/STHM BS10 .... **49** C4
Briarwood School
  MANG/FISH BS16 .... **79** C4
Bridge Farm Junior &
  Infant School
  HGRV/WHIT BS14 .... **107** D3
Brislington Retail Park
  BRSG/KWL/STAPK BS4 .... **99** D2
Brislington School
  BRSG/KWL/STAPK BS4 .... **100** A3
Brislington Trading Estate
  BRSG/KWL/STAPK BS4 .... **100** A1
Bristol Baptist College
  CFTN/FAIL BS8 .... **18** A4
Bristol Business Park
  MANG/FISH BS16 .... **70** A2
Bristol Cathedral
  CBRIS/FH BS1 .... **28** B3
Bristol Cathedral School
  CBRIS/FH BS1 .... **28** A3
Bristol City Council
  AVONM BS11 .... **58** B2
Bristol City Council
  AVONM BS11 .... **60** A4
Bristol City Council
  AVONM BS11 .... **61** D1
Bristol City Council
  AVONM BS11 .... **61** D4
Bristol City Council
  BMSTR BS3 .... **37** E2
Bristol City Council
  BMSTRD/HC/WWD BS13 ...... **105** C3
Bristol City Council
  BRSG/KWL/STAPK BS4 .... **40** B2
Bristol City Council
  BRSG/KWL/STAPK BS4 .... **90** A4
Bristol City Council
  BRSG/KWL/STAPK BS4 .... **96** A4
Bristol City Council
  BRSG/KWL/STAPK BS4 .... **97** D1
Bristol City Council
  BRSG/KWL/STAPK BS4 .... **97** D3
Bristol City Council
  CBRIS/FH BS1 .... **21** E4
Bristol City Council
  CBRIS/FH BS1 .... **28** B2
Bristol City Council
  CBRIS/FH BS1 .... **28** B1
Bristol City Council
  CBRIS/FH BS1 .... **28** A2
Bristol City Council
  CBRIS/FH BS1 .... **29** E1
Bristol City Council
  CBRIS/FH BS1 .... **30** B4
Bristol City Council
  CBRISNE BS2 .... **21** E3
Bristol City Council
  CBRISNE BS2 .... **22** A2
Bristol City Council
  CFTN/FAIL BS8 .... **11** D4

Bristol City Council
  CFTN/FAIL BS8............................ 20 A5
Bristol City Council
  CFTN/FAIL BS8............................ 26 C4
Bristol City Council
  CFTN/FAIL BS8............................ 27 E1
Bristol City Council
  EVILLE/WHL BS5.......................... 15 E4
Bristol City Council
  EVILLE/WHL BS5.......................... 24 C5
Bristol City Council
  EVILLE/WHL BS5.......................... 31 F1
Bristol City Council
  HGRV/WHIT BS14.......................... 98 B3
Bristol City Council
  HGRV/WHIT BS14........................ 107 C2
Bristol City Council
  HNBRY/STHM BS10 .... 49 C4
Bristol City Council
  HNBRY/STHM BS10 .... 65 C3
Bristol City Council
  HNBRY/STHM BS10 .... 66 A1
Bristol City Council
  HORF/LLZ BS7.............................. 67 C2
Bristol City Football Club
  BMSTR BS3 .... 34 B3
Bristol Civil Service Sports Club
  HORF/LLZ BS7................................ 6 B1
Bristol Clifton & West of England
  Zoological Society
  CFTN/FAIL BS8............................ 18 B2
Bristol County Court
  CBRISNE BS2 .... 20 C5
Bristol County Sports Club
  CBRIS/FH BS1 .... 28 B1
Bristol Crown Court
  CBRIS/FH BS1 .... 28 C1
Bristol Dental Hospital
  CBRIS/FH BS1 .... 20 C5
Bristol General Hospital
  CBRIS/FH BS1 .... 29 D5
Bristol Grammar School
  CFTN/FAIL BS8............................ 19 F5
Bristol Harlequins RFC
  BRSG/KWL/STAPK BS4 .... 100 B1
Bristol Ice Rink
  CBRIS/FH BS1 .... 28 B1
Bristol Industrial Museum
  CBRIS/FH BS1 .... 28 B5
Bristol North Baths
  HORF/LLZ BS7.............................. 13 D2
Bristol Old Vic (New Vic
  Theatre & Theatre Royal)
  CBRIS/FH BS1 .... 28 C2
Bristol Old Vic Theatre School
  CFTN/FAIL BS8............................ 18 C1
Bristol Rovers Football Club
  BRSG/KWL/STAPK BS4 .... 100 A2
Bristol Royal Hospital for
  Sick Children
  CFTN/FAIL BS8............................ 20 B5
Bristol Royal Infirmary
  CBRISNE BS2 .... 20 C4
Bristol South Swimming Pool
  BMSTR BS3 .... 36 B2
Bristol Steiner Waldorf School
  CFTN/FAIL BS8............................ 27 E1
Bristol University
  CFTN/FAIL BS8............................ 28 B1
Bristol Vale Trading Estate
  BMSTR BS3 .... 95 C2

British Empire &
  Commonwealth Museum
  CBRIS/FH BS1 .... 30 A4
Broadlands School
  KEYN BS31.................................. 112 A1
Broadmead Lane
  Industrial Estate
  KEYN BS31.................................. 103 D4
Broadwalk Shopping Centre
  BRSG/KWL/STAPK BS4 .... 39 E5
Bromley Heath Infant School
  MANG/FISH BS16 .... 72 B3
Bromley Heath Junior School
  MANG/FISH BS16 .... 72 B3
Brooklea Clinic
  BRSG/KWL/STAPK BS4 .... 33 E5
Broomhill Infant School
  BRSG/KWL/STAPK BS4 .... 90 A4
Broomhill JM School
  BRSG/KWL/STAPK BS4 .... 90 A4
Burnbush Primary School
  HGRV/WHIT BS14 .... 109 C2
Burnbush School
  HGRV/WHIT BS14 .... 109 C1
Bush Industrial Estate
  EVILLE/WHL BS5 .... 24 C3
The Business Park
  BMSTRD/HC/WWD BS13 .... 106 B4
CAB & Guildhall
  CBRIS/FH BS1 .... 29 D1
Cabot Primary School
  CBRISNE BS2 .... 22 A3
Cabot Tower
  CFTN/FAIL BS8............................ 27 F2
Cadbury Heath Health Centre
  OLD/WMLY/WICK BS30 .... 93 D2
Callicroft Infant School
  BRSTK/PCHW BS34...................... 43 C3
Callicroft Junior School
  BRSTK/PCHW BS34...................... 42 B3
Canons House
  CBRIS/FH BS1 .... 28 B4
Carla Trading Estate
  BMSTR BS3 .... 34 A4
Carlyle Business Centre
  CBRISNE BS2 .... 31 D2
Carrick Business Park
  BRSG/KWL/STAPK BS4 .... 100 A2
Castle CP School
  KEYN BS31.................................. 112 A1
Central Trading Estate
  CBRISNE BS2 .... 39 E1
Chandag County &
  Infant School
  KEYN BS31.................................. 113 D2
Charborough Road CP School
  BRSTK/PCHW BS34...................... 67 C1
Charlotte Keel Health Clinic
  EVILLE/WHL BS5 .... 23 D2
Chatterton House
  CBRIS/FH BS1 .... 29 E4
Cheddar Grove Primary School
  BMSTRD/HC/WWD BS13 .... 94 B3
Chesterfield Hospital
  CFTN/FAIL BS8............................ 27 D2
Chester Park Primary School
  MANG/FISH BS16 .... 78 B4
Christchurch C of E
  Primary School
  CFTN/FAIL BS8............................ 18 C5

Christ Church C of E VC
Infant School
MANG/FISH BS16 .... **80** A2

Christchurch Junior School
MANG/FISH BS16 .... **80** A2

City Business Park
CBRIS/FH BS1 .... **29** D1

City of Bristol College
BMSTR BS3 .... **96** B1

City of Bristol College
CBRIS/FH BS1 .... **27** F3

City of Bristol College
HORF/LLZ BS7 .... **14** B2

City & Port of Bristol Social &
Sports Club
AVONM BS11 .... **74** A2

Civic Centre
KGWD/HNM BS15 .... **86** B3

Claremont Special School
RDLND/MONT BS6 .... **4** A3

Clifton Cathedral Church
CFTN/FAIL BS8 .... **19** D4

Clifton Clinic
CFTN/FAIL BS8 .... **26** C1

Clifton College
CFTN/FAIL BS8 .... **18** B3

Clifton College
Preparatory School
CFTN/FAIL BS8 .... **18** B2

Clifton College Sports Club
CFTN/FAIL BS8 .... **82** A4

Clifton Down Shopping Centre
CFTN/FAIL BS8 .... **19** E2

The Clifton Gallery
CFTN/FAIL BS8 .... **26** C1

Clifton High Junior School
CFTN/FAIL BS8 .... **18** C5

Clifton High School
CFTN/FAIL BS8 .... **18** C4

Clifton High School
CFTN/FAIL BS8 .... **18** B5

Clifton Rugby Club
HNBRY/STHM BS10 .... **48** A2

Clyde House Surgery
RDLND/MONT BS6 .... **11** F5

College House
MANG/FISH BS16 .... **78** B2

College of St Mathias
C of E (A) Infant School
MANG/FISH BS16 .... **78** B2

Colston Hall
CBRIS/FH BS1 .... **28** C1

Colstons Collegiate
Lower School
MANG/FISH BS16 .... **8** B4

Colstons Girls School
RDLND/MONT BS6 .... **21** E1

Colstons Primary School
RDLND/MONT BS6 .... **20** B1

Colstons School
MANG/FISH BS16 .... **8** B5

Community Health Authority
KEYN BS31 .... **112** B1

The Compton Clinic
RDLND/MONT BS6 .... **11** D1

Coniston Primary School
BRSTK/PCHW BS34............. **43** C2

Connaught Infants &
Primary School
BRSG/KWL/STAPK BS4 .... **96** B3

Conygre Medical Centre
BRSTK/PCHW BS34............. **51** D4

Corbett House Clinic
EVILLE/WHL BS5 .... **32** A1

Coroners Court
CBRISNE BS2 .... **21** E3

Cossham Memorial Hospital
KGWD/HNM BS15 .... **85** D1

Cotham Galleries
RDLND/MONT BS6 .... **19** F2

Cotham Grammar School
RDLND/MONT BS6 .... **20** B2

Cotham Road Surgery
RDLND/MONT BS6 .... **20** A3

Courtney Primary School
KGWD/HNM BS15 .... **87** C4

The Craft Gallery
HORF/LLZ BS7 .... **67** C2

Crofts End Industrial Estate
EVILLE/WHL BS5 .... **25** F1

Crown Court
CBRIS/FH BS1 .... **21** D5

Custom House
CBRIS/FH BS1 .... **29** D3

Cutlers Brook Junior School
CBRISNE BS2 .... **14** C5

David Hamiltons Practice
CFTN/FAIL BS8 .... **19** F2

Dean Lane Family Practice
BMSTR BS3 .... **36** B1

Deers Wood Primary School
KGWD/HNM BS15 .... **87** D1

Dixon Business Centre
BRSG/KWL/STAPK BS4 .... **100** A1

Downend Cricket Club
MANG/FISH BS16 .... **80** A1

Downend School
MANG/FISH BS16 .... **80** B2

Downend Surgery
MANG/FISH BS16 .... **80** A2

Downs Fitness & Health Centre
CFTN/FAIL BS8 .... **11** D5

Dr Bells C of E School
MANG/FISH BS16 .... **78** B3

Duckmoor Road Industrial Estate
BMSTR BS3 .... **34** C3

Dunmail Primary School
HNBRY/STHM BS10 .... **65** D1

Easton Business Centre
EVILLE/WHL BS5 .... **23** E3

Easton CE V A Primary School
EVILLE/WHL BS5 .... **23** D4

Easton Leisure Centre
EVILLE/WHL BS5 .... **23** D4

Eastpark Trading Estate
EVILLE/WHL BS5 .... **25** D1

Eastville Health Centre
EVILLE/WHL BS5 .... **15** F5

Elmlea Infant School
HNLZ/SM/SNYPK/WT BS9 ...... **2** B3

Elmlea Junior School
HNLZ/SM/SNYPK/WT BS9 ...... **2** B3

Elm Park School
FRCTL/WBN BS36 .... **56** B1

Embleton Junior School
HNBRY/STHM BS10 .... **65** C2

Exhibition Centre
CBRIS/FH BS1 .... **28** B3

Explore @ Bristol
CBRIS/FH BS1 .... **28** B3

The Eye Clinic
CBRIS/FH BS1 .... **21** E5

Fairfield Grammar School
RDLND/MONT BS6 .... **14** A5

Fair Furlong Primary School
  BMSTRD/HC/WWD BS13 .... **104** B3
Fairway Industrial Centre
  BRSTK/PCHW BS34 .... **51** C4
Falconride Primary School
  KGWD/HNM BS15 .... **86** B2
The Family Practice
  RDLND/MONT BS6 .... **20** A3
Family & Youth Court
  CBRIS/FH BS1 .... **29** D1
Ferry Steps Trading Estate
  CBRISNE BS2 .... **38** C1
Filton Avenue Junior School
  HORF/LLZ BS7 .... **67** D4
Filton Clinic
  HORF/LLZ BS7 .... **67** D1
Filton College
  BRSTK/PCHW BS34 .... **51** D3
Filton High School
  BRSTK/PCHW BS34 .... **53** C4
Filton Hill CP School
  BRSTK/PCHW BS34 .... **52** A3
Filton Park School
  BRSTK/PCHW BS34 .... **67** C1
Filton Recreation Centre
  BRSTK/PCHW BS34 .... **67** D1
Filton Shield Road School
  HORF/LLZ BS7 .... **67** D2
Filton Town Council
  BRSTK/PCHW BS34 .... **67** D1
Filwood Swimming Baths
  BRSG/KWL/STAPK BS4 .... **96** B3
Fire Station
  CBRIS/FH BS1 .... **29** F2
Fishponds Health Centre
  MANG/FISH BS16 .... **79** C3
The Florence Brown School
  BRSG/KWL/STAPK BS4 .... **96** A3
The Florence Brown School
  CBRISNE BS2 .... **22** A5
Flower Gallery
  FRCTL/WBN BS36 .... **56** A1
Folk House
  CBRIS/FH BS1 .... **28** B1
Fonthill Junior School
  HNBRY/STHM BS10 .... **66** B1
Foster Almshouses
  CBRIS/FH BS1 .... **28** C1
Frenchay C of E School
  MANG/FISH BS16 .... **71** C4
Frenchay Health Authority
  MANG/FISH BS16 .... **79** D2
Frenchay Hospital
  MANG/FISH BS16 .... **71** C3
Frenchay Village Museum
  MANG/FISH BS16 .... **70** A4
Fromeside Clinic
  MANG/FISH BS16 .... **78** A2
Fulford Special School
  BMSTRD/HC/WWD BS13 .... **105** D3
The Galleries Shopping Centre
  CBRIS/FH BS1 .... **21** E5
Gay Elms Junior & Infant School
  BMSTRD/HC/WWD BS13 .... **104** B3
Georgian House
  CBRIS/FH BS1 .... **28** A2
Glenfrome Primary School
  EVILLE/WHL BS5 .... **16** A1
Gloucestershire County Council
  KGWD/HNM BS15 .... **86** B3
Gloucestershire County Cricket Club
  HORF/LLZ BS7 .... **14** A2

Glynne Wickham Studio Theatre
  CFTN/FAIL BS8 .... **28** A1
Granby House Clinic
  BMSTR BS3 .... **36** B3
Grange Road Surgery
  BMSTRD/HC/WWD BS13 .... **104** A2
Grove Industrial Estate
  BRSTK/PCHW BS34 .... **44** A4
Grove Road Day Hospital
  RDLND/MONT BS6 .... **11** D4
Hambrook CP School
  MANG/FISH BS16 .... **56** A4
Hambrook Sports Club
  MANG/FISH BS16 .... **56** A4
Hanham Abbots Junior School
  KGWD/HNM BS15 .... **91** D3
Hanham Business Park
  KGWD/HNM BS15 .... **91** C2
Hanham C of E Primary School
  KGWD/HNM BS15 .... **91** C3
Hanham High School
  KGWD/HNM BS15 .... **91** D3
Hanham Surgery
  KGWD/HNM BS15 .... **92** A3
Hannah More Primary School
  CBRISNE BS2 .... **30** B2
The Happening Art Gallery
  RDLND/MONT BS6 .... **19** F2
Hareclive Primary School
  BMSTRD/HC/WWD BS13 .... **105** D3
Hartcliffe Health Centre
  BMSTRD/HC/WWD BS13 .... **105** D3
Hartcliffe School
  BMSTRD/HC/WWD BS13 .... **106** B3
Harveys Wine Museum
  CBRIS/FH BS1 .... **28** B2
Haslemere Industrial Estate
  AVONM BS11 .... **59** D1
Hayward Road Industrial Estate
  MANG/FISH BS16 .... **80** A4
Headley Park Primary School
  BMSTRD/HC/WWD BS13 .... **95** C4
Heath House Priory Hospital
  HORF/LLZ BS7 .... **7** E5
Henbury Court Junior &
  Primary School
  HNBRY/STHM BS10 .... **48** A4
Henbury Manor School
  HNBRY/STHM BS10 .... **63** D1
Henbury Old Boys AFC
  HNBRY/STHM BS10 .... **64** A1
The Henbury Surgery
  HNBRY/STHM BS10 .... **48** A4
Henbury Swimming Pool
  HNBRY/STHM BS10 .... **64** A1
Hengrove School
  HGRV/WHIT BS14 .... **98** A4
Henleaze Infant School
  RDLND/MONT BS6 .... **4** A3
Highbridge Infant School
  BMSTRD/HC/WWD BS13 .... **104** A1
Hillfields Park Primary School
  MANG/FISH BS16 .... **79** D4
The Hindu Temple
  EVILLE/WHL BS5 .... **24** B4
Hippodrome Theatre
  CBRIS/FH BS1 .... **28** C2
Holloway Dental Health Centre
  HGRV/WHIT BS14 .... **109** D2
Hollywood Bowl
  CBRISNE BS2 .... **32** A4

Holy Family RC Primary School
  BRSTK/PCHW BS34 .... **44** A3
Holymead Infant School
  BRSG/STAPK BS4 .... **41** D5
Holymead School
  BRSG/STAPK BS4 .... **40** C4
Holy Trinity Primary School
  ALMDB BS32 .... **44** B1
Homeopathic Hospital
  CFTN/FAIL BS8 .... **20** A3
Horfield C of E School
  HNBRY/STHM BS10 .... **66** A4
Horfield Health Centre
  HORF/LLZ BS7 .... **6** B1
Horfield Sports Centre
  HORF/LLZ BS7 .... **67** C4
Hospital
  PTSHD/EG BS20 .... **74** B3
Hotspots Indoor Sports Centre
  BRSG/KWL/STAPK BS4 .... **100** A1
Hotwells Primary School
  CFTN/FAIL BS8 .... **26** B3
Ilminster Avenue Junior School
  BRSG/KWL/STAPK BS4 .... **97** D3
Industrial Estate
  BRSG/KWL/STAPK BS4 .... **100** A2
The Institute of
  Cosmetic Surgery
  CFTN/FAIL BS8 .... **18** B1
John Cabot City
  Technology College
  KGWD/HNM BS15 .... **85** D4
The John Milton Health Clinic
  HNBRY/STHM BS10 .... **48** B4
Jubilee Public Baths
  BRSG/KWL/STAPK BS4 .... **98** A1
Keynsham County
  Primary School
  KEYN BS31 .... **112** A2
Keynsham Hospital
  KEYN BS31 .... **113** C3
Keynsham Leisure Centre
  KEYN BS31 .... **113** C2
Keynsham Rugby Club
  KEYN BS31 .... **102** A4
Keynsham Town Football Club
  KEYN BS31 .... **102** A4
Kings Business Park
  CBRISNE BS2 .... **32** A3
Kings Chase Shopping Centre
  KGWD/HNM BS15 .... **86** A3
Kingsdown Sports Centre
  CBRISNE BS2 .... **20** B3
Kingsfield School
  KGWD/HNM BS15 .... **87** D3
Kingsweston School
  AVONM BS11 .... **61** D3
Kingswood Borough Council
  MANG/FISH BS16 .... **80** A3
Kingswood District Council
  KGWD/HNM BS15 .... **86** A4
Kingswood Health Centre
  KGWD/HNM BS15 .... **86** B3
Kingswood Leisure Centre
  MANG/FISH BS16 .... **80** A4
Knowle Junior Mixed School
  BRSG/KWL/STAPK BS4 .... **39** D3
Knowle Park Junior School
  BRSG/KWL/STAPK BS4 .... **97** D2
The Lake Surgery
  HNBRY/STHM BS10 .... **65** C4

Lawnwood Road
  Industrial Estate
  EVILLE/WHL BS5 .... **23** E4
Lawrence Hill Health Centre
  CBRISNE BS2 .... **23** D5
Lawrence Hill Industrial Estate
  EVILLE/WHL BS5 .... **24** A4
Lawrence Hill Industrial Park
  EVILLE/WHL BS5 .... **23** E4
Lawrence Weston School
  AVONM BS11 .... **62** A2
Lewis Road Surgery
  BMSTRD/HC/WWD BS13 .... **94** B3
Liberty Industrial Park
  BMSTR BS3 .... **94** B2
Little Stoke Junior School
  BRSTK/PCHW BS34 .... **53** C1
Lockleaze School
  HORF/LLZ BS7 .... **68** B3
Lodge Causeway Trading Estate
  MANG/FISH BS16 .... **78** A4
Longbrook Trading Estate
  BMSTR BS3 .... **89** D4
Longwell Green CP School
  OLD/WMLY/WICK BS30 .... **93** C4
Lonsdale Business Centre
  KGWD/HNM BS15 .... **85** D1
Lord Chancellors Department
  CBRIS/FH BS1 .... **29** D1
Lord Chancellors Department
  CFTN/FAIL BS8 .... **26** A1
Luckwell Road School
  BMSTR BS3 .... **35** D4
Lyntony House Reading School
  HORF/LLZ BS7 .... **13** D2
Malago Surgery
  BMSTR BS3 .... **36** B3
Malago Vale Trading Estate
  BMSTR BS3 .... **36** B4
The Mall Gallery
  CFTN/FAIL BS8 .... **26** B1
The Mall
  BRSTK/PCHW BS34 .... **50** A1
Manor Farm Associated
  Football Club
  HNLZ/SM/SNYPK/WT BS9 .... **76** A2
Maritime Heritage Centre
  CBRIS/FH BS1 .... **27** F4
May Park Primary School
  EVILLE/WHL BS5 .... **16** B4
Merrywood School
  BRSG/KWL/STAPK BS4 .... **97** C2
Millpond Primary School
  EVILLE/WHL BS5 .... **23** D1
Minto Road Industrial Centre
  CBRISNE BS2 .... **14** B5
Monks Park School
  HORF/LLZ BS7 .... **67** C2
Monks Park Surgery
  HORF/LLZ BS7 .... **67** C3
Montpelier Health Centre
  RDLND/MONT BS6 .... **21** E1
Mount Zion School
  RDLND/MONT BS6 .... **20** C1
Natural Health Clinic
  RDLND/MONT BS6 .... **19** F2
Newbridge Industrial Estate
  BRSG/KWL/STAPK BS4 .... **32** C3
New Fosseway School
  HGRV/WHIT BS14 .... **98** A4
Northville Family Practice
  HORF/LLZ BS7 .... **68** A2

Novers Hill Trading Estate
BMSTR BS3 .... **95** D2
Novers Lane Jmi School
BRSG/KWL/STAPK BS4 .... **95** D4
Oakfield Business Park
KGWD/HNM BS15 .... **86** A4
Oatley Trading Estate
KGWD/HNM BS15 .... **86** A2
Odeon Cinema
CBRIS/FH BS1 .... **29** D1
Off Centre Gallery
BMSTR BS3 .... **36** C4
Oldbury Court Infant School
MANG/FISH BS16 .... **71** D4
Oldbury Court Jm School
MANG/FISH BS16 .... **71** D4
The Open University
CBRIS/FH BS1 .... **29** E3
Optimax Laser Eye Clinic
CBRIS/FH BS1 .... **28** C2
The Orchard Medical Centre
KGWD/HNM BS15 .... **86** A3
The Other Surgery
CFTN/FAIL BS8 .... **19** E2
Our Lady of Lourdes RC School
KGWD/HNM BS15 .... **86** B4
**Our Lady of the Rosary
RC Primary School**
AVONM BS11 .... **61** D3
The Park School
KGWD/HNM BS15 .... **86** B3
Parkwall CP School
OLD/WMLY/WICK BS30 .... **93** D3
Parkway Trading Estate
RDLND/MONT BS6 .... **14** B4
Parnall Road Industrial Estate
MANG/FISH BS16 .... **78** B4
Parson Street Primary School
BMSTR BS3 .... **95** D1
Patchway C of E Primary School
BRSTK/PCHW BS34 .... **44** B2
Patchway Health Clinic
BRSTK/PCHW BS34 .... **43** D3
Patchway High School
ALMDB BS32 .... **44** A2
Patchway Town Council
BRSTK/PCHW BS34 .... **43** C3
Patchway Trading Estate
BRSTK/PCHW BS34 .... **42** A3
Pembroke Road Surgery
CFTN/FAIL BS8 .... **18** C2
Pen Park School
HNBRY/STHM BS10 .... **66** A1
**Perry Court Junior &
Infant School**
HGRV/WHIT BS14 .... **107** D1
Petherton Road Infant School
HGRV/WHIT BS14 .... **98** A4
Phoenix Business Park
BMSTR BS3 .... **94** B1
Phoenix NHS Trust
KGWD/HNM BS15 .... **91** D3
The Picture House
CBRIS/FH BS1 .... **21** E4
**Portbury Sawmills
Industrial Estate**
PTSHD/EG BS20 .... **58** A4
Portrait Gallery
HORF/LLZ BS7 .... **67** C2
Portview Trading Estate
AVONM BS11 .... **59** C3

Portway School
AVONM BS11 .... **60** B4
Portway Trading Estate
AVONM BS11 .... **59** D4
The Practice
CFTN/FAIL BS8 .... **27** F1
The Priory Surgery
BRSG/KWL/STAPK BS4 .... **98** A1
QEH Theatre
CFTN/FAIL BS8 .... **27** E1
Quakers Friars
CBRIS/FH BS1 .... **21** F5
Queen Elizabeth Hospital
CFTN/FAIL BS8 .... **27** F1
Redfield Leisure Centre
EVILLE/WHL BS5 .... **24** B4
Redgrave Theatre
CFTN/FAIL BS8 .... **18** B4
Redhouse Primary School
BMSTRD/HC/WWD BS13 .... **104** B2
Redland High Junior School
RDLND/MONT BS6 .... **12** B4
Redland High School
RDLND/MONT BS6 .... **12** B4
**Redland High School
Sixth Form Centre**
RDLND/MONT BS6 .... **12** A4
Red Maids Junior School
HNLZ/SM/SNYPK/WT BS9 .... **3** D1
Red Maids School
HNLZ/SM/SNYPK/WT BS9 .... **3** D1
Register Office
CBRIS/FH BS1 .... **21** E5
Ridgeway Industrial Centre
EVILLE/WHL BS5 .... **17** E5
Ridings High School
FRCTL/WBN BS36 .... **56** A1
Riverside Business Park
BRSG/KWL/STAPK BS4 .... **33** C3
Riverside Leisure Centre
CBRISNE BS2 .... **22** B3
Riverside Surgery
BRSG/KWL/STAPK BS4 .... **90** A4
Robin Cousins Sports Centre
AVONM BS11 .... **59** D3
**Romney Avenue Junior
Mixed School**
HORF/LLZ BS7 .... **7** E2
Royal Navy & Royal Marines
CBRIS/FH BS1 .... **28** C1
Royal West of England Academy
CFTN/FAIL BS8 .... **19** F5
RSPCA & Dogs Home
BRSG/KWL/STAPK BS4 .... **38** B1
**Russell Town Avenue
Industrial Centre**
EVILLE/WHL BS5 .... **24** A5
St Andrews Trading Estate
AVONM BS11 .... **59** D1
St Annes Junior Mixed School
BRSG/KWL/STAPK BS4 .... **32** C4
St Annes Park Jmi School
BRSG/KWL/STAPK BS4 .... **33** F3
St Apollonias Surgery
KEYN BS31 .... **112** B3
**St Augustine of Canterbury
RC Primary School**
MANG/FISH BS16 .... **72** B4
**St Barnabas C of E V C
Junior Mixed Infant School**
RDLND/MONT BS6 .... **22** A1

St Bedes RC School
AVONM BS11 .... **61** D1

St Bernadette RC School
HGRV/WHIT BS14 .... **108** B1

St Bernadettes RC
Primary School
HGRV/WHIT BS14 .... **108** A1

St Bernards RC Primary School
AVONM BS11 .... **74** B1

St Bonaventures RC School
HORF/LLZ BS7 .... **12** B1

St Brendans Sixth Form College
BRSG/KWL/STAPK BS4 .... **100** A2

St Brendans Trading Estate
AVONM BS11 .... **59** C1

St Catherines Industrial Estate
BMSTR BS3 .... **37** D3

St Gabriels Business Park
EVILLE/WHL BS5 .... **23** E3

St George Health Centre
KGWD/HNM BS15 .... **84** B3

St George School
EVILLE/WHL BS5 .... **24** A4

St Georges Primary School
CFTN/FAIL BS8 .... **27** F3

St Johns Church & Old City Gate
CBRIS/FH BS1 .... **29** D1

St Johns C of E Primary School
KEYN BS31 .... **112** B2

St Johns C of E VC
Primary School
CFTN/FAIL BS8 .... **11** D5

St Johns Lane Health Centre
BMSTR BS3 .... **37** E5

St Josephs RC School
MANG/FISH BS16 .... **79** C4

St Katherines School
PTSHD/EG BS20 .... **74** B4

St Martins Surgery
BRSG/KWL/STAPK BS4 .... **98** A2

St Mary Redcliffe Primary School
BMSTR BS3 .... **37** E2

St Mary Redcliffe & Temple
C of E VA School
CBRIS/FH BS1 .... **29** F5

St Marys Hospital
CFTN/FAIL BS8 .... **27** F1

St Mary's Redcliff
CBRIS/FH BS1 .... **29** E4

St Marys Rugby Club
ALMDB BS32 .... **46** A1

St Michael on the Mount
C of E Primary School
CFTN/FAIL BS8 .... **28** B1

St Michaels C of E VC
Primary School
FRCTL/WBN BS36 .... **56** B1

St Michaels Hill Clinic
CBRISNE BS2 .... **20** B5

St Michaels Hospital
CBRISNE BS2 .... **20** B4

St Michaels Primary School
BRSTK/PCHW BS34 .... **53** D2

St Nicholas Market
CBRIS/FH BS1 .... **29** D2

St Nicholas RC Primary School
EVILLE/WHL BS5 .... **22** B4

St Patricks RC School
EVILLE/WHL BS5 .... **24** C5

St Peter & St Paul School
RDLND/MONT BS6 .... **20** A3

St Pius X RC Primary School
BMSTRD/HC/WWD BS13 .... **104** B2

St Stephens C of E VC
Junior School
KGWD/HNM BS15 .... **86** A1

St Teresas RC School
HORF/LLZ BS7 .... **66** B2

St Thomas More RC School
HORF/LLZ BS7 .... **15** D1

St Ursulas High School
HNLZ/SM/SNYPK/WT BS9 .... **3** D1

St Vincents Trading Estate
CBRISNE BS2 .... **32** B3

Salvation Army
BMSTR BS3 .... **36** B2

Samuel Whites Infant School
KGWD/HNM BS15 .... **91** D2

Saracens Rugby Club
HNBRY/STHM BS10 .... **48** A2

Satellite Business Park
EVILLE/WHL BS5 .... **33** C1

Saville Court Business Centre
CFTN/FAIL BS8 .... **26** C1

Sea Mills Infant School
HNLZ/SM/SNYPK/WT BS9 .... **62** B4

Sea Mills Junior School
HNLZ/SM/SNYPK/WT BS9 .... **76** A3

Sea Mills Surgery
HNLZ/SM/SNYPK/WT BS9 .... **76** A3

Sefton Park Infants School
HORF/LLZ BS7 .... **14** A2

Severnside Trading Estate
AVONM BS11 .... **59** D2

Sheene Court Industrial Estate
BMSTR BS3 .... **36** A4

Shirehampton Baths
AVONM BS11 .... **74** B1

Shirehampton Cricket Club
AVONM BS11 .... **61** C4

Shirehampton Health Centre
AVONM BS11 .... **74** B1

Shirehampton Infant School
AVONM BS11 .... **74** A1

Shirehampton Junior School
AVONM BS11 .... **74** A1

Showcase Cinema Bristol
CBRISNE BS2 .... **32** A4

Sikh Temple
EVILLE/WHL BS5 .... **16** A4

The Sisters of the Temple
CFTN/FAIL BS8 .... **18** A5

Sneyd Park Surgery
HNLZ/SM/SNYPK/WT BS9 .... **77** D4

Soaphouse Industrial Estate
EVILLE/WHL BS5 .... **25** E3

The Soga Gallery
CFTN/FAIL BS8 .... **26** C2

Soundwell College
CBRISNE BS2 .... **31** D2

Soundwell College
KGWD/HNM BS15 .... **86** B1

South Bristol College
BMSTRD/HC/WWD BS13 .... **106** A3

South Gloucestershire Council
BRSTK/PCHW BS34 .... **43** C2

South Gloucestershire Council
BRSTK/PCHW BS34 .... **52** A4

Southmead Health Centre
HNBRY/STHM BS10 .... **65** D1

Southmead Health
Services NHS Trust
HNBRY/STHM BS10 .... **66** A3

South Street Primary School
BMSTR BS3 .... **35** F4

South View Business Centre
MANG/FISH BS16 .... **80** B2

South View Business Park
MANG/FISH BS16 .... **80** B2

Southville Primary School
BMSTR BS3 .... **35** F2

Southville Surgery
BMSTR BS3 .... **28** B5

Speedwell School
EVILLE/WHL BS5 .... **84** B2

Speedwell Swimming Baths
EVILLE/WHL BS5 .... **84** A2

Springfield School
RDLND/MONT BS6 .... **13** F5

Springwater Park
Trading Estate
EVILLE/WHL BS5 .... **33** E1

SS Great Britain
CBRIS/FH BS1 .... **27** F4

Stanbridge CP School
MANG/FISH BS16 .... **81** C1

Staple Hill Primary School
MANG/FISH BS16 .... **80** A3

Steps Gallery
CBRIS/FH BS1 .... **28** C1

Stockwood Green
Primary School
HGRV/WHIT BS14 .... **109** D3

Stoke Bishop C of E
Primary School
HNLZ/SM/SNYPK/WT BS9 .... **77** C2

Stoke Gifford Medical Centre
BRSTK/PCHW BS34 .... **53** D3

Stoke Lodge Infant School
BRSTK/PCHW BS34 .... **44** B3

Stokes Medical Centre
BRSTK/PCHW BS34 .... **44** B4

Stoke View Business Park
MANG/FISH BS16 .... **78** A3

Stonehill Business Centre
OLD/WMLY/WICK BS30 .... **92** B3

Stuckeys Furniture Gallery
HNLZ/SM/SNYPK/WT BS9 .... **10** C4

Stuckleys Pine Gallery
HORF/LLZ BS7 .... **5** E4

Summerhill Infant School
EVILLE/WHL BS5 .... **25** F4

Sun Life Sports Club
HNBRG/STHM BS10 .... **48** A3

Sussex Place Surgery
RDLND/MONT BS6 .... **14** B5

Temple County Primary School
KEYN BS31 .... **113** C1

Temple House Doctors Surgery
KEYN BS31 .... **112** B2

Temple Trading Estate
CBRISNE BS2 .... **31** F4

Teyfant Primary School
BMSTRD/HC/WWD BS13 .... **106** B3

Totterdown Bridge Estate
CBRISNE BS2 .... **39** D1

Trinity College
HNLZ/SM/SNYPK/WT BS9 .... **77** D3

Two Mile Hill Junior &
Infant School
KGWD/HNM BS15 .... **85** C3

Twyford House Cricket Club
AVONM BS11 .... **61** C4

Tyning Junior & Mixed School
HGRV/WHIT BS14 .... **97** D4

The Tynings CP School
MANG/FISH BS16 .... **80** B3

United Bristol
Healthcare NHS Trust
CBRIS/FH BS1 .... **21** D5

University of Bristol
CBRIS/FH BS1 .... **28** B1

University of Bristol
CBRISNE BS2 .... **20** B4

University of Bristol
CFTN/FAIL BS8 .... **20** A4

University of Bristol
CFTN/FAIL BS8 .... **27** D2

University of Bristol
HNLZ/SM/SNYPK/WT BS9 .... **10** B1

University of Bristol
HNLZ/SM/SNYPK/WT BS9 .... **77** D3

University of Bristol
Childrens Hospital
CFTN/FAIL BS8 .... **20** B4

University of the West of
England
CBRIS/FH BS1 .... **29** D3

University of the West of
England
MANG/FISH BS16 .... **9** F3

University of the West of
England Bristol
BMSTR BS3 .... **89** D2

University of the West of
England Bristol
MANG/FISH BS16 .... **69** C2

University of the West of
England Bristol
MANG/FISH BS16 .... **78** B2

University of the West of
England Bristol
RDLND/MONT BS6 .... **11** E3

Upper Horfield Primary School
HORF/LLZ BS7 .... **67** D3

Victoria Park County
Infant School
BMSTR BS3 .... **37** E4

Victoria Rooms
CFTN/FAIL BS8 .... **19** E5

Wadehurst Industrial Park
CBRISNE BS2 .... **31** D1

Wallis Estate
CBRISNE BS2 .... **14** C3

Wansdyke School
HGRV/WHIT BS14 .... **107** C3

Watershed Arts Complex
CBRIS/FH BS1 .... **28** C3

Waycroft Primary School
HGRV/WHIT BS14 .... **109** D2

Wellsway School
KEYN BS31 .... **113** D2

Westbury Bazaar & Gallery
HNLZ/SM/SNYPK/WT BS9 .... **64** B4

Westbury on Trym C of E
Primary School
HNLZ/SM/SNYPK/WT BS9 .... **64** B4

Westbury on Trym Practice
HNLZ/SM/SNYPK/WT BS9 .... **2** B1

Westbury Park School
RDLND/MONT BS6 .... **11** E2

Weston Park Primary School
AVONM BS11 .... **61** C3

Westpoint Trading Estate
KGWD/HNM BS15 .... **86** A4

West Town Lane Infant School
BRSG/KWL/STAPK BS4 .... **98** B2

Page 21

D2
1 Thomas St North

D3
1 King Sq
2 Lower Gay St

D4
1 Barton St
2 Montague Hl South

D5
1 Blackfriars
2 Bridewell St
3 Lower Maudlin St
4 Silver St

E1
1 Armidale Av

E3
1 Hillgrove St

E5
1 Old King Street Ct
2 Quakers' Friars
3 Whippington Ct

F1
1 Woodmancote Rd

F2
1 Norrisville Rd

F4
1 Gloucester St

F5
1 George Whitefield Ct
2 Hanover Ct
3 Meadow St
4 Philadelphia Ct
5 Wellington Rd

Page 23

D1
1 Baptist St
2 Gable Rd

D4
1 Durbin Wk

E2
1 Moorhill St
2 Northcote St

E3
1 Combfactory La

E4
1 Pountney Dr

E5
1 Payne Dr

F1
1 Cato St
2 Henrietta St

F3
1 Brighton Pk
2 Elmgrove Av
3 Kilburn St
4 Lawnwood Rd
5 Owen St

F4
1 Cattybrook St
2 Windsor Gv

F5
1 Cattybrook St
2 Thomas St

Page 26

B3
1 Albemarle Rw
2 Cornwallis Av
3 Dowry Sq
4 Hope St
5 Hotwell Rd
6 Polygon Rd
7 South Green St

B4
1 Humphry Davy Wy

B5
1 Brunswick Pl

C1
1 King's Rd
2 Regent St

C2
1 Saville Pl

C3
1 Ambra V South
2 Camden Ter
3 Dowry Rd

C4
1 Rownham Mead

Page 28

A1
1 Park Street Av
2 There-and-back-
again La

A2
1 Brandon Steep

A3
1 Lower College St
2 Partition St

B2
1 Frogmore St
2 Gaunt's La
3 Hobb's La
4 Orchard Av
5 Unity St
6 Upper Wells St

C1
1 Christmas St
2 Lower Park Rw

C2
1 St Augustine's Pl
2 St Stephen's Av

C3
1 Assembly Rooms La
2 Middle Av

Page 29

D1
1 John St
2 Pithay Ct
3 Quay St
4 Small St

D2
1 All Saints' La
2 Coronation Pl
3 Queen Charlotte St
4 Rackhay
5 St Nicholas St

D3
1 King William Av
2 Little King St
3 Queen Square Av

D4
1 Jubilee Pl

E3
1 Ferry St
2 Long Rw

E4
1 Phippen St

E5
1 Mede Cl

F1
1 Marybush La

F4
1 Portwall La East

Page 36

A3
1 Graham Rd
2 Stanley St
3 Westbourne Gv

A4
1 Rowley St
2 Stanley St North

A5
1 Beaufort St
2 Buckingham St

B2
1 Booth Rd

B3
1 Eaton St
2 Kent St
3 New John St
4 Norfolk Pl

C1
1 Brook Rd
2 Dean Crs

C2
1 Leicester St
2 Lombard St

Notes

Notes

Notes